WASHINGTON PLANS AN AGGRESSIVE WAR

In memory of Bernard Fall, scholar and friend,
who gave his life to find out the truth about the
Indochina war

WASHINGTON PLANS AN AGGRESSIVE WAR

RALPH STAVINS
RICHARD J. BARNET
MARCUS G. RASKIN

VINTAGE BOOKS
A Division of
RANDOM HOUSE   New York

327.73
S 798 w

Acknowledgments

We wish to thank Erwin Knoll, who helped edit the final manuscript, Connie Austin, Linda Barnes, Nancy Bekavak, Janice Caroll, Jan Hackman, Cynthia Keen, Hilary Maddux, Tina Smith, Lynn Strong, Kathy Terza, Bethany Weidner, and those interviewed in preparation of this volume. "The Men Who Made the War" by Richard J. Barnet is an adaptation from a forthcoming book soon to be published by Atheneum.

Vintage Books Edition, August 1971

ISBN: 0-394-71697-3

Library of Congress Catalog Card Number: 70-171367

Designed by James McGuire

Manufactured in the United States of America by the Colonial Press, Clinton, Mass.

Preface

Washington Plans an Aggressive War is the result of an intensive study carried on by members of the Institute for Policy Studies over a twenty-month period. The findings have been the subject of continuous seminars at the Institute, which is building a collection of materials on the war. The study, however, is the responsibility of its authors and does not necessarily reflect the views of the Institute, its trustees, or Fellows. Two of the authors of this volume, Richard J. Barnet and Marcus G. Raskin, have been students and critics of U.S. policy in Vietnam for a decade. Both witnessed the crucial escalation of the war in the Kennedy Administration while serving as officials in the Department of State and the White House. In early 1970, Marcus Raskin conceived the idea of a study which would attempt to explain how the Vietnam disaster happened by analyzing the planning of the war. A study team directed by Ralph Stavins concentrated on finding out who did the actual planning which led to the decisions to bombard North Vietnam, to introduce over a half-million U.S. troops into South Vietnam, to defoliate and destroy vast areas of Indochina, and to create millions of refugees in the area. The purpose of the study was to understand how and why all this happened. We hoped to lay bare for the American people the operations of the national security bureaucracy so that the nation might take steps to ensure that the same political pressures, ideological delusions, and bureaucratic impulses do not push us into another catastrophic involvement in which the United States once more seeks to project its power by killing on a grand scale. Thus, while we believe the study makes a contribution to general understanding of the operations of the U.S. national security structures, our primary interest is in the transformation of those structures.

We approached the study with two explicit biases. The first was that the war was politically and morally wrong from the outset. That bias was completely confirmed for us in the course of the study by mountains of documentary evidence, much of which has now been made public. It is a bias which, according to recent public opinion polls, a majority of the country now shares. The second bias was that the lawlessness of the nation-state constitutes the greatest threat to peace and human survival. The only hope of subjecting the state to law is to hold individuals who act for the state responsible for their acts. Thus the establishment of personal responsibility of national security officials for what they do in the name of the American people is the key to any program of practical reconstruction.

Ralph Stavins, assisted by Canta Pian, John Berkowitz, George Pipkin, and Brian Eden, conducted more than 300 interviews in the course of the study. Those interviewed included many of the top presidential advisers to Presidents Kennedy and Johnson, generals and admirals, middle-level bureaucrats who occupied strategic positions in the national security bureaucracy, and officials, military and civilian, who carried out policy in the field in Vietnam. A number of informants backed up their oral statements with documents in their possession, including informal minutes of meetings as well as portions of the official documentary record now known as "the Pentagon papers." Our information is drawn not only from the planning operations in the Department of Defense but also from the White House, the Department of State, and the Central Intelligence Agency.

The study is being published in two volumes. Volume II, which will appear in May 1972, contains detailed accounts of the planning management of the air war, the defoliation program, the pacification program, and other military operations. It also contains an analysis of the character of the national security managers by Michael Maccoby, an account of the bureaucratic command structure by Leonard Rodberg, an account of the resettlement program by Milton Kotler, and a legal analysis of criminal responsibility by Richard Falk. Volume I is in three parts: The first, an historical essay by Ralph Stavins, is the story of how the war happened. The second, an analytical essay by Richard Barnet, is an explanation of why it happened. The third, an analysis of the erosion of Congressional power and a series of proposals by Marcus Raskin, is a program for demilitarizing the national security bureaucracy and introducing legal standards of individual responsibility. The emphasis throughout has been on naming names, not to be vindictive but to emphasize a fundamental point: The war in Vietnam was the product of individual decisions of identifiable men. It was more than the work of a faceless "system" or inexorable bureaucratic process. Much less can it be ascribed to the collective guilt of the American people, less than one percent of whom knew the facts. Under the national security system as it now exists, even the people's representatives in the Congress appear powerless to oppose an Executive bent on making war abroad whenever he is prepared to mislead the public to gain support for the effort.

We believe, however, that the basic question raised by this horrendous chapter in our history is not deception. Had the Congress been fully informed or had the people been told the truth, the destruction of Vietnam under the circumstances now on the record would still have been a crime. We are prepared to believe that many of the men who have persisted for more than a decade in destroying Indochina thought—at least when they started—that they were justified in what they were doing. But the judgment by the American people of what the planners of the war did in their name must be based not on the war managers' own rationalizations but on their acts. The world cannot afford to countenance acts of mass destruction because the men who give the orders claim to be sincere and upright men.

The record establishes that the top civilian leadership of our country planned and carried out an aggressive war against a people who did not and could not hurt the United States. Under precedents established by the United States and imposed upon other countries, this pattern of conduct constitutes a war crime. Despite the frequent insistence among those who have held positions in the national security bureaucracy that all talk of war crimes committed by high officials is a form of "witch hunt" or "McCarthyism of the left," that diversionary tactic is a poor defense. The enactment and enforcement of laws against war crimes can hardly be construed as McCarthyism. We believe that those who have brought dishonor to the American people by planning and executing an aggressive war must be publicly identified and barred, at least for a decade, from holding positions of public trust. Only if the American people confront the crimes that have been committed in their name and those responsible for them will it be possible to make a break with a collective past that has scarred each one of us.

Ralph Stavins
Richard J. Barnet
Marcus G. Raskin

Contents

Part III/ From Imperial War-making to a Code of
Personal Responsibility
By Marcus G. Raskin

PART I /

WASHINGTON DETERMINES THE FATE OF VIETNAM: 1954–1965

Ralph Stavins

1 /

BACKGROUND:
1954–1960

The Geneva Accords of 1954, negotiated and adopted by
the belligerents in the first Indochina war—France and
the Viet Minh—protected the existence of the embryonic
State of Vietnam for a period of two years by providing
that nationwide elections would be held in 1956. The
provisions were agreed upon because the Viet Minh expected that their reward for defeating the French—the
unification of Vietnam under their own banner—was
merely being postponed, and was not to be denied.[1] This
two-year interval between victory and its fruits represented a grace period during which the southern State
of Vietnam, now known as the Government of Vietnam
(GVN), would have to prove that it was capable of
rebuffing the northern Democratic Republic of Vietnam
(DRV), the successors to the Viet Minh, in elections.
Otherwise, Vietnam would be unified under the aegis of
the DRV.

1/See, Hannon, J. S., "A Political Settlement for Vietnam: The 1954
Geneva Conference and Its Current Implications," 8 Virginia Journal of
International Law, December 1967, pp. 4–93.

Washington had footed the economic bill for the French military debacle.[2] As spearhead of the anti-Communist world, the Eisenhower Administration was determined not to "lose" Indochina as the Truman Administration had "lost" China. The French had been badly mauled, Washington was convinced, because they had stubbornly relied on a discredited colonial system and had been unable to streamline their military posture with sufficient jet aircraft. The United States would be victorious where the French had failed by avoiding the pitfalls of a blatant colonial attitude and by modernizing the Southern army. Simply stated, Washington needed to create a nationalist alternative in the South to the nationalist reality in the North.

Before the concepts of nation-building and self-defense could be put into effect, however, Washington had to deal with the legacy it had inherited at Geneva. It had to ease the French out of the picture, generate support for a new and untried leader to ensure his survival for at least two years, and circumvent the scheduled elections without becoming embroiled in another war with the North.

It was a tall order of business. By the end of 1954, the French were still commanding the territory south of the seventeenth parallel, and the writ of the GVN barely extended beyond the palace gates in Saigon. Intelligence reports circulating in Washington in the fall of 1954 estimated that the GVN would be unable to attain the level of popularity necessary to score an electoral victory by 1956. A National Intelligence Estimate (NIE) prepared by the Central Intelligence Agency in August 1954 declared:

Unless Mendes-France is able to overcome the force of French traditional interests and emotions which have in the

2/Robert Shaplen, *The Lost Revolution*, rev. ed. (Harper & Row, 1966), p. 94.

4

past governed the implementation of policy in Indochina, we do not believe there will be the dramatic transformation in French policy necessary to win the active loyalty and support of the local population for a South Vietnam Government. . . .

A subsequent NIE issued three months later concluded that the GVN "almost certainly would not be able to defeat the Communists in country-wide elections."

On the basis of CIA estimates and the famous Eisenhower prediction that Ho Chi Minh would capture 80 percent of the vote, it is safe to assume that Washington fully expected a Communist victory if elections were to be held in 1956. But by the fall of 1955 the CIA did not expect the elections to be held. In a NIE dated October 1955, the agency stated:

Diem will almost certainly not agree to hold national elections for the unification of Vietnam by July 1956. Although Diem, under pressure from the Western powers, might reluctantly agree to indirect consultations with the DRV concerning elections, he would insist on conditions which he felt certain the Communists would be unable to accept.

In fact, Ngo Dinh Diem did not even "reluctantly agree" to consult with the DRV as required by the Geneva Accords, and in 1956 he refused to hold the scheduled elections.

In 1954, however, Washington only marginally concerned itself with the dim prospects of a GVN electoral victory two years hence. Instead, attention was focused on the more immediate problem of maintaining the GVN as a governing body between 1954 and 1956. By August 1954, the CIA speculated that the survival of the GVN was open to doubt:

Although it is possible that the French and the Vietnamese, even with firm support from the U.S. and other powers, may be able to establish a strong regime in South Vietnam, we believe that the chances for this development are poor and, moreover, that the situation is more likely to continue to deteriorate progressively over the next year.

The agency noted that should Diem "lose army or U.S. support, his regime would probably collapse."

It is clear that Diem held the same view. Were he to risk elections against the DRV, he would lose. Were he to circumvent the elections, he would still have to convince a foreign power to grant him full military assistance. He lacked popular support at the ballot box and military support on the battlefield. His following in South Vietnam was restricted to his own family, a circle of opportunists, and a handful of technicians. His rule could be preserved only through the intercession of a foreign power. His personal crisis, then, acted as a templet for American foreign policy.

This is not to suggest that Diem hoodwinked the United States into supporting him. Diem had been identified by the U.S. government as the South Vietnamese leader most likely to serve as the "chosen instrument" of American policy in Indochina. He had lived in the United States and enjoyed the support of some of the U.S. Catholic hierarchy. But American support was, at first, conditional, contingent on his ability to demonstrate that he could rule. By 1955, this condition had not been met. The CIA reports, prepared under the direction of Allen Dulles, had not gone unread by the Secretary of State. The chances for success were gloomy. General J. Lawton Collins, President Eisenhower's personal envoy to Vietnam, disapproved of Diem's tactics and, in April 1955, advised Washington to remove Diem from power. Partly in deference to Diem's American supporters, Washington decided on a compromise: in the midst of the Binh Xuyen[3]

_____

3/The Binh Xuyen were an armed gang who were in the business of political murder. They would switch allegiance to whoever paid a higher price.

crisis the State Department instructed the Saigon Embassy that Diem was to be stripped of power and kicked upstairs to the presidency of Vietnam, a symbolic office at the time, while Dr. Phan Huy Quat, a Northerner, was to be appointed as functioning Premier. To Washington's surprise and consternation, Diem was able to repulse the attack before the decision was made known to him. The State Department cable was burned. By suppressing the Binh Xuyen gangster sect in pitched battle, Diem was able to meet the condition that Washington had imposed. He proved he could rule.

For the remainder of 1955 and well into the spring of 1956, Diem devoted his time and energy to crushing the other sects who competed with him for power in the South. Relying on military force, he dealt with the three remaining sects—the Hoa Hao, Cao Dai, and Binh Nuyen —one by one, in bloody combat. Relying on electoral fraud (although it was unnecessary, as his opponent was Bao Dai, the former French puppet), he was overwhelmingly elected President. Five months later, in the first national elections for Parliament, the CIA reported that "no anti-Diem Deputy was elected . . . due in part to government manipulation of the election campaign and in part to a boycott of the elections by most of the opposition parties." Thus, by the spring of 1956, the proper mixture of force and fraud had invested Diem with virtual dictatorial powers.

By the summer of 1956, Diem's strength in the South had reached its peak. Having destroyed the regional sects and intimidated the loyal opposition; having wrapped himself in the mantle of legitimacy and armed himself with American military and economic aid, Diem turned to his chief task: By refusing to hold elections for unification in July 1956, Diem threw down the gauntlet to the Communists in the North and in the South to do battle with him. It was the *casus belli* for the second Indochina war.

The events of the year stimulated hopes in Washington that Diem would be able to overcome the Communist challenge and extend national sovereignty over the whole of the South. Perhaps, it was believed, he would even fulfill Washington's deepest (though unexpressed) wish and extend his dominion over the North as well. Gazing into the future at this time, the CIA observed:

Diem's success in by-passing the July 1956 election date without evoking large-scale Communist military reaction will reassure many Vietnamese and encourage them to cooperate with GVN programs to expose and root out Communists. Continued improvement in internal security will depend in some measure on the government's ability to deal with economic and social problems and on the effectiveness of the administrative apparatus.

If the Communists were to undertake large-scale guerrilla action in South Vietnam they probably would not be able to develop widespread popular support, especially if the VNA [Army of Vietnam] were to register some early military success. The GVN is being increasingly accepted as a nationalist alternative to Communist leadership. Public confidence in the GVN, combined with general war-weariness, may have already reached the point where any effort to upset the government by force would lead to a strong popular reaction against the guerrillas.

This CIA assessment of Communist strength—that "any effort to upset the government by force would lead to a strong popular reaction against the guerrillas"—represents the only occasion when the intelligence agency led the policy-makers down the primrose path. All other estimates throughout the period from 1954 to 1956 argued to the contrary—that the Communists possessed the capability to seize control in the South.

When Diem assumed office in July 1954, for example, the CIA had divined that "the most significant particular political sentiment of the bulk of the population was an antipathy for the French combined with a personal regard for Ho Chi Minh as the symbol of Vietnamese National- ism. . . ." The popularity of Ho south of the seventeenth parallel was such that "the Viet Minh apparently exerts political influence in many areas scattered throughout South Vietnam." Given this Southern base of support, the CIA believed that Ho would be able to unify all of Viet- nam under his leadership. More significantly, he would be able to accomplish this objective without engaging Diem in armed combat. In a NIE circulated in November 1954, the agency wrote:

> The Viet Minh probably now feels that it can achieve con- trol over all Vietnam without initiating large-scale warfare. Accordingly, we believe that the Communists will exert every effort to accomplish their objectives through means short of war. . . .

Thus, the Viet Minh, according to the CIA, had the capacity to unify Vietnam through peaceful means. More- over, the agency, in the quotation cited above, presumed that the Viet Minh's objectives were identical with their capacity. But the CIA also believed the Viet Minh had the capacity to seize power in the South through a violent upheaval. Appraising Viet Minh strength in October 1955, the CIA wrote:

> The Viet Minh, *despite their relative quiescence*, present the greatest *potential* threat to Diem. Should the Viet Minh elect openly to invade the south with regular forces, they are capable of defeating the VNA and any French forces (if committed) now present in South Vietnam. (emphasis added)

> Should the Viet Minh initiate large-scale guerrilla opera- tions supported by substantial infiltration from the north, the South Vietnamese government would be hard-pressed to do more than maintain control in the Saigon–Cholon area and in a few other major urban centers. If the operation

9

were prolonged, the government probably could not survive without military assistance from outside.

Determining, then, that the Viet Minh had the capability to seize power through either peaceful or violent means, and acknowledging their past quiescence and their future threat, how did the agency assess the intentions of the Viet Minh?

The DRV would unleash guerrilla warfare only if "South Vietnam should appear to be gaining in strength or if elections were postponed over Communist objections." Of these two contingencies, the refusal to hold elections was considered next to inevitable, while a gain in GVN strength was considered virtually impossible. The upshot of the CIA findings was that Ho's intentions would remain peaceful unless and until Diem violated the Geneva Accords by nullifying the scheduled elections.

In fact, Ho had good reasons to be peaceful. Having fought the French from 1946 to 1954 and defeated them, the DRV secured the right to gain control over the entire South at the Geneva conference, but the exercise of that right was to be deferred and conditional. The Accords postponed that right for two years and restricted its exercise to the will of the people through the mechanism of the ballot box. Since, as we have seen, the North had the capacity to comply with the Geneva Accords, one would have every reason to expect that their intentions would be consistent with their capacity. Indeed, they were. There is nothing in the historic record of this period to suggest that the DRV activated its guerrilla apparatus in the South. In fact, the evidence suggests the contrary. Having inherited a war-wearied population, compelled to quell a peasant uprising in the North, and shorn of the productive rice fields of the South, Ho might even have tolerated the uninterrupted existence of the GVN after 1956, if Diem would have agreed to economic trade and practiced a foreign policy of neutralism.

In contrast to Ho's "relative quiescence," Diem, beginning early in 1956, set in motion a series of acts, the sum total of which effectively reopened the Indochina war. First, the Can Lao Party was organized. A secret police apparatus, relying exclusively on terror and murder, the Can Lao was a Vietnamese version of the Gestapo and the NKVD. Contrary to popular opinion, this party was not a mere creation of Diem and his fanatical brother, Nhu. Brigadier General Edward Lansdale, Diem's trusted American adviser, writing with remarkable candor, has explained the genesis of the Can Lao Party:

> Ambassador Durbrow seemed genuinely surprised when I told him that the Can Lao Party in Vietnam was originally promoted by the U.S. State Department and was largely the brain-child of a highly respected, senior U.S. Foreign Service professional. Several weeks after this action was undertaken originally, I learned of it and warned that the benefits were extremely short-term and that great lasting harm could result by a favored party forcing older parties to go underground.

> However, the real point is that we don't seem to have very long memories or enough solid feeling of responsibility for our acts. Many U.S. Foreign Service officials leap into attacks on the Can Lao Party. I agree with their reasons. Any thinking American would. But I sure would feel better about it if they could only remember the consequences of their own actions for a few short years—and learn from that memory. *I cannot truly sympathize with Americans who help promote a fascistic state and then get angry when it doesn't act like a democracy.* (emphasis added)

Second, in the spring of 1956, Diem secured the final commitment of U.S. military assistance for reorganizing, training, and expanding the Vietnamese army. This was accomplished through the efforts of several hundred American officers and enlisted personnel attached to the Military Assistance Advisory Group (MAAG). Drawing his strength from the twin pillars of the secret police and the regular army, the direct products of Washington's policies, Diem then initiated a campaign to locate, root out, incarcerate, and murder the members of the Communist Party of South Vietnam. At the same time, Diem's family rounded up whatever other opposition they could identify, until Diem's rule was virtually at war with all other political elements in the South, Communist and non-Communist alike. Joseph Buttinger—one of Diem's earliest supporters—speaking of the "takeover" period, stated:

The manhunt against the Viet Minh began only after the regime's military and police apparatus was sufficiently developed and firmly under government control. Two major campaigns were made with massive participation of the army. The first one swept through the provinces west of Saigon, lasting from June 8, 1956, to October 31, 1956. The second one was much longer—from June 17, 1956 to December 15, 1957. . . .

But there can be no doubt, on the basis of reports by the few impartial observers who have treated the subject, that innumerable crimes and absolutely senseless acts of suppression against both real and suspected Communists and sympathizing villagers were committed. Efficiency took the form of brutality and total disregard for the difference between determined foes and potential friends. Most of the real Communists escaped and, in hiding, prepared themselves for the day when conditions for successful insurrection would be ripe. Those who were caught were usually killed, and judging by the treatment the South Vietnamese Army later accorded to captured guerrillas, most likely also were tortured. The American public, which a little while later was told of the many Diem officials murdered by the so-called Vietcong, learned nothing at all about these earlier events, not so much because of Saigon censorship but rather because of the West's reluctance openly to condemn crimes committed in the name of anti-Communism.[4]

4/*Vietnam: A Dragon Embattled,* II (Praeger, 1967), pp. 975–976.

In the month following Diem's undeclared war against the Viet Minh, as the curtain of terror rapidly descended on the South, Diem canceled the elections scheduled by the Geneva Accords. In October 1956, he also abolished local elections, the traditional and time-honored method of selecting leadership throughout rural Vietnam. Finally, in the same month, Diem promulgated the Constitution of the Republic of Vietnam, a document which invested the President with power "to rule by decree in any emergency—a condition he could more or less define himself—and suspend any laws."[5] A dictator in lawful dress, Diem narrowly escaped an assassination attempt in February 1957. Reviewing the sordid history of the GVN, the CIA reflected:

> The prospects for continued political stability in South Vietnam depend heavily upon President Diem and his ability to maintain firm control of the army and police. . . .

> Diem's regime reflects his ideas. A façade of representative government is maintained, but the government is in fact essentially authoritarian. The legislative powers of the National Assembly are strictly circumscribed; the judiciary is undeveloped and subordinate to the executive; and the members of the executive branch are little more than the personal agents of Diem. No organized opposition, loyal or otherwise, is tolerated, and critics of the regime are often repressed. . . . The exercise of power and responsibility is limited to Diem and a very small circle mainly composed of his relatives, the most important being Nhu and Can.

The conclusion is inescapable. Diem—hand-picked and propped up by the U.S. government, his rule dependent upon the army and police—was the one who violated the Geneva Accords and commenced aggressive warfare against the Viet Minh, and the loyal opposition as well. Buttinger, summarizing the history of this period, writes:

5/Shaplen, *op. cit.*, p. 133.

While it is likely that the Communists, deprived of the chance of winning the South through elections, would sooner or later have resorted to terror and guerrilla warfare, the historical fact is that force in the struggle for the South was first used by the Diem regime, not by the Communists.[6]

Throughout this period, Hanoi stood idly by. As late as May 1957, almost one year after the scheduled elections had been canceled and the apparatus of the Can Lao Party had been unleashed to destroy the Communist Party of South Vietnam, the CIA could find no evidence of aggressive activity on behalf of the DRV, despite its acknowledged potential for seizing power in the South. In a NIE entitled "Prospects for North Vietnam," the agency wrote:

> The DRV continues to maintain its apparatus for subversion within SVN and has the capability to infiltrate fairly large numbers of military and political personnel into SVN. Although the Communists in the South have been largely quiescent, some trained military personnel remain, loosely organized in small units that presumably could be reactivated for missions of assassination, sabotage, or limited guerrilla activity.

> Because the country-wide elections envisaged by the Geneva Agreements have not been held and because military action has been prevented, the DRV has been frustrated in its hopes of gaining control of SVN. This has caused some discontent among cadres evacuated from the South in the expectation that they would soon return. Unification of the country remains a principal objective of the DRV regime.

> The DRV will probably continue for the next year or two to restrict its campaign for reunification to "peaceful" means. However, the DRV will continue its efforts to infiltrate and to subvert official and nonofficial organizations and to

---

6/Buttinger, *op. cit.*, p. 982.

exploit dissident and dissatisfied groups in SVN. It would probably not use its paramilitary forces in SVN to initiate widespread guerrilla activity unless it estimated that the situation in SVN had so deteriorated that such action could overthrow the government.

In 1958, the Viet Cong, without active support from the North, and as an act of survival in the South, retaliated against the GVN. A campaign was launched to kidnap and assassinate government officials. Southern peasants were taxed and recruited to support the VC. Non-Communist groups were enlisted to broaden the base of the resistance. Pressures were increasingly exerted upon Hanoi to lend active support to the fledgling rebellion in the South.

While Hanoi was weighing its alternatives, Washington issued a National Security Council paper declaring its policy objectives for Vietnam. The language in NSC 5809, dated April 2, 1958, clearly indicates Washington's aims toward the North as well as the South. The document recited U.S. objectives in Vietnam, including "work toward the weakening of the Communists of north and south Vietnam in order to bring about the eventual peaceful reunification of a free and independent Vietnam under anti-Communist leadership."

Washington, in its policies from 1954 to 1958, was determined to partition the South by force. By 1958, satisfied with the method and efficacy of Diem's rule below the seventeenth parallel, Washington expressed its deepest, yet publicly unacknowledged, wish to unify all of Vietnam under Diem.

Three years after Washington and Saigon had denied Hanoi the exercise of its right to unify Vietnam through a nationwide referendum, and one year after Washington had advocated its own policy of unifying all of Vietnam under the leadership of Diem, Hanoi entered the Southern struggle. In May 1959, the DRV, through the Central Committee of the Lao Dong Party, passed a resolution declaring that the struggle for reunification would have to be carried out by all apppropriate measures. The U.S. Mission in Saigon noted with approval that "British observers have taken this to mean measures other than peaceful." In the same Mission report, two conversations by Premier Pham Van Dong were repeated for Washington consumption. Speaking to French Counsel Georges-Picot on September 12, 1959, the Premier of North Vietnam was quoted as saying, "You must remember we will be in Saigon tomorrow, we will be in Saigon tomorrow." In November 1959, the Mission added, Pham Van Dong twice told Canadian Commissioner Erichsen-Brown that "we will drive the Americans into the sea."

Buttinger dates Hanoi's forceful intervention in the South from September 1960. Reviewing the policies issued at the Third Congress of the Lao Dong Party, Buttinger argued that "not until September 1960 . . . did the policy of overthrowing the Diem regime by force and of liberating the South receive quasi formal endorsement." The Third Congress, in approving the formation of the National Liberation Front, stated that the aim of the Front was to create a "democratic coalition," one "not necessarily pledged to early unification with the North."

In retrospect, Hanoi's motives for entering the struggle seem reasonably clear. Although the Viet Cong took up arms against Diem in order to survive and sought Northern support to keep the resistance alive, Hanoi was motivated to join the issue not out of sympathy for the plight of its Southern brethren but by the prospects that the GVN would deteriorate. Only after the Viet Cong proved to Hanoi that the Viet Cong had survived and that the GVN might fall did Hanoi actively enter the struggle. This proof required time—at least three to four years. If the probable collapse of the GVN represented the signal for Hanoi to move—and the CIA invariably underscored this prospect as the single factor that would sway Hanoi[7] —then Hanoi had good reasons to hold back. It was reluctant to enter the struggle until it felt that it could tip the scales decisively as a result of its own intervention. Hanoi, therefore, was regarded as dilatory and overly cautious by its own Southern cadre.

The early history of South Vietnam strongly suggests that Diem was the aggressor in commencing the second Indochina war, and that the United States had full complicity in that act of aggression. The United States wanted the territory of South Vietnam within its own sphere of power and was willing to pay a heavy price to realize that goal. In the fifties, the price was to build a fascist regime in the South and violate international law abroad. Washington picked Diem to rule and gave him unconditional support from the spring of 1955 onward. Washington had full knowledge of Diem's incapacity to preserve his political writ except through recourse to violence and terror. The Army of Vietnam (ARVN) and the Can Lao Party, both conceived and designed by Washington, were the two institutions directly responsible for administering the desired dosages of force and repression. The army and the police were not used to defend the South from a potential attack by the North, but rather to unleash aggression against the Southern-based Viet Minh as well as the loyal opposition. Thus, the United States produced a fascist regime in the South. It also fully subscribed to Diem's cancellation of the nationwide elections, a mandatory requirement of the Geneva Accords. Washington's public rationale was that the Communists would have performed fraudulently in the North, though it knew

7/"It would probably not use its paramilitary forces in SVN to initiate widespread guerrilla activity unless it estimated that the situation in SVN had so deteriorated that such action could overthrow the government." *Supra*, p. 13.

privately that the GVN had already committed fraud in the South. The elections were prohibited not because of the possibility of Communist fraud, but rather because of the certainty of Communist victory.

In the 1960's, the resistance of the Viet Cong and the recalcitrance of Diem motivated the decision-makers in Washington to go beyond the installation of a fascist regime and the flouting of law. The Kennedy and Johnson administrations distinguished themselves from Eisenhower's by undertaking aggressive war directly against the North.

2 /

THE TRANSITION FROM EISENHOWER TO KENNEDY: 1960–1961

In April 1958, Washington had expressed the hope that Diem would be able to conquer all of Vietnam. By January 1960, Washington became alarmed over the possibility that the Viet Cong might overthrow Diem, and that the North would extend its domain over the South. What was most shocking about conjecture was that it had been inspired by the accomplishments of a handful of guerrillas. In a report describing the internal security in Vietnam, Saigon authorities estimated that as of January 1960 the strength of the Viet Cong throughout South Vietnam did not exceed 3,000 to 5,000 men. The report added that the Southern cadre had been infiltrated from the North, and then repeated Pham Van Dong's remark that Hanoi would drive the Americans into the sea.

Washington was in the grip of the Domino Theory, which argued that the end of the American presence in

South Vietnam entailed the prospective exit of America from Southeast Asia. This, in turn, raised the specter that American interests would be rolled back to the edge of the Orient—perhaps even to the mid-Pacific region.

The decade of the sixties dawned on Washington with these two clouds on the horizon: Hanoi would overthrow Diem with a few guerrilla bands, and the United States, as a direct consequence, would be forced to retire from the arena of world politics.

The objective situation in the South did not conform to Washington's apprehensions. After six turbulent years of rule, Diem did not have his own constituency. In such nonindustrialized countries as South Vietnam, there are three possible constituencies that a leader can draw upon as support for his politics: the peasantry, the elite, and the army.

Diem, Mandarin in outlook, nationalist in policy, Catholic by belief, had little sympathy and no understanding for the plight of the peasants whose station in life was one of unremitting toil, narrow political views, and Buddhist upbringing. Economics, politics, and religion, three exceptionally powerful influences on human behavior, came together to place Diem and the peasants on opposite sides of a great divide. Diem's policies conformed to his attitudes toward the peasantry. For the peasant, there were two issues of vital importance: village democracy and land reform. Were Diem to have simply preserved the ancient heritage of village democracy, and to have introduced the modern idea of land reform, the peasant class would have laid down their lives for him. Instead, he unilaterally intervened in 1956 to prohibit local elections, and he refused to introduce a reasonable program of land reform. He terminated the peasants' political existence and cast aside their economic hopes. Their relationship to each other and their relationship to the land were under assault. With no attempt at rebuttal, the U.S. Mission in Saigon submitted to Washington the Viet Cong estimate that 70 percent of the people in the countryside were openly hostile or silently indifferent to the GVN. In the period following this estimate, Diem added insult to injury by compelling the peasants to leave their tiny plots of land and ancestral villages to enter strategic hamlets or work on government projects as corvée labor, without pay.

Another possible constituency for Diem would have been the burgeoning class of urban elitists. Professionals, skilled technicians, religious leaders, and journalists— those whom Edward Lansdale had referred to as the loyal opposition—could have been formed into a rival political party, as recommended by Lansdale, or invited into the official political party of the South, the National Revolutionary Movement, and offered positions in Diem's cabinet, as envisioned by the State Department. But Diem was adamant in his refusal to reform the structure of the GVN. General reform would have to begin with the termination of Diem's rule and the installation of a leadership that believed in and could command the power to reform. Diem did not believe in reform and barely had the power to defend his own rule. Instead of recognizing a loyal opposition—the prerequisite for reform—Diem insisted upon blind loyalty, though it could be achieved only through intimidation and terror. The potential loyal opposition was systematically hunted down and persecuted.

This meant that the loyal opposition was placed on the same footing as the Viet Cong. The logical circle was closed with the proposition that all opposition was Communist-inspired, though it was obvious that the urban elitists eschewed violence and were deeply committed to a non-Communist South Vietnam.

The ground swell of resentment which had accumulated over the years in the elite class surfaced early in 1960 among Saigon intellectuals, labor and business groups, and the official bureaucracy. Their grievances encompassed the unbridled power of Diem's family, the clandestine activities of the Can Lao Party, the corruption in high places, and the rampant extortion practiced by local police. In April 1960, the urban elites, approaching an open breach with the regime, organized themselves through the process of public petition and pleaded with Diem to "liberalize the regime, expand democracy, grant minimum civil rights, and recognize the opposition in order to let the people speak without fear." Their plea fell on deaf ears.

The ARVN was the only constituency that had supported Diem. He relied on his 170,000 troops—a force he had steadily expanded in the 1950's—to maintain his rule over the non-Communist South, peasant and elite alike. But the test for appointment and promotion in the army was no different from that in the civil order. When competence is sacrificed for loyalty in government, the predictable result is inefficiency and mounting discontent. But when political loyalty becomes the standard of an army—an army, moreover, which is engaged in combat with a trained, determined, and hardened foe—the result can easily be the overthrow of the government. Until 1960, the ARVN's loyalty was pointed to with pride, though it merely concealed its gross incompetence. The army's enemy, by and large, was the civilian South, where loyalty was generally lacking but where there was little organized resistance. But once the Viet Cong had been organized into a fighting unit, the façade of the ARVN was penetrated and its incompetence disclosed for all to see.

On September 26, 1959, the Viet Cong successfully engaged two ARVN companies and exposed a number of their weaknesses. These deficiencies in the ARVN, present but hidden before 1960, became commonplace in the 1960's—security leaks, poor planning, and a lack of aggressive leadership. The Viet Cong, on the other hand, scored high in each of these areas. The result was that the Viet Cong possessed confidence and high morale, while the ARVN was timid and shamefaced.

Following their initial success, the Viet Cong overran a government outpost at Tay Ninh on January 26, 1960, displaying other factors which were to become recognized as characteristic of the Vietnam war. At Tay Ninh, the Viet Cong were able to infiltrate directly into the ARVN because of the active cooperation of the local people. It was now abundantly clear that the Viet Cong had the immediate support of the peasantry and could march from hamlet to hamlet as a people's army, while the ARVN was little more than a praetorian guard of a distant tyrant.

The ARVN responded to its initial series of defeats by turning against Diem. The middle-echelon officer corps began to object openly to Diem's handling of internal security problems, and this discontent soon spread to the generals. In September 1960, General Minh told the U.S. Mission that for every Viet Cong killed by the ARVN, the policies of the GVN were creating ten more Viet Cong in their rear. By November 1960, part of the ARVN was in open revolt. General Thi, an officer believed to have been most loyal to Diem, led his paratroopers into Saigon and staged an attempted coup.

During this same period, the intelligence community in Washington argued that further coups and revolts were likely to occur, but they would not originate from the Viet Cong. Instead, insurrection would emerge somewhere in the non-Communist South, most likely from the army or the urban elites. Washington was further advised that the Viet Cong, still numbering under 10,000, did no more than aggravate the government's problems.

The Saigon Embassy supported the estimate of the intelligence community. Ambassador Durbrow expected a coup, but doubted that the Viet Cong would have a hand in it. The coup would spring from non-Communist sources, and the Viet Cong would exploit the coup for their own purposes.

The objective circumstances in the South thus directly contradicted the myths current in Washington. Reality, as perceived by the Embassy, the State Department, and the intelligence community, showed that a handful of guerrillas did not create the revolutionary climate, nor did they possess the power to stage an uprising against the GVN. They could do no more than feed on the despair generated by Diem's own policies. The extinction of village democracy and the failure to introduce a land-reform program had alienated the peasantry. The intimidation and terror practiced by the Can Lao Party, and Diem's persistent refusal to include the loyal opposition in the legitimate organs of government had turned the urban elites against the GVN. The emphasis on loyalty and the daily reality of structured graft and corruption had exposed the inability of the ARVN to maintain internal security. Bereft of its esprit de corps, the army moved into opposition. The defection of the foot soldiers spread to the officer corps, resulting in an attempted coup against Diem.

By the end of 1960, Diem stood almost alone in Saigon. Surrounded by his immediate family, he was at odds with the peasantry, the elite, and part of the army. Without a constituency at home, Diem had no recourse but to expand his constituency in Washington. His xenophobia caused him to resist this until the fall of 1961, but, from November 1960 on, his rule was absolutely dependent on Washington's good graces. This was made clear by Ambassador Durbrow who, as early as September 1960, reminded Washington that its objective was an anti-Communist South Vietnam, and that the United States was not committed to any particular ruler. Diem's policies were such that Washington should begin to consider "alternative actions and leaders in order to achieve our objective." The puppet was getting in the way. The sacrifice was being prepared.

POLITICAL REFORM

From the fall of 1960 to the spring of 1961, the emphasis in both Washington and Saigon was on reform. Reform, it was felt, could be designed to capture a modicum of support from the constituencies Diem had alienated. Ambassador Durbrow, by no means certain of his government's willingness to pressure Diem to institute widespread reform, thought it prudent first to pressure the State Department into supporting him in this enterprise. Durbrow told State that Diem was in "serious danger" and "drastic action was called for." Popular resentment of Diem's family had mounted to the point where Diem's political position was in great jeopardy. State was reminded of analogous situations in other countries, where "useful government personalities have had to be sacrificed for political reasons," and Durbrow suggested that Diem's hated brother Nhu be appointed an ambassador and sent abroad. A similar course was recommended for Tran Kim Tuyen, the head of Saigon's secret intelligence. Other proposed reforms included two cabinet seats for the loyal opposition; disbanding of the Can Lao Party; wider powers to the National Assembly, including the right to investigate any public official except the President; compelling government officials to make public disclosures of their financial holdings; granting to the peasant a direct subsidy and payment for his corvée labor. Durbrow suggested that these new charges on government could be financed through deficit spending.

State concurred with Durbrow's assessment but advised him to proceed cautiously in gaining Diem's consent to remove Nhu and Tuyen from the offices of government. State further recommended that Diem restore local elections in the countryside, at least for some officials. But State declined to abolish the Can Lao Party, noting that to eliminate both Can Lao and Tuyen would be too much. The logic of the State Department's position was that the totalitarian Can Lao Party should exist simultaneously with the expansion of democratic rights.

Durbrow visited Diem on October 14 and proposed these reforms. After listening to Durbrow read a fourteen-page paper, Diem said his own ideas conformed with Durbrow's suggestions. He added, however, that the stepped-up activity of the Viet Cong made the time inopportune for reforming the countryside. Durbrow begged Diem's indulgence and asked if he could bring up a sensitive and delicate matter—the growing criticism of Nhu and Tuyen and the possibility that they might be assigned abroad. Diem, obviously offended, replied that allegations against Nhu and Tuyen amounted to little more than malicious gossip circulated by the Communists to slander the regime. Durbrow closed the discussion by apologizing for having brought up the subject, and for the other suggestions he had made.

MILITARY REFORM

Since Diem would not agree to political reforms that might attenuate his power, Washington turned its attention to possible military reforms. On September 16, 1960, the same day that Ambassador Durbrow recommended to State that Diem begin to reform the GVN, the Joint Chiefs of Staff informed the Commander-in-Chief for the Pacific (CINCPAC) and the Chief of MAAG that they and the Deputy Secretary of Defense had approved a CINCPAC draft plan for counterinsurgency operations by the Government of Vietnam. The draft plan recommended national emergency organizations to reduce Communist influence in Laos and Vietnam. These organizations would integrate civil and military resources under centralized direction, and U.S. agencies in the field would support the training for the conduct of emergency operations. The JCS viewed the counterinsurgency plan in the same light as the Ambassador saw the reforms of the GVN. Both would obviate the necessity for American involvement in a land war in Asia. In a memo to the Secretary of Defense, the JCS asserted that

> encouraging the Government of South Vietnam to adopt a national course of action designed to reduce the growing threat of Communist insurgent actions was vital to the continued freedom of that country and an important action to preclude the necessity for implementing U.S. or SEATO war plans.

The draft plan forwarded to MAAG stressed organizational matters, including the formation of a National Emergency Council and a Director of Operations to integrate civil and military efforts and formulate the Vietnamese National Counter-Insurgency Plan, with subcouncils at regional, provincial, and village levels. The plan concluded with concepts of political and military operations. The concept of political operations stated that:

> In order to provide protection which the people require, it is necessary to exercise more than an ordinary degree of control over the population. Among the more important operations required are those for exercising control in such a manner as to isolate insurgents and sympathizers from the support of the populace. Such techniques as registration and identification, food control, and control of movement, should be implemented as offering the best prospects for success. Control measures instituted should require support by

psychological warfare and information programs to gain and maintain popular confidence and support.

Military operations called for the training and equipment of home guards and civil guards as a means of reinforcing the permanent local security establishment. The regular army, the militia, and the police should be placed under centralized direction and the operations in Vietnam "should also be coordinated with Cambodia, and Laos, as feasible."

The Counter-Insurgency Plan was reviewed by the Chief of MAAG and the Ambassador. The Plan, consistent with the political and military concepts cited above, was forwarded to Washington on January 4, 1961. To execute the Plan, it was recommended that the force level of the ARVN be expanded by 20,000 and that logistical support be provided for 32,000 of the Civil Guard.

Assumptions underlying the Plan were made explicit: The greatest threat to the GVN is the expansion of guerrilla war by the Viet Cong; Diem offers the best hope for defeating the insurgency; U.S. policy is to create government stability by eradicating the insurgency; North Vietnam has the capability of supporting guerrilla operations by infiltrating regular forces and cadres (guerrilla forces have increased from 3,500 to an ARVN estimate of 9,800 during 1960); the gravity of the threat will continue until a maximum offensive and coordinated retaliatory effort is made by civil and military authorities.

The Counter-Insurgency Plan represented the first opportunity for the new president, John F. Kennedy, to make policy toward Vietnam. On January 30, 1961, ten days after assuming office, he authorized the increases in the ARVN and the Civil Guard. Kennedy, according to Chalmers Wood, the Vietnam desk officer in 1961, personally approved of the Plan.

A controversy arose, however, over who should bear the costs for the increases in the size of the ARVN. The recently appointed Ambassador, Nolting, recommended to Kennedy that he "withhold the green light" until Diem agreed to offer the non-Communist loyal opposition two seats in the cabinet of the GVN. The State Department, having cast aside its hope of a broad-based reform, wanted some liberalizing measures adopted by Diem and attempted to use the increases in the ARVN as leverage toward this end. Kennedy held back for a few months, but as the United States entered negotiations over Laos —a matter that raised doubts in Diem's mind as to the sincerity of Washington's commitment to South Vietnam —Kennedy relented. If Diem would accept the Plan, then Washington would foot the bill and back him wholeheartedly.

In point of fact, the only significant military changes that would be instituted in connection with the Plan would be in the U.S. chain of command, not in the GVN. Early in 1961, Lieutenant General T. J. H. Trapnell visited Vietnam on behalf of the JCS and, upon his return on March 28, submitted a series of recommendations. Trapnell argued that the United States should bear the full costs of the Counter-Insurgency Plan, in exchange for which it should simply seek Diem's acceptance of the Plan and not bother to insist on political change. This view was accepted by Kennedy. Simultaneously, Trapnell called for a change in the U.S. chain of command. He defined the situation as a "hot war" and objected to the concept of the "Country Team," which placed the MAAG mission under the authority of the Ambassador. In his report to the JCS, Trapnell observed:

> The problem is one of military problems being reviewed by the Country Team and changes made—not for political or economic reasons—but on purely military grounds. This over-control and coordination of pure military matters by the Country Team has sometimes delayed, thwarted or precluded military plans or recommendations of Chief MAAG

which he, in his considered professional opinion, felt were necessary in the best interest of the U.S. in furthering U.S. goals. When the internal security situation of a country deteriorates to the point where it is obvious that military action of intervention is the only answer, I feel that the Country Team concept of control and coordination under the Ambassador should not apply and that pure military matters should be the responsibility of the senior U.S. officer in the country concerned. Military directives should not come through the Ambassador for his review but directly through military channels in order that military directives and policy decisions will not be influenced by non-military thinking and direction in a hot war situation.

Kennedy concurred. Although the issue was not resolved immediately, by the end of 1961 the MAAG mission had been quietly dropped in favor of MACV, the Military Assistance Command, Vietnam. Hereafter, the chief U.S. officer would have direct access to U.S. military channels and the President for military matters. What is striking about Trapnell's statement and Kennedy's decision to create MACV is the absence of any consideration of the fact that the "hot war" in Vietnam differed from the hot wars of the past in ways that made "non-military thinking and direction" relevant and desirable even in the tactical military sphere. Indeed, the premise of counterinsurgency argued directly against the dominance of a military solution. The creation of MACV reinforced Washington's tendency to think of Vietnam in terms of a military solution—and a military solution based on conventional warfare. With the creation of MACV, power shifted from the Ambassador to the chief military officer in the field, and the commitment to counterinsurgency was shattered beyond repair.

At the end of March 1961, the CIA circulated a NIE on the situation in South Vietnam. This paper advised Kennedy that Diem was a tyrant who was confronted with two sources of discontent, the non-Communist loyal opposition and the Viet Cong. The two problems were closely connected. Of the spreading Viet Cong network, the CIA noted:

> Local recruits and sympathetic or intimidated villagers have enhanced Viet Cong control and influence over increasing areas of the countryside. For example, more than one-half of the entire rural region south and southwest of Saigon, as well as some areas to the north, are under considerable Communist control. Some of these areas are in effect denied to all government authority not immediately backed by substantial armed force. The Viet Cong's strength encircles Saigon and has recently begun to move closer in the city.

The people were not opposing these recent advances by the Viet Cong; if anything, they seemed to be supporting them. The failure to rally the people against the Viet Cong was laid to Diem's dictatorial rule:

> There has been an increasing disposition within official circles and the army to question Diem's ability to lead in this period. Many feel that he is unable to rally the people in the fight against the Communists because of his reliance on virtual one-man rule, his tolerance of corruption extending even to his immediate entourage, and his refusal to relax a rigid system of public controls.

The CIA referred to the coup attempted the previous November and concluded that another coup was likely. In spite of the gains by the Viet Cong, the Agency predicted that the next attempt to overthrow Diem would originate with the army and the non-Communist opposition.

> The Communists would like to initiate and control a coup against Diem, and their armed and subversive operations including united front efforts are directed toward this purpose. It is more likely, however, that any coup attempt which occurs over the next year or so will originate among

non-Communist elements, perhaps a combination of disgruntled civilian officials and oppositionists and army elements, broader than those involved in the November attempt.

In view of the broadly based opposition to Diem's regime and his virtual reliance on one-man rule, it was unlikely that he would initiate any reform measures that would sap the strength of the revolutionaries. Whether reform was thought of as widening the political base of the regime, which Diem would not agree to, or whether it was to consist of an intensified counterinsurgency program, something the people would not support, it had become painfully clear to Washington that reform was not the path to victory. But victory was the goal, and Kennedy called upon Deputy Secretary of Defense Roswell Gilpatric to draw up the victory plans. On April 20, 1961, Kennedy asked Gilpatric to:

a) Appraise the current status and future prospects of the Communist drive to dominate South Vietnam.
b) Recommend a series of actions (military, political, and/or economic, overt and/or covert) which will prevent Communist domination of that country.

THE GILPATRIC TASK FORCE

Gilpatric organized an Interdepartmental Task Force with representatives from State, Defense, the CIA, the International Cooperation Agency, the U.S. Information Agency, and the Office of the President, with Brigadier General Edward Lansdale as operations officer. The report was to be completed in one week.

The final version, "A Program of Action to Prevent Communist Domination of South Vietnam," was submitted to Kennedy on May 6. The victory plans recommended by the Gilpatric Task Force called for the use of U.S. ground troops and a bilateral treaty between the United States and the GVN. Both proposals stood in direct violation of the Geneva Accords, but were required because "it is essential that President Diem's full confidence in and communication with the United States be restored promptly."

Diem suspected that the United States was wavering in its commitment to the GVN on several grounds, some rational, such as the negotiations for a Laotion settlement, others irrational, such as his belief that the United States had played a role in the November coup attempt. But it was Diem's suspicions, not the justifications for them, that compelled Washington to give serious consideration to using ground troops and to signing a treaty with the GVN, even though Diem's policies were demonstrably bankrupt and the suggested remedies violated international law. The feeling was beginning to take hold in Washington that if the United States took over the job, Diem's policies would not matter. This belief was to be reinforced during the crisis in the fall of 1961, when Secretary of State Dean Rusk recommended that the United States simply take over the machinery of government in the South, should ground troops be introduced into the combat theater.

Circumventing international law was viewed by the Kennedy Administration as a problem far less significant than that of building support for a bankrupt GVN. Nevertheless, the question exercised the minds of officials in Washington. In his report to Kennedy, Gilpatric, for example, advanced the following argument to meet the charge that the United States was flouting the law:

On the grounds that the Geneva Accords have placed inhibitions upon free world action while at the same time placing no restrictions upon the Communists, Ambassador Nolting should be instructed to enter into preliminary discussions with Diem regarding the possibility of a defensive security alliance despite the inconsistency of such actions with the Geneva Accords. This action would be based on the premise that such an undertaking is justified in international law as representing a refusal to be bound by the Accords in a degree and manner beyond that which the other party to the Accords has shown a willingness to honor. Communist violations, therefore, justify the establishment of the security arrangement herein recommended. Concurrently, Defense should study the military advisability of committing U.S. forces in Vietnam.

This was the explanation that would be given to the American public: Communist violations of the Accords justified the bilateral treaty and the use of U.S. ground forces. But would this explanation also convince official Washington of the need to deploy troops? Indeed not. In the same report, Gilpatric informed Kennedy why U.S. troops were needed in Vietnam. "U.S. forces are required," Gilpatric wrote, "to provide maximum psychological impact in deterrence of *further* Communist aggression from North Vietnam, China, or the Soviet Union." They would also serve an additional purpose: "to provide significant military resistance to *potential* North Vietnam Communist and/or Chinese Communist action." (emphasis added)

The U.S. public was to be told that Washington had a legal right to deploy troops in response to actual Communist transgressions, while privately Washington would decide to act because of "potential" Communist action. Of course, "further" aggressions from China or the Soviet Union could hardly be equated with past violations, especially since neither country had set foot in South Vietnam. Indeed, Russia had sponsored the two Vietnams for membership in the United Nations as late as 1959. "Further" aggressions from the North, such as reactivating the guerrilla apparatus in the South, an apparatus manned by Southern cadres and fed by Southern peasants, were

34

Hanoi's delayed response to the initial transgression by the GVN, which in collusion with Washington, had refused to consult with the North or hold elections in the South, as required by the Geneva Accords.

Thus, Washington's reason for deploying combat troops directly contradicted the explanation that would be given to the press and to Congress. Washington had decided that the way to manipulate international law was to fool the American people.

On May 11, President Kennedy, after reviewing the findings of the Gilpatric Task Force, issued a National Security Action Memorandum (NSAM) which contained several important decisions on Vietnam. Such memoranda, written by the Special Assistant to the President for National Security Affairs, McGeorge Bundy, were used to convey Presidential orders to all agencies that were to carry them out, or needed to know about them. The NSAM of May 11 stated:

1. The U.S. objective is to prevent Communist domination of South Vietnam.
2. A further increase in GVN forces from 170,000 to 200,000 is to be assumed.
3. Defense Department is directed to examine the size and composition of U.S. forces in the event that such forces are committed to Vietnam.
4. The United States will seek to increase the confidence of Diem.
5. The Ambassador should begin negotiations for a bilateral arrangement with Vietnam.
6. The program for covert action is approved.

Gilpatric asked the JCS their opinion on the desirability of deploying U.S. forces to Vietnam. They recommended immediate deployment of a sufficient number to achieve the objectives set forth in the Gilpatric report. To set the machinery in motion, the JCS added, Diem should "be encouraged to request that the United States fulfill its SEATO obligations. . . . Upon receipt of this request, suitable forces could be immediately deployed."

Vice President Johnson was dispatched to Vietnam to shore up Diem's confidence in the U.S. commitment by "encouraging" him to request U.S. ground troops. Referring to Diem as "the Winston Churchill of the Orient," Johnson asked him to make this request. But much to Washington's chagrin, Diem told Johnson that he did not want foreign troops on Vietnamese soil, except in the event of overt aggression. Moreover, he pointed out, the presence of U.S. troops would contravene and nullify the Geneva Accords. The semblance of legality could be preserved, he added, if American troops were channeled through the MAAG screen.

After Johnson's visit, Diem sent a letter to President Kennedy expressing gratitude for Johnson's offer of assistance. "I was most deeply gratified by this gracious gesture by your distinguished Vice President, particularly as we have not become accustomed to being asked for our own views as to our needs," he wrote, concluding with the reminder that "we can count on the material support from your great country which will be so essential to achieving final victory." Material support, not U.S. troops, would be furnished by Washington; otherwise, Diem would make himself even more vulnerable to the Communist charge that he was a colonialist.

During the summer of 1961, when the situation in Indochina deteriorated, Diem changed his mind and requested a treaty and troops from the United States. On October 1, Nolting reported that Diem wanted a bilateral defense treaty with the United States; on the thirteenth, Diem requested ground troops. These requests coincided with the conclusion of Defense Department and JCS studies, both of which advised the President to dispatch

U.S. troops to Vietnam, as well as with the announcement of a forthcoming "fact-finding mission" to Vietnam by two White House advisers, General Maxwell Taylor and Walt W. Rostow.

The Defense Department's study of the Viet Cong movement produced the discovery that the men and material originated in the South, not the North. The Department found that although the level of infiltration from the north was increasing, the "vast majority of Viet Cong troops are of local origin." If Hanoi was not furnishing the troops, was it at least furnishing the supplies? "There is little evidence of major supplies from outside sources," the Defense Department study found, "most arms being captured or stolen from GVN forces or from the French during the Indochina war." The North had given moral support to the insurgents, but little else. What should the United States do?

Having determined that the Viet Cong movement was local in origin, the Defense Department recommended that 11,000 U.S. combat troops and 11,800 support troops be deployed to Vietnam for the purpose of sealing the border against any possible future infiltration from the North. But, the Department added, these troops would be insufficient to establish an anti-Communist government in the South. "The ultimate force requirements [for that purpose] cannot be estimated with any precision," the Department stated. "Three divisions would be a guess."

The Joint Chiefs of Staff, in their reply to Gilpatric, reasoned that the North would rely still further upon a policy of infiltration if SEATO and U.S. troops were deployed in the South. The JCS speculated that it would be uncharacteristic of the North to respond with an overt invasion of the South, but, in the event that it did, the United States would have to send in three divisions. If China threw its weight into the struggle, then six U.S.

divisions, or a total of 205,000 men, would be required, and the use of nuclear weapons would become a distinct possibility.

The CIA took the Viet Cong threat less seriously than the Defense Department did, and identified the non-Communist (perhaps one should say anti-Communist) South as the immediate danger to Diem. The agency wrote:

> Most immediate threat to Diem is not a military takeover by the Communists but the mounting danger of an internal coup by disgruntled military and civilian members of the government who are critical of Diem's leadership. These critics hold that Diem's heavy hand in all operations of the government is not only hampering the anti-Communist military effort but is steadily alienating the populace.

Should a SEATO task force be dispatched to Vietnam as an alternative to, U.S. troops—one of the contingency plans circulating in Washington at the time—the CIA, like the JCS, discounted the likelihood of a Northern invasion. Hanoi's strategy, the Agency believed, would be "to play upon possible SEATO weariness over maintaining substantial forces." Once this weariness became evident, "the Asian members would soon become disenchanted and look to the U.S. to do something to lessen the burden and to solve the problem." Whether this something would be a sizable number of U.S. ground troops, as favored by the JCS, or the use of nuclear weapons, as contemplated by CINCPAC, was left undecided.

If the CIA analysis was correct, the United States faced the possibility of a major war on the Asian mainland for the purpose of defending the narrow base of the Diem regime against its own people. Even the anti-Communist opposition in the South was rapidly being transmuted into a Communist monolith, located either in Moscow or Peking.

Nevertheless, some advisers began to argue for war. William Bundy, who had recently changed position from the CIA's Far East expert to Deputy Secretary of Defense for International Security Affairs, echoed Walt Rostow's belief that the fall of 1961 was the "now or never" period for the United States. If America acted promptly and aggressively, Bundy argued, there was a 70 percent chance that it would "clean up the situation." There was a 30 percent chance that "we would wind up like the French in 1954; white men can't win this kind of war." Having weighed the options, Bundy concluded that a preemptive strike was advisable, and recommended "early and hard hitting operations."

THE TAYLOR–ROSTOW MISSION

On October 11, 1961, President Kennedy authorized the Taylor–Rostow mission to Vietnam. Its purpose was to examine the feasibility of dispatching U.S. troops; Kennedy specifically recommended that the mission look into the question of troop requirements. One option would be to send fewer U.S. combat troops than the 22,800 identified in the Defense Department plan, but enough to "establish a U.S. presence in Vietnam." A second dispensed with U.S. combat forces entirely, and envisioned a stepped-up version of what is now called the "Vietnamization" program. According to this plan, the United States would increase its training of Vietnamese units and furnish more U.S. equipment, "particularly helicopters and other light aircraft, trucks, and other ground transport."

Two days after Kennedy announced the Taylor–Rostow mission, Diem, who had heretofore refused to "request" U.S. combat troops, met with Ambassador Nolting, and asked that the U.S. government provide South Vietnam with the aid that had been secretly discussed when the

Taylor–Rostow mission was being planned. Vice President Thuan, speaking for President Diem, requested an additional squadron of AD-6 fighter bombers, U.S. civilian contract pilots for helicopters, transport planes to be used for noncombat operations, and U.S. combat units to be introduced into South Vietnam as combat-trainer units.

Diem had changed his mind. Originally ashamed to be dependent upon a U.S. presence and afraid to scuttle the Geneva Accords, he set aside these considerations once it became clear that a neutral Laos was about to emerge from the negotiations then under way. According to Diem, a neutral Laos would be useful to the Communists. They could then cross the western border at will, infiltrate into the South, and crush him. The terrain in Laos was more difficult to defend, and the Communists were strong enough there to strike a final blow. Laos he argued, had been used to trap the Americans into conceding South Vietnam. Having enticed the Americans into a settlement that made it look as if the Americans had lost nothing, the Communists could concentrate all of their energies on seizing South Vietnam. To counter this strategy, Diem wanted some immediate assurance that the United States would remain committed to the South. Such assurance would require a bilateral treaty and the presence of U.S. combat troops. Only this would dissuade the North from pursuing a militant policy and convince those elements in the South that were still loyal to Diem that a Laotian settlement was not the death warrant for the GVN.

The Kennedy Administration had discovered that it was impossible to avoid war. The only question was where and when. If Laos was not settled quickly, the United States would have to pour in troops, with small chance of success. But to negotiate a neutral Laos meant that U.S. troops would have to be deployed to South Vietnam, thus increasing the likelihood of a direct confrontation. Washington had painted itself into a corner—either war in Laos now or war in Vietnam in the future. Kennedy chose the latter.

The Taylor–Rostow mission stopped at Hawaii on the way to Vietnam and discussions were held with Admiral Felt, head of CINCPAC. Rostow asked about contingency plans in the event that open warfare broke out with the North. One question in particular concerned the use of nuclear weapons. Felt replied, "Plans were drawn on the assumption that tactical nuclear weapons will be used if required and that we can anticipate requests being made for their use if action expands into a Phase 4 situation." (Phase 4 involved a North Vietnamese and Chinese invasion of the South.)

Once in Vietnam, Taylor and Rostow explored ways of introducing U.S. ground troops. They had decided that Diem needed them to preserve his rule, but they also recognized that such a course would damage America's image as a peacekeeper. The general and the professor wondered how the United States could go to war while appearing to preserve the peace. While they were pondering this question, Vietnam was suddenly struck by a deluge. It was as if God had wrought a miracle. American soldiers, acting on humanitarian impulses, could be dispatched to save Vietnam not from the Viet Cong, but from the floods. McGarr, the Chief of MAAG, stated that Taylor favored "moving in U.S. military personnel for humanitarian purposes with subsequent retention if desirable." He added, "This is an excellent opportunity to minimize adverse publicity."

Taylor himself viewed the flood-relief task force more ambitiously. It would be the most efficient way to deal with world opinion, assuage Diem's fears, and allay Kennedy's reservations. World opinion would be swayed by humanitarian considerations. The colonial stain would not unduly tarnish Diem's image because the flood-relief program clearly was not intended to "take over the respon-

sibility for the security of the country." Finally, and perhaps most important, Taylor's plan contained a built-in
excuse to withdraw—a feature intended to overcome
Kennedy's objections. The President, it was well known,
believed that it was far more difficult to remove troops
than to introduce them. Taylor wrote to Kennedy, "As
the task is a specific one, we can extricate our troops when
it is done if we so desire. Alternatively, we can phase
them into other activities if we wish to remain longer."

Having invented a scheme that would enable the leaders in Saigon and Washington to placate their respective
constituencies, Taylor then turned his attention from his
preoccupation with politics to the military consequences.
He recommended that the President deploy 8,000 ground
troops and acknowledged that most of them would be
used for logistical purposes. Such a token gesture could
not be expected to have great military significance, but it
surely involved the risk, as Taylor put it, of "escalating
into a major war in Asia." Even if this danger did not
materialize, the initial commitment would make it "difficult to resist the pressure to reinforce." Once the blood
of a single American soldier had been spilled, the President would assume the role of Commander-in-Chief and
would be obliged to discharge his constitutional duty to
protect the troops in the field. This obligation made it
unlikely that troops would be removed and far more
likely that additional troops would be sent over. The
technical device of a built-in exit might be superseded
by the political reality of a built-in escalation. And with
the DRV and the Viet Cong committed to a policy of
attrition, the United States would then be locked into a
long struggle at the edge of the Communist world. Such
a struggle would take place, unfortunately, at a time when
"the strategic reserve of the U.S. forces is presently so
weak that we can ill afford any detachment of forces."
Taylor, in effect, told Kennedy to dispatch a few thousand

combat troops which could not turn the tide of military battle, which invited a major war, provoked an indefinite and indecisive conflict, and depleted the U.S. reserve. Why should Kennedy do this? Because, as Taylor said, "I do not believe that our program to save South Vietnam will succeed without it."

The symbolic gesture of stationing a few thousand U.S. troops would save South Vietnam, Taylor argued, because it would inform the Communists of the "seriousness of the U.S. intent to resist" and would raise the "national morale" of the South. Taylor predicted that the North would back down if the United States exhibited a fixed resolve to defend the South. That resolve had to be conveyed in the form of a clear message to Hanoi that the United States would take offensive action against the North if it did not stop supporting the Viet Cong. A small task force was a harbinger of greater devastation. The North would desist once it understood this message because, in Taylor's words, "North Vietnam is extremely vulnerable to conventional bombing, a weakness which should be exploited diplomatically in convincing Hanoi to lay off South Vietnam."

The small task force, along with other forms of United States–GVN cooperation, not only would alarm Hanoi, but in the South would "reverse the present downward trend, stimulate an offensive spirit and build up morale." As Rostow commented to Diem at this time, "That secret of turning point is offensive action."

The twin purposes of discouraging the North and encouraging the South became the strategy that was to be relied upon throughout the Vietnam war. The same arguments that were advanced for the first time in 1961 were repeated in 1965 when Washington made the decision to embark on Operation Rolling Thunder. By the summer of 1965, however, lifting Southern morale was no longer viewed as necessary to win the war. The decision to send in the first 500,000 combat troops was justified solely by the need to convince the Communists that the United States was serious.

The strategy has remained surprisingly constant, guiding American policy for the better part of a decade. The architects of the strategy, Taylor and Rostow, did not envision the small task force of 8,000 men as the "final word." It was simply the first lesson they planned for the leadership in Hanoi.

By its major premise—that Hanoi would back down only if it *knew* the United States was prepared to attack North Vietnam directly—the strategy entailed a built-in escalation. Events had to follow in a monotonous but natural order: increase the size of U.S. support troops in the South; institute covert operations against the North; threaten to bomb the North; bomb the North; pour U.S. combat troops into the South as rapidly as possible; invade Cambodia; invade Laos; invade the North?; destroy the North?; etc.

The strategy required not only that the United States make it known that it would attack the North directly, but also that the United States not obliterate the North. To threaten to destroy the Communist regime in Hanoi would risk a direct encounter with China or Russia, a risk that the national security managers wished to avoid. They did not want to fight a nuclear war. They wanted to fight a safe war. The strategy therefore demanded a combination of escalation and moderation.

America would exercise its power in a deliberate and calculated manner in order to hold Hanoi hostage. The term "Hanoi" here is to be taken literally: the rest of Vietnam, indeed all of Indochina, was to become a target. One could say that U.S. strategy was to kill the people while preserving the Hanoi government. Once surrounded by devastation, isolated, and abandoned by her socialist allies, Russia and China, Hanoi would be left with no choice but to submit to a "moderate" but triumphant America.

Although the creation of the task force was its most far-reaching recommendation, the Taylor–Rostow report urged the President to adopt a number of other measures. These were mainly of a military and administrative nature. The report recommended that the personnel in the MAAG mission be increased from 1,103 to 2,612. Moreover, U.S. aircraft, consisting of several helicopter companies, and U.S. crews for supporting or operational missions were to be introduced no later than mid-November. The combat troops, the increase in the size of MAAG, and the use of U.S. aircraft and crews were all violations of the limits on troops and armaments set by the Geneva Accords. The International Security Agency (ISA), reviewing the legality of these recommendations, noted that the additions to MAAG, although a violation of international law, could not easily be proved: discussion between the International Control Commission, which was charged with enforcing the Geneva Accords, and the Embassy could be extended for months, during which time the value of the increase in MAAG's size would be realized.

The use of U.S. helicopters was of a more serious nature, requiring some groundwork to pacify Congress and the press. But combat troops could not so easily be disguised. Their only justification would be their subsequent success, not prior propaganda, and ISA viewed them with deep skepticism. It predicted that the North would respond by infiltrating 15,000 men, which would in turn require three U.S. divisions to offset them. Thus an indefinite war of attrition would be ensured.

The administrative recommendations of Taylor and Rostow were designed to place a number of Americans on four specific levels of the South Vietnamese bureaucracy. First, Americans would work as high-level government advisers. Taylor envisioned "a limited number of

Americans in key ministries." This would mean that U.S. advisers would, in effect, become cabinet officers in the Diem government. Next, "a joint U.S.–Vietnamese Military Survey, down to the provincial level, in each of three corps areas," would engage in a number of tasks, including intelligence, command and control, the build-up of reserves for offensive purposes, and mediation between the military commander and the province chief. The other two functions would be border control operations and "intimate liaison with the Vietnamese Central Intelligence organizations."

The ostensible purpose of giving Americans critical roles in government was that "Vietnamese performance in every domain can be substantially improved if Americans are prepared to work side by side with the Vietnamese." Taylor designated these administrative changes as representing a "shift from U.S. advice to limited partnership." The concept of "limited partnership," in fact, meant that the GVN had been negligent in reforming itself in the past, and suggested that the only way to reform the GVN in the future would be for the United States to take it over. With U.S. ground troops in the field, U.S. aircraft controlling the skies, and U.S. civilian personnel administering the cities and provinces, Vietnam would be reformed. Only Washington's own people could fulfill Washington's wishes.

The administrative changes meant that the national security managers had decided that the most effective mechanism for processing reforms through the GVN was for America to take over the government. They were also beginning to understand that the surest way to take over a client state was to introduce ground troops who would ultimately become responsible for the defense of the country. Under such circumstances, the native leader no longer serves as a puppet but rather, in the managers' words, as a "platform" upon which the American military and administrative personnel would be able to operate. Reduced from a leader to a platform, the local ruler of the client state is robbed of the last vestiges of his political life. His value to the mother country is no longer measured by the speed and economy with which he is able to bring about the changes suggested by Washington (the core of his bargaining power). Since the local leader is no longer the source of change, he is not expected to do anything; he is merely expected not to undo anything. The mother country is less interested in gaining than in not losing. That desirable feature of leadership, charisma, gives way to banality. The worth of the leader is now measured by the number of followers he does not lose, the number of riots that do not occur, the number of battles that are not fought.

The leader's role in his own country is purely custodial. His task is to hold things together. To the degree that he performs this function, he has built the platform upon which the troops from the mother country may enter. His obligation to the mother country is to serve as the official greeter of the foreign troops. He is a janitor at home and a master of ceremonies abroad.

The problem with Diem was that he was unable to play a custodial role at home or a ceremonial one abroad. By 1961, he was beginning to lose his followers faster than the United States could increase its personnel in Vietnam. Were this inverse ratio to continue, the moment would come when there would be no platform for American troops to walk on. But this was not clearly perceived in Washington in 1961. When it did become obvious in 1963, Diem was dispensed with. Whereas Ambassador Durbrow had toyed with the idea of eliminating Diem because he was not a reformer, the Kennedy circle would remove him because he had been abandoned by the last of the faithful. Diem's failure to reform would be the alibi for, not the cause of, his downfall.

What was obvious in 1961 was that Kennedy was alarmed about Diem's public image in America. From the point of view of the President of the United States, the local leader must be palatable to the American people if American troops are to be ordered to Vietnam. One explanation for Kennedy's decision to veto the recommendation of all of his senior advisers to send troops to Vietnam was that Diem lacked the image that would qualify him to receive American ground troops. In a discussion of "the famous problem of Diem as an administrator and politician," Taylor suggested three choices that were available to Washington.

The first was to "remove him in favor of a military dictatorship which would give dominance to the military chain of command." The second was to "remove him in favor of a figure of more dilute power who would delegate authority to act in both military and civilian leaders." It was this option that foreshadowed the need for a local leader who could retain a rapidly diminishing constituency, so that the largest number of U.S. troops could be sent. Once the need became apparent, the second choice was axiomatic. Washington would then require someone to perform custodial services in Vietnam and act as an official greeter for American troops, roles played by General Khanh in 1964 and General Thieu after 1965. In 1961, however, Taylor opted for the third choice. He wished to retain Diem in order "to bring about a series of *de facto* administrative changes via persuasion at high levels . . . using the U.S. presence to force the Vietnamese to get their house in order in one area after another." In considering the first two choices, Taylor raised the prospect of a coup, but rejected it because "it would be dangerous for us to engineer a coup under present tense circumstances, since it is by no means certain that we could control its consequences and potentialities for Communist exploitation." In other words, the United States had not yet taken over enough of Vietnam to guarantee the irrelevance of the new leader.

The Taylor–Rostow report had a profound influence on Washington's policy toward Vietnam. The report fashioned the strategy of combined escalation and moderation. By establishing the principle of "limited partnership," a euphemism for American control, it resolved the conflict between the need for efficient prosecution of the war and the need for administrative reform. The previous aim of reform had been to broaden the base of the government to include elements of the loyal opposition. The new focus was on the pace at which American troops entered the field and American bureaucrats entered the government. Broadening the base came to mean turning the reins of government over to the Americans. Once Americans took over, they could juggle the concepts of warfare and welfare according to their own priorities. The battle between these concepts would be waged within the American establishment, with the pacifiers making feeble attempts to reform the military. Reform ultimately came to mean less indiscriminate killing instead of greater citizen participation. Finally, the report defined the qualities of the ideal leader that America would need in Vietnam after it stationed its troops in the field and its bureaucrats in office—qualities that were to be found eventually in the middling leadership of Thieu.

THE RECOMMENDATIONS OF McNAMARA AND RUSK

While the Taylor–Rostow report was circulating in Washington, Secretaries McNamara and Rusk were writing their own recommendations for Vietnam policy. McNamara picked up the thread of Taylor's strategic analysis and Rusk pondered the need for an American seizure of the Vietnamese bureaucracy.

Rusk believed the President should carefully weigh the decision to send in U.S. troops against Diem's unwillingness to "give us something worth supporting." Diem's failure to trust his own commanders and his obstinate refusal to broaden the base of government made it unlikely that a "handful of American troops can have decisive influence." Rusk noted the vital importance that U.S. policy attached to Southeast Asia, but he cautioned against "committing American prestige to a losing horse." His recommendations, however, also presumed a seizure of the internal bureaucracy, the process described by Taylor as "limited partnership." Rusk directed the State Department to draw up a list of expectations "from Diem if our assistance forces us to assume *de facto* direction of South Vietnamese affairs."

While Rusk was elaborating on Taylor's report from the civil side, McNamara accelerated the recommendations from the military side. He accepted the strategy recommended by Taylor, but criticized him for not putting enough muscle behind that strategy. In McNamara's view, the 8,000-man task force would help Diem but would not "convince the other side (whether the shots are called from Moscow, Peiping, or Hanoi) that we mean business. Moreover, it probably will not tip the scales decisively. We would be almost certain to get increasingly mired down in an inconclusive struggle." Since the aim of the strategy was to make the enemy know that the United States would attack directly if it did not disengage itself from the Southern struggle, McNamara concluded:

> . . . the other side can be convinced we mean business only if we accompany the initial force introduction by a clear warning commitment to the full objective stated above, accompanied by a warning through some channel to Hanoi that continued support of the Viet Cong will lead to punitive retaliation against North Vietnam.

McNamara presumed that the other side would attack, not withdraw, in spite of the presence of U.S. troops and a clear statement of intent. The United States would then reply with 205,000 men, or six divisions. Public opinion in America, McNamara believed, "will respond better to a firm initial position than to courses of action that lead us in only gradually."

What is striking about the recommendations by the Secretary of State and the Secretary of Defense is that each, within his particular domain, went beyond the suggestions made by General Taylor. Whereas Taylor spoke of a limited partnership between the GVN and the United States government, Rusk operated on the assumption of a "*de facto* direction of South Vietnamese affairs." With respect to military policy, Taylor boldly conceived a strategy that could well lead to genocide, but he was rather timid in applying it. He wanted to avoid the impression that the United States would send its troops into actual combat, and urged the flood-relief idea upon the President as a cover to preserve a peaceful image. McNamara, however, not only was willing to embrace the need for 8,000 combat troops, but seemed to be devising a preemptive strategy by calling on a second-strike capability of six divisions as a response to the Northern invasion that would be touched off by the initial force. While Taylor saw the flood-relief task force as a humanitarian cover to avoid a larger war, McNamara viewed it as a way to provoke the North into that larger war. Taylor, moreover, counseled the President on the importance of a peaceful image for domestic public opinion. At best, Taylor reasoned, the American public would have to be led to accept a gradual involvement. McNamara, on the other hand, believed that America would much more likely support a firm hand. Taylor either eschewed war altogether by projecting such logical incompatibilities as a bold strategy and a quiescent task force, or equivocated by never pulling out or pushing in. McNamara, just recovering from his personal revulsion at the possibility of a nuclear holocaust over Berlin, seemed to be willing to prosecute a large conventional war. In view of the advanced state of U.S. technology, such a war, if carried on for years, could produce effects amounting to nuclear devastation.

KENNEDY'S DECISION

In spite of the agreement among his senior advisers that ground troops should be dispatched, Kennedy refused. He could have cited many reasons to support his decision. One was that the introduction of U.S. combat forces in Vietnam would cripple the discussions for a negotiated settlement in Laos. British Ambassador Ormsby-Gore had told Rusk on November 7 that "the introduction of U.S. troops would not only complicate the situation, but make it impossible to get anywhere on Laos." A week later, Ambassador Alphand of France told Rusk that further escalation would undermine the Geneva negotiations and compound the risk of "mass intervention" by the Soviet Union. Alphand also reminded the Secretary of "difficulties for the West of fighting in Vietnam." Rusk, however, took this to mean that Europe and America might have to part ways. Rusk explained that it "would be difficult for U.S. opinion and friendly countries to accept a repetition of Laos in Vietnam." Southeast Asia, he concluded, was "more important to the United States than to Europe." Indeed, "if the loss of Southeast Asia was at stake, and Europeans did not agree with our policies, there might have to be a divergence." Rusk's attitude demonstrates a fundamental shift in the direction of American foreign policy. Hereafter the national security managers, except for George Ball, were to reject the need for a multilateral response and affirm the will to proceed alone in Asia. The first sign of this shift occurred on January 19, 1961, just before Kennedy's inauguration when, during discussions with the President-elect, Eisenhower told him, "It is imperative that Laos be defended. The United States should accept this task with our allies, if we could persuade them, and alone if we could not. Our unilateral intervention would be our last desperate hope in the event we were unable to prevail upon the other signatories to join us."

Kennedy's advisers wholeheartedly supported Eisenhower's position, but had to wait for Johnson to apply it to Vietnam, not Laos. Kennedy himself, in 1961, seemed to be more impressed with the arguments advanced by the British and French Ambassadors than with Eisenhower's position or with Rusk's acceptance of it. Kennedy, it could be argued, was yet to be persuaded that U.S. foreign policy was destined to go it alone in Asia. In addition to shattering the Laotian settlement, the dispatch of troops to Vietnam at a time when the Berlin crisis could again erupt increased Kennedy's "expressed concern over a two-front war." This does not mean, however, that Kennedy was willing to preside over the liquidation of the fledgling American Empire in Southeast Asia. The fear of a two-front war, according to Arthur Schlesinger, Jr., would have to be weighed against the fear "that an American retreat in Asia might upset the whole world balance."

Other factors must be considered to explain Kennedy's veto of combat troops. One way to understand the President's motives is to recall the decisions he made and try to discover what light they shed on decisions that he did not make. We do know, for example, that Kennedy sent troops to Vietnam, referring to them as support troops, though their combat role was extensive. Therefore, we can conclude that Kennedy saw the need to disguise their combat function. We also know that the number sent during his administration ultimately doubled the initial figure of 8,000 recommended by Taylor and Rostow. Therefore, Kennedy saw the need to introduce them into Vietnam gradually instead of at one stroke. Finally, we know that Kennedy began a campaign of covert activities against North Vietnam—a campaign that marked the switch to direct offensive actions but was disguised so that Washington could publically disavow its own role.

Kennedy's policy toward Vietnam, then, was to accelerate the war while denying that he was doing it. His policy was to prosecute a private war. He was willing to go it alone in Asia, but not to admit it. He disregarded the counsel of his advisers only to the extent that they preferred a public war.

The President, clearly, did not believe the American people would support him in his decision to escalate the level of combat. This does not mean that Kennedy thought the American people would have been opposed to a war in Indochina under any circumstances. It simply means that in 1961 the American public would not support a war whose ostensible purpose was to preserve the Diem regime. The war would be repulsive because the leader was odious. In 1963, when the self-immolation of protesting Buddhist monks became a daily event, Diem's image abroad deteriorated and became incompatible with the American presence. The American people could resign themselves to an indefinite war, but not when the character of the regime, personified by Diem, Nhu, and Madame Nhu, was so obnoxious. Washington concluded that Diem would have to be eliminated before the war could be escalated.

While Diem was too repellent to be given American combat troops, he was not pliable enough to accept American bureaucrats. Rusk, as we have seen, presumed that America would undertake a *de facto* direction of South Vietnamese affairs." The Taylor–Rostow report had anticipated a "limited partnership" between the GVN and the United States government. Diem quickly dashed these hopes. Vice President Thuan told Ambassador Nolting that Diem's "attitude seemed to be that the United States was asking great concessions of GVN in the realm of its sovereignty, in exchange for little additional help." When Nolting pressed Diem directly on the need for a close partnership, Diem informed him that "Vietnam did not want to be a protectorate."

By word and deed, Diem demonstrated that he would no more broaden his decision-making councils to include Americans than he would do so to include other Vietnamese. To turn over the internal bureaucracy to the Americans, Diem had told the Ambassador to Thailand, Kenneth Young, would "give a monopoly on nationalism to the Communists." The only conditions under which Diem would accept a U.S. directorate were the dispatch of U.S. combat troops and a bilateral treaty. If he was certain that the Americans would openly defend him, then he could afford to come out openly as their puppet. But Washington would not openly defend Diem because he did not seem worth defending in public.

In these circumstances Kennedy made the decision not to send in combat troops, or rather, to fight a private war. In NSAM 111, Kennedy, observing widespread criticism of Diem's regime, stated that U.S. support would be conditional upon whether real reforms were instituted by Diem. The President said:

Rightly or wrongly his regime is widely criticized abroad and in the U.S., and if we are to give our substantial support, we must be able to point to real administrative, political, and social reforms and a real effort to widen its base that will give maximum confidence to the American people, as well as to world opinion that our efforts are not directed towards the support of an unpopular or ineffective regime, but rather towards supporting the combined efforts

55

of all the non-Communist people of the GVN against a Communist takeover.

In the very next clause of the NSAM, however, Kennedy made the decision to send U.S. troops and informed the American Ambassador that these troops should be seen as the equivalent of combat forces.

It is anticipated that one of the first questions President Diem will raise with you after your presentation of the above joint proposals will be that of introducing U.S. combat troops. You are authorized to remind him that the actions we already have in mind involve a substantial number of U.S. military personnel for operational duties in Vietnam, and that we believe that these forces performing crucial missions can greatly increase the capacity of GVN forces to win their war against the Viet Cong.

U.S. firepower and U.S. troops would be immediately sent to Vietnam without the necessity of any "real administrative, political and social reforms." What was desirable was that Diem's image be improved.

In the next clause of the memorandum, Kennedy dispensed with the need for the GVN "to widen its base . . . towards supporting the combined efforts of all the non-Communist people of the GVN against a Communist takeover." Kennedy admonished the Ambassador:

You should inform Diem that, in our minds, the concept of the joint undertaking envisages a much closer relationship than the present one of acting in an advisory capacity only. We would expect to share in the decision-making processes in the political, economic and military fields as they affected the security situation.

Reform, to Kennedy, ultimately meant that Diem needed an attractive image in America, and that Washington needed to seize the bureaucratic machinery in Vietnam. If neither was forthcoming, Diem would be eliminated, and a "genuine and real" puppet put in his place.

3 /

WASHINGTON MANAGES THE PRIVATE WAR: 1962–1963

The private war required dispatching U.S. combat troops to Vietnam to perform "operational duties" and withholding that fact from the American public. The troops were put under the jurisdiction of the newly-organized Military Assistance Command, Vietnam (MACV), but their combat role was disguised. The public was told that U.S. personnel would only "advise" the South Vietnamese army.

Another component of the private war was the initiation of covert activities. Begun in the spring of 1961, only six weeks after John F. Kennedy had assumed the Presidency, these activities continued without interruption up to the launching of Operation Rolling Thunder in February 1965, the beginning of the overt war by Lyndon Johnson.

In March 1961, Kennedy instructed the national security agencies to "make every possible effort to launch guerrilla operations in Viet-Minh territory at the earliest possible time." He directed the Secretary of Defense and the Director of the CIA to furnish plans for covert programs against the North both in the near term and in the "longer future periods." Two months later, Kennedy approved the program for covert actions that had been proposed by the Vietnam Task Force, a group working out of the State Department and then under the leadership of Sterling Cottrell. Cottrell had accompanied Taylor and Rostow on their mission to Vietnam in the fall of 1961 and had urged the President not to introduce combat troops into the South. In the spring of 1961 he recommended that the President use South Vietnamese troops for commando raids and sabotage in North Vietnam and Laos.

The President agreed. One hundred days after he was elected President, he ordered agents to be sent into North Vietnam who were to be resupplied by Vietnamese civilian mercenary aircrews. Special GVN forces were meanwhile to infiltrate into Southeast Laos to locate and attack Communist bases, and other teams trained by the Special Forces were to be used for sabotage and light harassment inside North Vietnam. Finally, Kennedy ordered flights over North Vietnam to drop leaflets. Two days after Kennedy authorized the Taylor–Rostow mission and before the mission arrived in Vietnam, the President ordered guerrilla ground action, "including the use of U.S. advisers if necessary against Communist aerial resupply missions in the vicinity of Tchepone, Laos." In December, immediately after he shelved Taylor's proposal to deploy 8,000 combat troops in the South, Kennedy adopted a CIA-sponsored program to recruit South Vietnamese personnel for the purpose of "forming an underwater demolition team to operate in strategic maritime areas of North Vietnam."

By the end of 1961, the private war consisted of covert operations directed against North Vietnam and Laos, and the concealed use of U.S. air and ground combat personnel against the Viet Cong in South Vietnam. Each element of the private war increased in tempo and intensity throughout 1962 and 1963. By the time Kennedy was assassinated, the United States had 16,500 troops in South Vietnam pretending they were not fighting, and the Special Forces were executing a host of covert programs in North Vietnam and Laos.

During its thirty-three months in office, the Kennedy Administration managed and directed an illicit war. By sending an additional 1,000 troops to Vietnam in 1961, Kennedy broke through the MAAG ceiling and violated the Geneva Accords, which had set firm limitations on the outside men and materiel which could be introduced into Vietnam. Speaking to Rusk at a National Security Council meeting in November 1961, Kennedy defined the Presidential manner proper to breaching international laws: "Why do we take onus, say we are going to break the Geneva Accords? Why not remain silent? Don't say this ourselves!"

The Accords, of course, had been violated before. But the decision to conceal violations—and the developing war—from the American public was new. That the Bay of Pigs, the U-2 flights over the Soviet Union, and attempted coups in various parts of the world had also been covert enterprises does not diminish the special significance of the Vietnam undertaking. Here, for the first time, covert activity no longer crystallized into a single event, as with the Bay of Pigs. In Vietnam, the "black stuff" became the usual way of doing business; the war itself was covert. Nor does it suffice to say that the U-2 flights were stretched out through time. The purpose of these flights was spying; they were repetitions of a single act; and they were placed under the jurisdiction of the CIA, an agency restricted to covert acts. In Vietnam, as we shall see below, several covert programs were put together to create a pattern of warfare, rather than spying, and these programs were instituted and managed by the government itself.

ROOM 303

In 1962 and 1963, two agencies in Washington managed the Vietnam War—the 303 Committee and the Special Group Counter-Insurgency (SGCI).

The 303 Committee, taking its name from the room number at the Executive Office Building where it met once a week, came into being as a direct consequence of the egregious blundering at the Bay of Pigs in the spring of 1961. Kennedy, appalled at the military incompetence shown by the fiasco and embarrassed by the public image it created, was determined to make sure that the covert activities of the CIA did not contradict U.S. foreign policy and that they were not beyond the capabilities of the military. Thereafter, CIA programs had to be cleared in advance. This was the task of the 303 Committee, whose jurisdiction came to include every important covert program conducted anywhere in the world, including Vietnam. The membership of the Committee included the Deputy Secretary of Defense, the Deputy Undersecretary of State, the Special Assistant to the President for National Security Affairs, and the Deputy Director of Intelligence of the CIA. During the Kennedy years, these offices were held, respectively, by Roswell Gilpatric, U. Alexis Johnson, McGeorge Bundy, and Richard Helms. The Chairman of the Committee was McGeorge Bundy, who had been given his choice between chairing the Special Group Counter-Insurgency and the 303 Committee.

To the extent that Vietnam was a covert war in 1962 and 1963, the 303 Committee managed the war. It did this by approving and revising the programs that defined American covert participation in the war. At least four major programs were authorized and supervised by the 303 Committee—Operation Farmhand, the training of the Montagnards, DeSoto patrols, and 34a operations.

Operation Farmhand was the first covert program approved by the 303 Committee for Vietnam. Under this program South Vietnamese personnel were airlifted into North Vietnam in the spring of 1961, to "commit sabotage, spy and harass the enemy." Trained by the army's Special Forces, who were themselves detached and put under the control of the CIA, the commandos were invariably arrested as soon as they landed in the North. In many instances, personnel would have to be conscripted to accept an assignment. Frequently, they would show up drunk or fail to appear at all. In the field the program was a total failure, but, strategically, it informed the North that direct measures were to be taken against it.

The second major program authorized by the 303 Committee was the training of the Montagnards in South Vietnam, who had managed to preserve their ethnic identity over the centuries. They were local tribesmen whose loyalty never extended beyond their own clan, and who were as opposed to the encroachments of the GVN as they were to the solicitations of the Viet Cong. Because they inhabited an area that bordered an infiltration route from North to South, the CIA believed that they could be trained into a force of warriors to be used in attacks against the Viet Cong. The CIA felt that the bonds of affiliation among ethnic minorities could be easily nourished and exploited; that nomadic tribes, rather than landed peasants, could be made into warriors and moved more easily from one assignment to another. As warriors, the Montagnards took their orders directly from the

Agency, in return for which they were liberally paid and promised autonomy from the GVN. The GVN neither consented to nor complied with this promise. By the end of 1963, 30,000 local tribesmen had been armed and trained. This work had been contracted out from the CIA to the Special Forces. Eventually, the Montagnards were formed into units known as Civilian Irregular Defense Groups (CIDG). They were used for various types of operations, and were noted primarily for their brutality and terrorism. CIDG units were used to repress the Southern peasantry as well as for armed incursions into the North. As soon as the program registered a degree of success, the Military Assistance Command, Vietnam, in an attempt to break the autonomy of the Special Forces, removed the program from the CIA and placed it under its own jurisdiction.

CIA training of the Montagnards in South Vietnam had its counterpart among the Meo tribesmen in Laos. The Meo, too, were a local clan whose latent warrior tendencies and antipathy toward central rule were carefully nurtured by the Agency. By training and paying the Montagnards and Meo tribesmen, the CIA, in effect, created a force of warriors directly under its command. The conflict between the local tribesmen and the central government, fostered by the CIA, ran parallel to a larger conflict within the U.S. structure—a conflict between the Special Forces and the Joint Chiefs of Staff. Just as the local tribesmen were promised their autonomy from the central government by the CIA, so the Special Forces had been established as an autonomous force, to take their commands directly from the President and circumvent the JCS. During the course of the Indochina war, the local tribesmen were eventually reduced to subservience by the central government and the Special Forces were taken over by the JCS. The "guerrillas" within the host country and the "guerrillas" within the mother country were broken and absorbed by the host and mother, respectively. But the idea of developing a guerrilla force within the host country, originated by the CIA, may well prefigure a structural development for the imperial army of the future. The conflict between the Special Forces and the JCS, on the one hand, and the local tribesmen and the central government, on the other, reflects a larger conflict between the client state and the imperial power. The United States, as the imperial power, has encountered grave difficulties in developing effective and loyal armies within its client states. Neither the Royal Laotian Army nor the ARVN has been able to hold its own against the people's army embodied by the Viet Cong and the Pathet Lao. It was as a direct result of this difficulty that the CIA attempted to build an army of local tribesmen. This guerrilla army was an astonishing success when measured against the regular armies of the client states. When the JCS set out to break the autonomy of the Special Forces, it fortuitously picked up the guerrilla army of local tribesmen under its own command. The structural development, then, was one whereby JCS, the military organ of the mother country, was able to employ local tribesmen directly as its new army. With this one stroke the JCS offset the twin difficulties of relying upon a client army and relying upon troops conscripted at home. Neither American boys nor the client's boys wished to fight in a people's war. What could be better cannon fodder to use against the people than a pre-people, i.e., clansmen? The courage of the local tribe and the technology of the imperial power were in the process of uniting to do battle with the people and their guerrilla organizations.

The third program begun by the 303 Committee was the use of DeSoto patrols. Originated in 1962 and approved by the President, it authorized U.S. destroyers to operate along the North Vietnamese coast and to stimulate the radar of the enemy so that the position and type of radar could be fixed and identified.

After the DeSoto patrols had been approved by Kennedy and the policy had been formulated by the 303 Committee, the program was submitted to the JCS for implementation. The JCS put the program under the jurisdiction of the Joint Center for Intelligence at JCS headquarters in Washington. The Ops Center, as it was called, made up the tentative schedules and forwarded them to CINCPAC (Commander-in-Chief, Pacific) in Hawaii. CINCPAC selected the precise dates for the DeSoto patrols and sent orders to the Seventh Fleet. Informational copies of these orders were also sent to MACV in Saigon. The question of who selected and kept track of the timing of DeSoto patrols was to assume critical importance in the Gulf of Tonkin incident of August 1964.

CINCPAC plan 34a, drawn up in the fall of 1963 as an annex to the entire CINCPAC plan for all of Southeast Asia, was the covert plan directed against the North. It consisted of two parts: psychological operations and hit-and-run attacks. The latter included amphibious raids by the Vietnamese in areas "south of the Tonkin Delta having little or no security." This part was subsequently expanded to encompass the use of Swift torpedo boats to shell the Northern mainland and kidnap Northern personnel. Plan 34a, too, was assigned by the 303 Committee to the JCS for implementation.

THE SPECIAL GROUP FOR COUNTER-INSURGENCY

The second agency in Washington that managed the private war from 1961 to 1963 was the Special Group Counter-Insurgency (SGCI). Organized in response to Khrushchev's speech on wars of national liberation, the

SGCI was created by President Kennedy in NSAM 124, issued in late 1961. The SGCI, like the 303 Committee, met once a week. In fact, its membership was identical to that of the 303 Committee and it met in Room 303 at the Executive Office Building immediately after the Committee adjourned its meetings. Members of the 303 Committee would complete their discussions, sign the orders for the covert programs, and then call the SGCI to order, invite in additional deputies, and turn their attention to the problems of counterinsurgency.

Nonetheless, there were substantial differences between the 303 Committee and the SGCI. The 303 Committee managed the covert operations of the United States government in every area of the world. The programs themselves generally originated with the CIA, although other agencies of government such as the Defense Department, the JCS, and the State Department did submit proposals, many of which became operational. The only requirement for a 303 hearing was that the program be significant and covert. When a program did become operational, it generally involved the services of the Special Forces. The SGCI, on the contrary, never managed covert operations, had a very limited relationship to the CIA, and did not employ the services of the Special Forces. It dealt exclusively with the overt programs of the U.S. government in any nation around the globe that was deemed to be threatened by an insurgency. These programs were under the special jurisdiction of the several national security agencies, including the Defense Department, AID, the State Department, USIA, and the CIA. The purposes of SGCI were to coordinate the overseas programs of the national security agencies, eliminate duplication of effort, and ensure that those projects relating to counterinsurgency were completed. The SGCI supervised the overseas programs of each of the national security agencies.

A counterinsurgency doctrine was written in 1962 and was technically known as "The Overseas Internal Defense Policy of the USA." In NSAM 182, President Kennedy adopted it as the official policy of the United States government. The main premise of the doctrine was that the counterinsurgents should help themselves, but a saving clause was added to the doctrine instructing: "where necessary, introduce U.S. troops."

Thus the 303 Committee was, by and large, responsible for the unofficial policy of the U.S. government toward Vietnam during the period of the private war—the covert activities in North Vietnam and Laos, and the disguised use of U.S. combat troops within South Vietnam. The SGCI, on the other hand, was in charge of the official policy—the policy that was reported in the press and otherwise made known to the American public.

The official policy consisted of a strategic plan which, consistent with the counterinsurgency doctrine, called upon the GVN to defend itself, to win its own war, and to employ Americans in the role of teachers. There were three parts to the plan:

(1) The U.S. government officially accepted Diem as the Premier of South Vietnam, and all aid and assistance were channeled through him.

(2) The strategic hamlet program was devised as the principal weapon to defend the South against further encroachments by the Viet Cong. Strategic hamlets were to provide a method of organizing the rural peasants into larger territorial units to increase their defense capability and weed out Viet Cong. As envisioned by the planners, the hamlets were to expand in accordance along the pattern of an oil blot—dense in the center, blurred at the perimeter. Ideally, a second hamlet would not be built until the first was satis-

factorily organized and properly defensible. Diem's brother, Nhu, was placed in charge of the program and built the hamlets in total disregard of the oil-blot theory. Instead of securing one hamlet before proceeding to the next, Nhu emphasized numbers of hamlets, with the result that none was secure. When Diem was assassinated in 1963, thousands of strategic hamlets collapsed overnight.

(3) The ARVN was to be built into a powerful army which could take the offense against the Viet Cong and regain the territory then held by the Communists. The ARVN, trained by MACV, working in conjunction with the strategic hamlet program under the charismatic leadership of Diem, would, it was anticipated, extend the national sovereignty of the GVN throughout all of South Vietnam.

The national security agencies of the U.S. government devoted all of their efforts to the plan. Their programs were supervised by the SGCI and their projects were completed under the whip of a Special Agency, which ostensibly possessed a blueprint of victory.

The countries under the jurisdiction of the SGCI included Vietnam, Laos, Thailand, Iran, and a half-dozen Latin American nations. Vietnam and Laos were at the top of the list. By the end of 1962, entire meetings were devoted to Vietnam alone. The principal input to the SGCI were weekly reports furnished by the Vietnam Task Force. In time, however, these reports, prepared by Sterling Cottrell and Ben Wood, were considered too meager; other national security agencies, such as the Pentagon, AID, and CIA, began to supply supplementary reports on Vietnam. The reports, whether from the Task Force or the other national security agencies, were discussed at the opening of each meeting. Then, expert witnesses who had just returned from Vietnam would brief the Special Group. Some of the witnesses who appeared before the SGCI on a regular basis were John Richardson, the CIA station chief in Vietnam; Victor Krulak, the head of SACSA (Office of the Special Assistant for Counter-Insurgency and Special Activities); William Jordan, a former *New York Times* reporter and the author of two white papers on Vietnam; Ted Sarong, the Australian attaché; Robert Thompson, the British expert on counterinsurgency and moving force behind the strategic hamlet doctrine; and a Mr. Walton, an ex-marine and head of the police safety division in Vietnam.

Shorthand notes on the discussions at these meetings have been made available to the author. The highlights of these discussions deserve consideration, since they reflect the information that guided official Washington during the period of the private war and the reaction to that information.

The year 1962 has been referred to as the optimistic period in Vietnam. The insurgency was coming under control, persuading McNamara that the United States had turned the corner in Vietnam and American boys would soon be returning home. On May 3, 1962, Sterling Cottrell reported to the Special Group that the United States had "reached the bottom" in Vietnam. Cottrell, it should be recalled, was the head of the Vietnam Task Force, had accompanied Taylor and Rostow on their mission to Vietnam, and had opposed their advice on the issue of ground troops. He supported a low-keyed approach to Vietnam and obviously had a stake in the continuation of the current Vietnam policy. General Lyman Lemnitzer, the Chairman of the JCS, reported on May 17, 1962, that the build-up in defense areas was going well. The military, to a man, could only see benign effects flowing from U.S. policies. On May 31, Cottrell informed the Group that the GVN was increasing the number of strategic hamlets at an "ambitious and uncontrolled rate." On June 20, John McCone, Director of the CIA, warned that the Viet Cong were in the process of moving up to larger-unit action. They were employing heavier weapons, he added, to wipe out strategic hamlets before help could arrive. On November 5, the Task Force told the Group that Viet Cong forces were as strong as ever. They were able to recruit new personnel at a high rate, even though their morale had begun to slip. Cottrell added that the "situation was still in balance."

In 1963, the United States tried again to document its charge that the Viet Cong were being aided by massive infiltration from the North. One task confronting the Special Group was to determine the accuracy of the charge. On January 17, 1963, the Task Force downgraded the infiltration argument by explaining that local recruitment and local supplies were furnished the Viet Cong in the South; the insurgents had little need to be dependent upon the North for either. Taylor, complying with orders from "higher up," said it was important to get information on Northern infiltration and authorized William Jordan to go to Vietnam and develop a substantial report. Washington was becoming embarrassed over the fact that it was increasingly committing itself to intervention in a civil war. On April 5, 1963, the famous meeting of the Special Group was held in which Jordan reported, after spending three months in Vietnam, that "we are unable to document and develop any hard evidence of infiltration after October 1, 1962." Evidence prior to that date strongly indicated the absence of any infiltration. At the same meeting, Robert Thompson attempted to counter Jordan's pessimistic appraisal by forecasting that "U.S. forces are adequate. By the end of the year, troops can begin to be withdrawn."

A State Department representative on the Special Group culled through the various remarks of the U.S. army officers who returned from Vietnam in 1962 and paraphrased their observations thus: "If free elections were to be held in South Vietnam in 1962, Ho would get 70 percent of the popular vote." Because of Ho's popularity, he added, wholesale supplies in the South and ready recruitment of personnel were available to the Viet Cong. Only a trickle of supplies plus the original covert apparatus had been furnished by the North. The State Department official pointed out that all insurgencies receive some outside help. A devotee of military history, he observed that there "has never been a case of an isolated insurgency. Not even the U.S. War of Independence was an isolated insurgency."

This same official was one of the authors of the Counter-Insurgency Doctrine of the U.S. government. He contrasted Communist Party doctrine with U.S. doctrine on the necessity of outside help for an insurgency, noting that Communist doctrine

> emphasizes the fact that the insurgency should be home-grown, and that major communist powers, especially China, do not pour in masses of outside assistance. This enables the insurgents to retain their own independence so that they can sustain themselves over the long haul. Communist Party doctrine stands in radical contrast to the U.S. doctrine of counter-insurgency, which demands massive support by us and which turns the counter-insurgents into our dependents, sapping their morale and capacity to fight.

He supported this comparison with the evidence accumulated by the Special Group showing that all weapons captured by the United States during the period of the private war were either homemade or had been previously captured from the GVN/USA. "Throughout this time," he stated, "no one had ever found one Chinese rifle or one Soviet weapon used by a VC." His conclusion was that the great weight of evidence and doctrine proved "that the massive aggression theory was completely phony."

The Special Group devoted part of its attention to some of the programs conducted in the field. As early as 1961, the defoliation program, originally designated Operation Hades and subsequently accorded the euphemism Operation Ranchhand, was granted Presidential approval. Limited at first as an experimental measure, it soon became an exercise in wholesale crop destruction. The expanded program received strong financial and political support. Discussions of Operation Ranchhand in Washington were instructive, especially as they illuminated the amount of bureaucratic concern for the consequences of their own decisions. There was none. Indeed, what was most striking about the discussions of the defoliation program at the Special Group meetings was the total absence of inquiry into the nature of the program. No limits were ever established, no results examined, no damage surveyed. Concern about the program focused on the single question of whether the South Vietnamese military had given their consent. Apparently, it was felt that if the GVN recommended the program and the ARVN consented to it, bureaucratic responsibility in Washington ceased. Though the program was the brain-child of ARPA (the Pentagon's Advanced Research Projects Agency), and was placed under the operational command of the U.S. Chemical Corps, the highest-level bureaucrats in Washington, including Roswell Gilpatric, U. Alexis Johnson, Maxwell Taylor, Robert Kennedy, Michael Forrestal, and Richard Helms, along with a host of their deputies, evinced no interest in their own policies. The forced migration, sterility, and hunger that followed in the wake of defoliation were not matters that preoccupied those who had already approved the program. Such consequences were left to the concern of the GVN. The imperial relationship between the United States and its client was employed by the policy-makers in Washington to remove every vestige of personal responsibility from their shoulders and lay it at the door of the GVN officials. Thus, Washington was able to authorize atrocious acts of war and evade any responsibility for them. Maxwell Taylor's concern for Operation Ranchhand was summed up by him in an interview in the following words: "We used it for crop destruction and foliage. It was only useful along the highways. It was not at all criminal. It was simply ineffective. The entire program was irrelevant." Defoliation was indeed irrelevant to Washington, but it was not irrelevant to the peasants turned into migrants, to the women turned sterile, to the children turned hungry.

KENNEDY IN CONTROL

Although the bureaucracy in Washington was not concerned with the fruits of its labor in Vietnam, the President was massively concerned with his capacity to command the bureaucracy in Washington. In his quest for control, he introduced four structural innovations in the office of the Presidency—the Special Group Counter-Insurgency, the 303 Committee, the Country Team, and the Green Berets. Although all of these were fashioned to meet specific deficiencies in the execution of foreign policy, and in this sense may be viewed as ad hoc measures, an extraordinary pattern emerges when the four are grouped together—an expansion of the war-making powers of the Executive to a degree never before contemplated in the history of the Republic. For the first time, total command over the several national security agencies was concentrated in the office of the President.

The SGCI was a special agency created by Kennedy to supervise the programs of the national security agencies. The centralization of the state apparatus was completed through the appointment of a chairman and a co-chairman whom the President personally trusted and who would report directly to him. Thus, Kennedy selected Maxwell Taylor, then occupying a special office in the White House as the President's military adviser, to be chairman of the SGCI, and his brother, Robert Kennedy, to be co-chairman. Taylor acted as a broker among the various power blocs to ensure that the agencies responded to the President's bidding. Robert Kennedy was considered the moving force behind the SGCI. He attended every meeting and, through his personal tactics, managed to transform them into courtroom spectacles. Officers of the agencies presented their findings from a witness chair, and Kennedy would zealously and relentlessly cross-examine each witness. Witnesses were often intimidated by Robert Kennedy's ferocity. When William Jordan testified on the issue of massive infiltration from the North, for example, he was excused prematurely in order to avoid further embarrassment at the hands of Kennedy. Another witness, reminded that the President's brother was simply trying to get the facts, replied that Kennedy was "guilty of over-kill." Kennedy's function, it seems, was to instill a modicum of fear into the agencies —to persuade them that they were being watched closely by the President and should act accordingly.

Defenders of the Kennedy Administration contend that the purpose of these exertions was to keep America out of an unnecessary war in Southeast Asia. The Kennedys, it is suggested, believed that the only way to avoid a deepening and perhaps irreversible commitment to Vietnam was to expose the inflated statements offered by officials who wished to draw the nation into a wider war. These rationalizations seem to fall by the wayside when it is recalled that the purpose of the SGCI in general, and Robert Kennedy's purpose in particular, was to centralize control of the national security state machinery in the hands of the President.

The CIA had displayed its power to make foreign policy at the Bay of Pigs, forcing the President to assume responsibility for events he had not initiated and could not control. After Cuba, Kennedy fired Allen Dulles and appointed John McCone as Director of the CIA, perhaps reasoning that the latter would be more manageable. At the same time, he created the 303 Committee to break the independent power of the Agency and place it within an institutional setting managed by the President. From that time on, the CIA had to clear each of its programs in advance and report directly to McGeorge Bundy, the Chairman of the 303 Committee and the National Security Adviser to the President. Bundy, Maxwell Taylor, and Robert Kennedy were the trusted lieutenants who took their orders directly from the President and who were placed in charge of special agencies to centralize command in the national security apparatus on his behalf.

Just as the 303 Committee and the SGCI were designed to unify the state apparatus directly under President Kennedy in Washington, every effort was made to centralize Presidential control in the field. When Kennedy assumed the Presidency, one of the problems plaguing American foreign policy was the fact that each agency in the field acted as if it were a self-contained system, staking a claim against the Pentagon for its own resources, moving from one area of the globe to the next according to its assessment of where the action was, insulating itself from supervision above, and extending its imperial writ below. The armed services offered the prime examples of separate fiefdoms run wild, but the civil agencies in the field, including the CIA, State, USIA, and others, also made their own rules and circumvented all attempts at direction from above. The CIA, for example, had a percentage of all shipping to Vietnam assigned directly to it, set up its own chain of communications in the field, and had a back channel to Washington. Laos simply became competitive turf for the several agencies, each moving in with personnel and materiel, then seeking a program first to justify its presence and second to expand its domain. Aircraft stationed in Korea were forwarded to Vietnam on Air Force orders which had not been cleared at higher levels, and when such clearance became necessary, front committees were created at the Pentagon to clear automatically any material request from below. As far as the agencies in the field were concerned, the state was a political fiction. The sole reality was the state economy, which was viewed as an infinite source of supply to feed the agencies' appetites.

The origin of Operation Ranchhand, under the expert guidance of William Godell, offers a classic example. ARPA appropriated surplus funds to begin the defoliation program, and then by-passed the original guidelines to expand the program in order to justify a further increase in its budget. Just as feudal war lords had waged war against each other within fledgling nations, so the modern agencies looked upon each other as rivals, trying to preempt the power and resources within the fledgling empire.

The Country Team was created to cope with this problem. In 1961, Kennedy invested U.S. Ambassadors with plenary power to control the national security agencies in the field. Thus, all of the agencies were required to clear their programs with and be supervised by the Ambassadors to the countries in which they were operating. The Ambassador received his authority directly from Kennedy and reported directly to him. Just as Kennedy had hoped to subjugate the national security agencies in Washington to the command and control of the SGCI, so he relied upon the concept of the Country Team to achieve the same level of control in the field.

However, the Joint Chiefs of Staff—in contrast to the other national security agencies—have an independent base of support both in Congress and in the public. Working through the chairmen of key Congressional committees, the Chiefs have a Congressional format to articulate the proposals they deem important, regardless of whether or not they have the support of the President or his senior advisers. Once these proposals are vented in a public forum, the Chiefs can count on the right wing constituency in the country to lend their support. Since the Chiefs formulate, express, and then personify the national interest on any issue concerning national security, they rival the President's claim to sovereignty. By virtue of their Congressional support, political constituency, and claim upon the flag, the Chiefs, unlike anyone else, can even level the charge of treason at the President. Because of their formidable power, the President must respond to any proposal put forward by them.

The President, of course, is not without his own resources in persuading the Chiefs to champion his own causes. But he must always bargain with the Chiefs and grant certain concessions if they oppose him or if he needs their overt support. This uneasy balance between the President and the Chiefs gradually tips in favor of the Chiefs once the state embarks on war. The Joint Chiefs of Staff, not the Commander-in-Chief, are presumed to know how to manage a war. For the President to oppose their programs is to lay himself open to the charge that he is playing with American lives. Thus, when the President expands a war on the grounds that he is protecting the lives of U.S. troops in the field, either he has, in effect, borrowed the Chiefs' argument and is proclaiming for all to hear that his policies are in full accord with those of the military or, in the alternative, he is anticipating just such a challenge by the Chiefs and is laying the ground-work for his own defense. The policies of the Chiefs, moreover, invariably extend the zone of combat until victory is achieved. The Chiefs depart from the civilian leadership in that they are willing even to wage nuclear war, if that is considered necessary to avoid defeat.

But if the war can be interpreted as a police action, or can proceed under cover of a private affair, then the power of the Chiefs can be sharply circumscribed. Thus, Kennedy had an obvious stake in keeping the war private. And while it was private, he was not passive. It was during the period of the private war that Kennedy set about building the elite corps of the Green Berets. Sorenson wrote:

> But the President's pride was still the Army Special Forces, rapidly growing to a level some five or six times as large as when he took office, although still small both in total numbers and in relation to the need for more. The President directed—again over the opposition of top generals—that the Special Forces wear Green Berets as a mark of distinction.

Kennedy wanted to prosecute the Vietnam war exclusively through the organization of the Special Forces, and thereby seize command of the military organ of the state apparatus. The ultimate vision was of the Green Berets as a praetorian guard, an elite army directly under the command and control of the President. The Green Berets represented Kennedy's attempt to curb the power of the Chiefs and institutionalize the military directly under the Presidency.

Edward Lansdale, a devout believer in the Special Forces and in the concept of counterinsurgency, was quietly assigned an office under McNamara and vested with the power to keep Vietnam under Presidential control. It was a case of bad judgment. Lansdale was immediately perceived as a potential threat by the JCS, and they created their own branch of counterinsurgency by establishing the position of Special Assistant for Counter-Insurgency and Special Activities (SACSA). Victor Krulak, the first "SACSA," a former Marine Corps General and an astute politician, referred to as "the brute," undercut Lansdale at every turn until Lansdale was labeled a "paper tiger." Once he gained control over the concept of counterinsurgency, General Krulak was able to restore some of the power of the Chiefs. The military first employed the concept of counterinsurgency as a cover to gain control over part of the covert programming, then expanded it to encompass conventional warfare which the military was organized to pursue. In this respect, there was an implicit accord between the military and civilian leadership.

Every one of Secretary McNamara's famous visits to Vietnam was a guided tour carefully stage-managed by the JCS. He would stop off at Hawaii and pick up a briefing book prepared by Krulak, replete with impressive charts and graphs displaying the progress of the war. McNamara would scan the book to obtain the information he needed for press conferences to be held in Saigon. After the trip the information would be converted into a hard-cover volume containing references to McNamara's recent findings in Vietnam, but again written by Krulak. This book would then be handed to President Johnson as the final report. The book had been written in advance of the trip and the trip itself had been staged in advance.

With the concept of counterinsurgency in their hip pocket, the management of some of the covert programming well in hand, and McNamara under close scrutiny and partial guidance, the JCS turned their attention to the thorny problem of the Special Forces. Operating in the field under the supervision of the CIA, the Special Forces were successful in training the Montagnards. In 1964, Operation Switchback was approved in Washington to break up the Special Forces as an autonomous force, remove them from the CIA's direction, and place them under the command of MACV. In one stroke, the JCS picked up control of the Special Forces and the local tribesmen. The totality of the state apparatus was concentrated in the hands of the Chiefs and the President. The question left hanging in the balance—and still unanswered—was whether the Chiefs and the Commander-in-Chief would share the total power equally, or whether one would make a claim against the other.

Centralization of the state apparatus—except for the JCS—directly under the command and control of the President greatly enhanced the power of the President. The effects of this transfer of power are profound. Through the auspices of the 303 Committee and the mobilization of the Green Berets, the President now makes the decisions on matters of espionage and military strategy. To the extent that he has control over the CIA and shares the power of the military, he is in effect a super-spy and field marshal. The time and energy he is normally expected to devote to his duties as Chief Executive are now absorbed by these new offices. How much time Kennedy actually devoted to supervising covert activities and personally managing the activities of the Special Forces remains a matter of speculation, but it was certainly a significant proportion.

Though the 303 Committee and the Special Group were successful in centralizing the state apparatus under the Executive, neither the Green Berets nor the Country Team approached such success. Nonetheless, the concept of centralizing the state apparatus was advanced by Kennedy and the reality partly measured up to the concept. What emerged, then, was a budding totalitarian state under the control of a Leader. Simultaneously, that very state apparatus prosecuted a private war. The thirty-three months of Kennedy's Presidency marked the makings of a totalitarian state structure and a private war.

The fact that the war was private meant that it was not the principal preoccupation of the nation, but rather the chief task of the state; that it was conducted not in the interests of the nation, but in the interests of the state. Indeed, one could now say that it was conducted against the interests of the nation, because it destroyed the orderly processes of the Republic.

WOULD KENNEDY HAVE WITHDRAWN?

American national security was never at stake. Through the Special Group, the state had intimate knowledge of the fact that there was no infiltration from the North, nor any Chinese or Soviet support for the Southern struggle. Kennedy knew therefore that the war in South Vietnam was a civil war. How was American national security threatened by the outcome of their civil war? The probable impact of a Viet Cong victory on the international interests of the United States was never systematically studied during the Kennedy years. When the issue did surface, the CIA fudged its assessment. It suggested, for example, that Southeast Asia would be demoralized if South Vietnam went Communist, and that this demoralization might even spread to India. But what is demoralization? How is it measured? How are its consequences determined in terms of national security? Is demoralization the sort of thing that causes a nation to switch sides or does it impel it to attach itself ever more closely to the mother country? Would a Viet Cong victory have created a revolution in Thailand? In India? In Cambodia? In Japan?

According to the Bureau of Intelligence and Research (INR), the intelligence branch of the State Department, "there was no serious analysis of what we could expect throughout Southeast Asia if we failed to support

South Vietnam." The state was not the least bit interested in determining whether the national security was at stake. What was constant about U.S. policy in Southeast Asia was that there was never any discussion of why we should be there. Only in 1969 did the intelligence community attempt a detailed and exhaustive study of the consequences to be expected if South Vietnam were to become a Communist nation. According to INR, this estimate, prepared by the CIA and recently made public, concluded that:

> We would lose Laos immediately. Sihanouk would preserve Cambodia by a straddling effort. All of Southeast Asia would remain just as it is at least for another generation. Thailand, in particular, would continue to maintain close relations with the U.S. and would seek additional support. Simultaneously, Thailand would make overtures and move toward China and the Soviet Union. It would simply take aid from both sides to preserve its independence. North Vietnam would consume itself in Laos and South Vietnam. Only Laos would definitely follow into the Communist orbit.

This estimate suggests, therefore, that if the United States had been defeated in open warfare by a "fourth-rate nation," there would have been no international consequences to U.S. interests. It is reasonable to assume, therefore, that if the United States had not fought and not been defeated, its stock of goodwill might have risen. Laos and South Vietnam would have gone Communist whether or not the United States intervened.

The events of the early 1960's, however, strongly suggest that had John F. Kennedy lived, he would not have pulled out of Southeast Asia and would have taken any steps necessary to avoid an ignominious defeat at the hands of the Viet Cong. In a nationwide interview on NBC television two months before he was assassinated, when asked whether the United States was likely to reduce its aid to Vietnam, Kennedy replied:

I don't think we think that would be helpful at this time. If you reduce your aid, it is possible you could have some effect upon the government structure there. On the other hand, you might have a situation which could bring about a collapse. Strongly in our mind is what happened in the case of China at the end of World War II, where China was lost—a weak government became increasingly unable to control events. We don't want that.

What I am concerned about is that Americans will get impatient and say, because they don't like events in Southeast Asia or they don't like the Government in Saigon, that we should withdraw. That only makes it easy for the Communists. I think we should stay. We should use our influence in as effective a way as we can, but we should not withdraw.

A week earlier, in another nationwide interview with Walter Cronkite, Kennedy had said:

But I don't agree with those who say we should withdraw. That would be a great mistake. . . . We took all this—made this effort to defend Europe. Now Europe is quite secure. We also have to participate—we may not like it—in the defense of Asia.

Kennedy would not withdraw, but he was plagued by the American public's impatience and dislike for what he had decided to do. To stay in Vietnam without arousing public opposition, he waged the war as privately as possible.

THE "BRUSH-FIRE" WAR

There is a counterargument to this interpretation of Kennedy's Vietnam policy which advances the premise that Vietnam was an example of a new concept officially and publicly identified as brush-fire war. Congress freely debated this policy and appropriated huge sums of money in support of it. The war, then, was a public, not a private, matter. Under Kennedy, American manpower in Vietnam never exceeded 16,000, a figure clearly within the bounds of a brush-fire war.

The problem with this thesis is that there were only a handful who seriously propounded the brush-fire war doctrine in the highest councils of the state. Hilsman and Thompson come to mind as officials closely associated with a counterinsurgency strategy for Vietnam, but the dominant positions in the Kennedy Administration were held by exponents of conventional war, whose recommendations were withheld from the public. Walter Rostow, who publicly enunciated the doctrine of brush-fire war in behalf of the Administration in 1961, was privately recommending "offensive action" and aerial strikes against the Northern mainland. McNamara, too, called for public support for brush-fire wars and simultaneously urged in private that the United States be fully prepared to deploy 260,000 troops in a conventional role. The public statements of the Kennedy Administration invited public support for a brush-fire war, but the private recommendations presupposed the use of heavy firepower.

This does not necessarily mean that the officials were simply and deliberately deceiving the public. To some extent, they were also deceiving themselves. The contradiction between their public rhetoric and their private recommendations was blurred, at the time, both by their language and by the variety of military technology available to them.

It became fashionable in the early 1960's to speak of "surgical air strikes," a term coined by Walt Rostow, Aerial warfare is, of course, the apex of conventional warfare. To speak of air strikes is to evoke the bombing of London, Dresden, and Hiroshima. Brush-fire war, on the other hand, involves the rhetoric of limited hostilities, pacification, and nation-building. The concept of a "surgical air strike," then, tends to blur the distinction between conventional and brush-fire warfare. It implies that friend can be distinguished from foe in the air and that conventional weapons can be used selectively to wage brush-fire war. It suggests a lower level of violence than conventional warfare, a means of protecting our friends and destroying our enemies.

When asked to comment on the feasibility of using "surgical air strikes" within the bounds of brush-fire war, McGeorge Bundy called the question "naïve." "Professors know that bombs kill people," he said. Yet such naïveté helped to preserve a posture of innocence, permitting the decision-makers to believe that they had not embarked on a course of systematic deception.

The type of ordnance financed during the Kennedy period also helped the policy-makers to blur the distinction between the two types of war. Preparations for both conventional warfare and brush-fire war simultaneously made dramatic advances. Within two years there was a sixfold increase in counterinsurgency forces and a 45-percent increase in the number of combat-ready army divisions. Hence, the managers were equipping the state to fight either kind of war. This produced an element of doubt and ambiguity as to which kind of war the United States was fighting and would continue to fight. Since brush-fire signified a lower level of involvement and could be prosecuted without interfering with the normal business of everyday life, it was functional to point to the counterinsurgency preparations as consistent with Kennedy's Vietnam policy. The dual defense capability could be cited as justification for both the public rhetoric and the private recommendations.

What remains unequivocal when one examines the over-all changes introduced by the Kennedy managers at the Pentagon is the decision to prepare for waging any type of war, at any place, at any time. Not only did the brush-fire and conventional capabilities make giant strides in a peaceful era, but the nation's strategic and tactical nuclear capabilities were similarly expanded. Strategic nuclear weapons were increased 100 percent, and tactical weapons 60 percent. The capacity to fight any type of war was called the doctrine of "flexible response."

Not only was a conventional war anticipated and recommended by the Kennedy government, but Kennedy himself authorized the first use of heavy firepower when he sent the newly-armed helicopters to Vietnam in 1962. The MAAG mission, moreover, had trained the ARVN to prosecute a conventional war. Would the Americans, when need beckoned and opportunity knocked, renounce their own training, firepower, and private urgings?

The United States proceeded one step at a time, and Kennedy took the first giant step. If the Viet Cong could not be defeated at a lower level of violence, why not proceed to the next level? That was the precise purpose of flexible response. We have Kennedy's public statement that he would not withdraw. We have Kennedy's policy of gradual escalation. Finally, we have Maxwell Taylor's statement, when asked what Kennedy would have done in Vietnam had he lived: "Far be it for me to read the mind of a dead man, but let me just say this, Kennedy was not a loser."

4 /

WASHINGTON PLANS
AN AGGRESSIVE WAR:
NOVEMBER 1963
TO FEBRUARY 1965

By early 1963 the private war had not yielded the necessary results. The Viet Cong could not be defeated at a
lower level of violence. At the battle of Ap Bac in
December 1962, the Viet Cong again proved their superiority over the ARVN. Evading a carefully-laid trap, the
Viet Cong "fought their way inside the perimeter of a
U.S. Special Forces training camp at Plei Nrong, killing
39 of the trainee defenders and capturing 114 weapons."
Moreover, the ARVN refused to do battle. A revitalized
ARVN, American firepower, and the Special Forces did
not constitute a formula for victory.

Michael Forrestal and Roger Hilsman arrived in Vietnam at the close of this battle, having been dispatched
by Kennedy to investigate the progress of the war. Their
report, filed with the President on their return, stated that

the Viet Cong had increased "their regular forces from 18,000 to 23,000 over this past year." During this same time span, the Government of Vietnam had claimed that 20,000 VC were killed in action and 4,000 were wounded. Forrestal questioned these figures. "No one really knows," he wrote, "how many of the 20,000 'Viet Cong' killed last year were only innocent, or at least persuadable villagers."

This incipient practice of including civilian casualties in the citations of Viet Cong deaths held untoward policy implications for the U.S. government, which was willing to live with the reality of growing complicity in the killing of innocent civilians precisely because it began to discount their innocence.

Kennedy was informed by Forrestal that "the vast bulk of both recruits and supplies come from inside South Vietnam itself." The civilians in the South represented the essence of the Viet Cong movement; the only question was whether they joined the movement freely or out of coercion. "At the very least," Forrestal judged, "the figures on Viet Cong strength imply a continuing flow of recruits and supplies from these same villages and indicate that a substantial proportion of the population is still cooperating with the enemy, although it is impossible to tell how much of this cooperation stems from fear and how much from conviction." Yet Forrestal underscored the fact that "the Viet Cong continue to be aggressive and extremely effective." It would seem that he had answered his own question. Like many other officials and agencies, he had discovered that the Viet Cong were actively assisted by the rural population, and that they fought with dedicated spirit, high moral fervor, and extreme effectiveness. These observations, cited in every document that examined the "progress" of the war, should have allowed Forrestal and Kennedy to draw the obvious conclusion—that the rural populace cooperated out of conviction because it, in fact, was the Viet Cong. But, to draw this conclusion, Washington would have had to admit to the ugly fact that the civilians in the South were the enemy. Washington was reminded of this time and again, but would not admit to, or act on, that knowledge.

The United States could not act effectively in this situation. The civil war ravaging in Vietnam pitted the people of Vietnam against the government of Vietnam, and the United States had committed itself to support the government. To win such a war, a military strategy was needed to separate the people from the areas controlled by the Viet Cong. The most effective way to detach the people from the movement would be to create widespread civilian casualties and a wholesale number of civilian refugees. Only a conventional war could fit the people into the three neat categories of corpses, refugees, and VC. After the dead and the refugees had been removed from the areas controlled by the VC, the VC would be isolated and could be "wasted" by heavy firepower.

Yet even a conventional war, the only strategy that held out a hope for victory, posed desperate problems. To kill indiscriminately in the countryside and uproot the peasants from their ancestral homes would create many more active VC. Furthermore, the regular troops from the North would throw their weight behind the movement and match any American build-up. A conventional war would not close off the infiltration routes from the North, and would recruit manpower for the VC in the South. The strategy was self-defeating. There was no way that America could win in Vietnam.

In 1963, the Viet Cong were simply demonstrating to Washington that they could not be defeated within the framework of the present strategy. The amalgam of Special Forces, heavy firepower, and covert activities was being rapidly discredited. It was clear that Washington would have to devise a new strategy in light of Kennedy's decision not to withdraw. But before a new strategy could

88

be devised, Diem's regime began to totter. The Buddhist uprisings throughout the spring and summer of 1963 proved beyond doubt that Diem could no longer guarantee a stable government, the sole element that justified his dictatorial rule. Were Washington to raise the war to a higher level of violence, it would need a government in Vietnam capable of supporting an increased American presence.

Although Washington had not yet divined the new strategy, it knew it could no longer keep the war private. Whatever the new strategy would be, Ap Bac, as well as a series of other battles throughout 1963, demonstrated the need to break out of the constraints of a private war. Simultaneously, the Buddhist upheaval cast strong doubt on Diem's capacity to support a public war. Neither his rule at home nor his image abroad was adequate for the next level of violence. By the summer of 1963, Washington was without a strategy to fight the war and without a government in Vietnam to support a public war, whatever the strategy. Yet Washington was determined to stay. Thus, it began to consider the elimination of the Diem regime.

At a National Security Council meeting on July 4, 1963, the war planners first "discussed the possibility of getting rid of the Nhus." The combined judgment of the participants—John Kennedy, George Ball, McGeorge Bundy, Roger Hilsman, and Michael Forrestal—"was that it would not be possible." But this judgment was immediately colored by their estimate that "there would be coup attempts over the next four months." Hilsman inquired into the effects of a coup on the war effort. He noted that "everyone agreed that chances of chaos in the wake of a coup are considerably less than they were a year ago." Forrestal followed up Hilsman's observations by citing Krulak's notion that "even if there were chaos in Saigon, military units in the field would continue to confront the

Communists." The Hilsman point of view that the war "would eventually go badly if Diem remained in office, and his removal may not create chaos or civil war" began to gain adherents. It was a prescription for eliminating Diem.

The next day, July 5, Ball, Nolting, and Wood discussed the possibility of bringing Diem around. Nolting reported that he had extracted a promise from Diem to conciliate the Buddhists by granting their demands for greater equality. "Diem had given his word that the agreement would be carried out," Nolting said, and he drew upon his own experience in dealing with Diem to tell the group that "when Diem gave his word, he followed through although sometimes it was handled in his own way."

Six weeks later, Washington received vivid evidence of just how Diem carried out his promise "in his own way." On August 21, Vietnamese military units raided the main Buddhist pagodas in Saigon, Hué, and several other cities. Monks were shot down and grenaded. Religious statues and holy relics were desecrated.

The private breach of faith and the concomitant public outrage created a furor in Washington. Beginning the week of August 26, the National Security Council met on a daily basis to decide what to do with Diem. Although the results of these meetings proved to be inconclusive, the views of the participants are enlightening. At the August 31 meeting—attended by the full body except for Kennedy, who was at Hyannisport at the time—Rusk opened the session by favoring the retention of Diem. The fear of a wider civil war damaging the war effort still swayed him—and McNamara and Johnson—in this direction. Paul Kattenburg, Chairman of the Vietnam Working Group at the State Department, broadened the discussion by arguing unequivocally in favor of immediate American withdrawal from Vietnam. "At this juncture," Kattenburg informed the National Security Council, "it would be better for us to make the decision to get out honorably." His analysis was based upon the belief that "Diem will get very little support from the military and as time goes on it will get less and less support, and the country will go steadily downhill." America was wasting its prestige and staining its honor. He concluded his statement with the prediction that "we are going to be thrown out of the country in six months."

Other participants were appalled by Kattenburg's attitude. Rusk characterized his remarks as "largely speculative." The Secretary of State offered his own judgment that "it would be far better for us to start on the firm basis of two things—that we will not pull out of Vietnam until the war is won and that we will not run a coup." McNamara expressed agreement with this view. Rusk then invited Johnson to speak, and the Vice President said he agreed with Secretary Rusk's conclusions completely; that he had great reservations himself with respect to a coup, particularly as he had never really seen a genuine alternative to Diem. Johnson added that "it would be a disaster to pull out," that "we should stop playing cops and robbers and get back to talking straight to the GVN," and that "we should once again go about winning the war." He concluded his remarks with the recommendation that "someone talk rough to them—perhaps General Taylor." The dominant position remained to win the war and retain Diem.

In September, selective cuts were made in the aid program to Vietnam, but Diem was not notified of these. More students and monks were arrested in the South. NSC meetings were conducted throughout the month. McNamara was dispatched to Vietnam to get more facts. In Saigon a meeting was held on September 29 with Diem, Thuan, Lodge, McNamara, and Taylor. Diem and Thuan claimed successes for both the strategic hamlet program and the war against the VC. McNamara immediately got to the nub of the matter. He told Diem that he was concerned over the political unrest in Saigon and the evident inability of the government to provide itself with a broad political base. He was also troubled, McNamara said, by the probability that the war effort would be damaged by the government's political deficiencies and the attendant loss of popularity.

McNamara, until then an unswerving supporter of Diem, had finally realized that an increased war effort would require a reasonably popular regime, or at least one that kept dissent within tolerable limits. He told Diem that the "recent wave of repressions have alarmed the public opinion both in Vietnam and in the United States." Washington needed the support of the American public if the war was to become a matter of public policy, but Diem's behavior was drying up that source of support. McNamara warned Diem that public opinion in the United States seriously questioned the wisdom or necessity of American support for a government that was so unpopular at home. Could the situation be turned around? Could Diem offer some reasonable hope for conciliation? McNamara waited for a reply. "Diem offered absolutely no assurances that he would take any steps in response," according to the firsthand notes drawn up by General Krulak. That sealed Diem's fate.

Kennedy permitted Lodge to work out the details. Kennedy did not want Diem killed, but merely removed from the country. On November 1, when the coup had begun, Diem called Lodge from the palace to ascertain the position of the U.S. government. The following conversation took place:

Diem: Some units have made a rebellion and I want to know what is the attitude of the U.S.?

Lodge: I do not feel well enough informed to be able to tell you. I have heard the shooting, but am not acquainted with all the facts. Also it is 4:30 a.m.

	in Washington and the U.S. Government cannot possibly have a view.
Diem:	But you must have some general ideas. After all, I am a Chief of State, I have tried to do my duty. I want to do now what duty and good sense require. I believe in duty above all.
Lodge:	You have certainly done your duty. As I told you only this morning, I admire your courage and your great contributions to your country. No one can take away from you the credit for all you have done. Now I am worried about your physical safety. I have a report that those in charge of the current activity offer you and your brother safe conduct out of the country if you resign. Had you heard this?
Diem:	No. (And then after a pause) You have my telephone number.
Lodge:	Yes. If I can do anything for your physical safety, please call me.
Diem:	I am trying to re-establish order.

Diem escaped from the palace, only to be captured and killed the following morning, November 2. On November 19, cross-border operations into Laos were resumed. Washington was informed that "the first results were just coming in."

On November 20, Lodge, Harkins, Rusk, McGeorge Bundy, McNamara, and Taylor met at Honolulu and underscored U.S. support for the new regime. Two days later, Kennedy was assassinated.

On November 26, after Johnson had told the nation, "Let us continue," he issued NSAM 273, based in large measure on the consensus reached at the Honolulu conference a week earlier. This NSAM provided that "planning should include different levels of possible increased activity, and in each instance there should be estimates of such factors as (a) Resulting damage to NVN; (b) The plausibility of denial; (c) Possible NVN retaliation; (d) Other international reaction."[1]

The "possible increased activity" referred to covert operations directed against the North. Just as Kennedy's initial decision had been to begin the covert war, Johnson's first decision was to widen it. His second decision, however, represented a point of significant departure—to begin planning for an overt war. Between December 1963 and February 1965, these twin policies were managed by Washington. The covert strikes increased in intensity and scope as Washington began to draw up plans for a conventional war to be waged directly against North Vietnam.

PLANS FOR COVERT WARFARE

NSAM 273 authorized Krulak to form a committee and develop a coherent program of covert activities to be conducted during 1964, while the rest of the national

---

1/NSAM 273 also indicated Washington's intention to withdraw 1,000 U.S. advisers by the end of the year. This provision has been described by the Pentagon's historians as "essentially an accounting exercise," offset in part by troop rotations. What was most peculiar about NSAM 273 was the dual stipulation that, on the one hand, the war would be won by December 1965, and, on the other, that increased activity, of both an overt and covert variety, would have to be undertaken. Did the war-makers take this to mean that the proposed escalation would result in an early victory? This would seem to have been the last occasion when some high-level decision-makers were still able to believe in the possibility of imminent victory. Throughout 1964, proposals for escalation increasingly assumed the grim prospects of a long, drawn-out struggle, possibly lasting ten years. In retrospect, then, Diem's assassination drove home the need for escalation as well as the reality of an indefinite struggle. The end of Diem meant the end of the unfounded optimism that had previously characterized some official thinking. Finally, Diem's removal from power was encouraged by Washington to abort any possibility of an understanding between Nhu and the NLF. Escalation, obviously, could not take place if the GVN had entered into a coalition with the NLF. In making such a deal, the government of the South would have joined with the people of the South in constructing a total obstacle to U.S. interests in Indochina.

security apparatus explored the feasibility of initiating a wider war against the North. Drawing upon operation plan 34a, the Krulak committee recommended that the program of covert activities, consistent with Johnson's directive in NSAM 273, was to be conducted along lines which would commit the United States to the least risk. In a report issued by Krulak on January 2, 1964, a twelve-month program of covert activities to be performed in three phases was recommended to Johnson. The operational control of the program was assigned to MACV. The CAS (a code name for the CIA's operational work) and CINCPAC were to train and equip the ARVN. Phase one of the program, scheduled for the months of February to May, was to consist of intelligence collection and twenty destructive acts against the North. The second and third phases were to increase the tempo and magnitude of the first phase, and extend the destructive operations to targets identified with North Vietnam's economic and industrial well-being. President Johnson approved the entire package on January 16.

General Krulak appended his own set of expectations to the report submitted to Johnson. The question facing the Johnson Administration was whether threats and punishment would alter the will of the DRV. "Toughened as they have been by long years of hardship and struggle," Krulak wrote, "they will not easily be persuaded by a punitive program to halt their support of the VC insurgency unless the damage visited upon them is of great magnitude."

Covert 34a operations began on February 1, 1964. Six months later they were to play a dramatic role in the Gulf of Tonkin incident and the subsequent escalation of the war. The 303 Committee assigned the program, like the DeSoto destroyer patrols, to the JCS for implementation. The JCS put the 34a program under the jurisdiction of SACSA, then under the leadership of Major General

Rollen H. Anthis. SACSA invested MAC-SOG (Military Assistance Command—Special Operations Group) in Saigon with authority to draw up the monthly schedules and the specific targets to be destroyed in North Vietnam. MAC-SOG would send the schedule of operations back to SACSA for approval along with the results of the previous month's operations. SACSA would evaluate the results for the JCS and deposit a copy of the proposed schedule for the following month with the 303 Committee.

Although SACSA and the Joint Intelligence Center, the agency that had jurisdiction over the DeSoto program, are both parts of the JCS complex in Washington, it seems that neither agency knew the dates, targets, or areas of operation directed by the other agency. Each was involved in covert operations, but neither knew the specifications of the other's work. It would have been possible for an official to put the DeSoto and 34a schedules together at SACSA and the Joint Intelligence Center—the information was available—but no one did.

Similarly, there was no coordination at MACV. Informational copies of the DeSoto schedules were deposited at MACV and the 34a schedule was drawn up by a subsidiary of MACV, MAC-SOG. The information was available in Saigon just as in Washington. However, no one at MACV knew that a 34a operation and a DeSoto patrol were scheduled to occur almost simultaneously at Tonkin in August. At CINCPAC headquarters in Hawaii, where the DeSoto schedule was drawn up, the existence of the 34a program was known, but no schedule of operations was available. Admiral Sharp, the head of CINCPAC, had the prerogative to order a 34a operation, and he made references to 34a programs in his DeSoto orders. Whether he personally knew that a 34a operation was scheduled for July 31, 1964, when he ordered the destroyer *Maddox* on a DeSoto patrol for August 1, is unclear. No one in Washington or Saigon knew, but Sharp might have had this information. What is important is that there was no deliberate *conspiracy* in Washington or in Saigon to bring these two programs together to make it look as if a U.S. destroyer had been innocently attacked on the high seas.

There was no reason to expect that the two would come together. Generally operating in different areas, they were planned on unrelated cycles. The 34a operation was scheduled one month in advance. There were lapses of several months between DeSoto operations. DeSoto was an updating program, designed to examine the defenses of the enemy and identify his rader. Hence, it was not a daily activity. Listening to the mainland radio traffic, another function of a DeSoto patrol, was also accomplished by a listening station north of Danang. This was not essential to the DeSoto program. Furthermore, the two programs had been going on for quite some time prior to Tonkin, and they had never intersected before.

It would have been a simple matter for someone to discover that the *Maddox* would enter the same waters less than one day after a Swift torpedo boat had shelled the Northern mainland, but no one did. The *Maddox* overheard Radio Hanoi describe the attack that had taken place the previous day, and heard the orders given to the Northern boats to attack the *Maddox*. The North thought the two operations were linked. In fact, they were not.

There was no conspiracy in Washington or Saigon to bring these two operations together, but the absence of a conspiracy does not mean that there was no intent to provoke the North. Every covert program was designed, in part, for this purpose. To shell the Northern mainland, whether or not the *Maddox* entered the same water at the same time, was an act of provocation.

Tonkin was significant because it taught the United States government that the North could be provoked. As Walt Rostow said in the State Department dining room two days after the Tonkin incident: "We don't know what happened, but it had the desired result."

The United States government had discovered the way to legitimize the war. By provoking the North in a way that made it look as if the United States had been innocently attacked, a wider war could be made palatable to the American public. The Gulf of Tonkin was a little Pearl Harbor. The question then was: Could the managers state a repeat performance? In a later examination of the overt programming for 1964, it will be noted that January 1, 1965, was referred to as D-Day. The United States was prepared to widen the war unilaterally, and justify it on the basis that the North was infiltrating troops into the South. But the infiltration argument, aside from its gross falsity, lacked the glamour attendant upon a surprise or shock attack. Infiltration was gray, dreary, and continuous. It was an issue that had to be researched and explained. The death of Americans, the sinking of a U.S. ship on the high seas, was dramatic, shocking, and unique. It was the stuff of headlines. The immediate dispatch of U.S. airplanes to bomb the North in response to the death of innocent American soldiers or the sinking of an innocent American ship could tap the romantic impulse of the American public and drum up sufficient support for a wider war. Even under these optimum conditions, however, Johnson was never able to count on the unswerving support of the American public. That problem would surface after 1965. In 1964, the problem was how to widen the war in a legitimate way. Tonkin furnished the answer; it was provocation.

A policy of provoking the North was not inconsistent with the immediate suspension of DeSoto patrols. Although the government knew that Tonkin was an accident, it suspected that vociferous segments of the American public felt otherwise. To avoid a charge of conspiracy and to preserve the aura of innocence, DeSoto was immediately suspended. As William Bundy said a week after Tonkin: "To maintain the credibility of our account of the events of last week, they [DeSoto] *must* be clearly dissociated from 34a operations, both in fact and in physical appearance."

But the patrols were suspended for only a month, and not until a controversy had been sparked at the highest levels of government. Most of Johnson's senior advisers wanted to extend the area of provocation, and DeSoto was seen as a convenient vehicle. The JCS preferred that DeSoto continue as an uninterrupted policy. Johnson disagreed. The argument developed when McNamara, shortly after the Tonkin incident, requested that the JCS furnish him with a list of U.S. actions which would be provocative. The JCS submitted a lengthy list which included the increased use of 34a operations, the continuation of DeSoto patrols, and supersonic overflights of Hanoi to break all the windows in the city. The JCS offered a graduated scale of options from extreme to less extreme acts. Taking DeSoto as an example, they suggested that some patrols approach the Northern mainland very closely, while others go no nearer than ten miles. Some would use destroyers, others pleasure yachts. Johnson ordered Harry Rowan, then of ISA (International Security Affairs, the advisory arm to the Secretary of Defense) and now president of the RAND Corporation, to study the need for DeSoto patrols, and learned that the Chiefs could muster only rather feeble arguments. Johnson, suspending DeSoto temporarily, explained his action in these terms to the Chairman of the JCS: "I myself can walk in that park across the street at three in the morning, but I don't have to send Lady Byrd and Linda Byrd to walk in that same park at three in the morning."

The DeSoto patrols were stopped for one month, not because the United States did not want to provoke the

North, but rather because the ten-day to two-week period after Tonkin "should be a short holding phase," according to the Department of State, "in which we would avoid action that would in any way take onus off the Communist side for escalation." Johnson had obtained his Congressional resolution and the North had escalated. The President had only to bask in the sun while American strength (we hit the North once because of Tonkin) and American moderation (we have done nothing to fan the fires) sank into the consciousness of the rulers in Hanoi and the public in America.

While a waiting strategy had been officially adopted, the advisers were determining how to translate a policy of provocation into a posture of legitimacy. John T. McNaughton, the first assistant to McNamara, recommended that the entire JCS package be approved. Speaking of extraterritorial actions, he argued that "they should be likely at some point to provoke a military DRV response." The "provoked response," McNaughton added, "should be likely to provide good grounds for us to escalate if we wished." He recommended that the DeSoto patrols be resumed. If a patrol was attacked, the United States "should apply the August 5 limited retaliation formula again." If by chance the DRV should sink a U.S. destroyer, then the U.S. should "commence a full-fledged squeeze on North Vietnam."

McNaughton had grasped the full potential of covert activity. It is in the nature of covert programs that one can place the onus of escalation on the other side while permitting his own side to disavow its acts by ascribing them to the client or by denying them altogether. It takes only a short step in either direction to establish a policy which can legitimize a wider war or allow for total withdrawal. "We can provoke a DRV response," McNaughton stated, or "if the worst comes and SVN disintegrates or their behavior becomes abominable, [the U.S.] can disown SVN."

An increasing reliance on covert activity is directly correlated with militant expansion of empire. Covert activity not only allows an imperial power to provoke a small enemy into acting like an equal, it also invests the imperium with powerful leverage over its client. If the client is neither willing nor able to fight, the imperium can simply abandon him by ascribing those covert acts to him. The imperial power uses covert activity to set the rules both for the enemy and for the client. Simultaneously, it buys time for itself (in Vietnam, it gave the United States four years to make up its mind) in which it can decide to widen the war or pull out. In an age of options and imperialism, covert programs become the normal business of the state. But this exacts a high price from the bureaucracy. Legitimate officers must operate within a state structure which increasingly compels them to make illicit decisions for which they must assume personal responsibility. Illicit decisions here refer to those which have not been authorized by Congress or acknowledged to the public, so that the official, when confronted by his decision, must dissemble. Illicit in the wider sense refers to the initiation of warfare for reasons peculiar to national security officials and not necessarily shared by other organs of government or the public. Illicit, in sum, means the application of force and fraud by national security officials acting according to their own rules and not subject to an institutional check by another organ of government or the public.

Before the lessons of Tonkin could be parlayed into greater gains for U.S. policy, the senior advisers had to obtain greater control over the covert programs. The 303 Committee tightened its reins over covert activities by adopting a policy requiring every member to approve personally each order for a 34a operation. Thus the highest level of Washington officialdom was made personally responsible for the planning of covert activity and the policy of provocation. Accordingly, McGeorge Bundy and Cyrus Vance, among others, initialed written orders for the execution of several specific covert programs against the Northern mainland: bombardments of Sam Son radar, the Tiger Island barracks, the islands Hon Ngu, Hon Matt, and Hon Me, and the destruction of a section of the Hanoi–Vinh railroad by an infiltrated demolition team. When questioned by Senator Church as to Washington's relationship to the 34a operations, Secretary Rusk claimed it was a South Vietnamese program and added that Washington "doesn't follow that in great detail." In fact, the reverse was true. The GVN didn't follow it in great detail.

After Washington had exercised closer management over covert operations and sufficient time had elapsed to tag the North with the onus for escalation, the possibility of manufacturing more Tonkins was given consideration. On September 8, Taylor, Wheeler, McNamara, and Rusk —Washington's heavy artillery on Vietnam policy— determined that henceforth the United States "should be prepared to respond on a tit-for-tat basis against the DRV," and a NSAM was issued to that effect. That statement, however, was simply a transformation of the Tonkin action into general policy. The critical question was whether the United States should seek out additional Tonkins. Should it manufacture as many incidents as possible to increase the likelihood that another Tonkin would occur? And should it seize upon the next Tonkin as an excuse for a wider war? "The main further question," Taylor, Rusk, McNamara, and Wheeler noted, "is the extent to which we should add elements that would tend deliberately to provoke a DRV reaction, and consequent retaliation by us. Examples of actions to be considered would be running U.S. naval patrols increasingly close to the North Vietnamese coast and/or associating them with the 34a operations." In other words, should the United States stage a repeat performance of Tonkin? The managers postponed consideration of the question until October because General Khanh, the head of the GVN, had not gained sufficient control over events in the South. Washington needed greater assurance that the GVN would not collapse at the precise time that Washington would embark upon a wider war. "By early October," the four decided, "we may recommend such actions."

Johnson did not wait. On September 10, he resumed the DeSoto patrols and ordered an increase in 34a activity. By October, he had personally ordered "ship-to-shore bombardment of radar sites." The United States was willing to provoke the North into a wider war. Massive intervention by the United States was made to depend upon "GVN progress." When the situation in the South looked somewhat more stable, the United States would commence the air war. The precise date would be determined by the enemy. By manufacturing enough Tonkins, the United States would paint the enemy into a corner. When an "ugly incident" occurred, the United States would begin continuous air raids against the North. Such an incident would be the killing of American boys or the sinking of an American ship. Tonkin was an accident. Pleiku would be the excuse.

PLANS FOR OVERT WARFARE

Six days after Johnson had approved the covert program for 1964, Maxwell Taylor, then Chairman of the Joint Chiefs of Staff, had cited NASM 273 as authority to initiate a wider war against the North. In a lengthy memorandum to the Secretary of Defense, dated January 22,

1964, Taylor argued that NSAM 273 "makes clear the resolve of the President to ensure victory over the externally directed and supported Communist insurgency in South Vietnam." If NSAM 273 could support a new program of covert activities, there was no reason why it could not serve also as the basis for a continuous bombing campaign against the North. "To achieve victory," Taylor wrote, the United States must "undertake bolder actions which may embody greater risks." The justification for launching direct aerial attacks against the North was, once again, the Domino Theory. In two brief paragraphs, without any argument or supporting evidence, Taylor sounded the clarion call by reading off the list of countries that would automatically fall into the Communist orbit if South Vietnam were lost. Laos, Thailand, and Cambodia would go immediately. The rest of Asia, including Burma, India, Indonesia, Malaysia, Japan, Taiwan, Korea, and the Philippines, would look unfavorably upon "U.S. durability, resolution, and trustworthiness." Taylor did not offer an opinion as to whether such despair would cause the rest of Asia to go Communist. Instead, he went on to claim that similar "unfavorable effects" would spread "to Africa and in Latin America." But the implication was clear. If South Vietnam went Communist, the United States was headed on a perilous course; it could be pushed out of three continents. South Vietnam was a symbol of "our worldwide confrontation with the Communists." Presumably, then, the Communists in Burma, India, Indonesia, Malaysia, Japan, Taiwan, Korea, the Philippines, all of Africa, and all of Latin America would be emboldened to strike out at once and push America back to its continental limits. The United States, Taylor concluded, "must prepare for whatever level of activity may be required and, being prepared, must then proceed to take actions as necessary to achieve our purposes surely and promptly."

Taylor called for aerial bombing of key North Vietnamese targets, using U.S. resources under Vietnamese cover, and with the Vietnamese openly assuming responsibility for the actions. He urged the simultaneous use of U.S. combat troops "in direct actions against North Vietnam." In effect, he was saying that inaction would make America look like a frightened schoolchild; that bombing the North openly would make America look like a bully; and that, in prosecuting the holy war against Communism, we must always look like men. Hence, we should acknowledge our land invasion of the North, but not our aerial attacks. How would air and ground attacks against the North affect the insurgency in the South? "It would be unrealistic," Taylor claimed, "to believe that a complete suppression of the insurgency can take place in one or even two years." How long would an overt war last? The best evidence, Taylor said, was the British effort in Malaya, "which required approximately ten years before the bulk of the rural population was brought under control of the government." The impact of Taylor's memo was shocking. The United States should wage a wider war, a war that should be fought at "whatever level of activity may be required," and a war that would probably continue for ten years.

Beginning in February 1964, almost every national security official supported some kind of contingency plan for overt war against the North. The JCS had started the bandwagon rolling, and everyone else was eager to climb aboard. There was absolutely no talk of withdrawal or accommodation, nor the barest hint of why the United States should remain in Vietnam. The whistle had been blown; the game was on. The United States was going to bomb North Vietnam. Whether to bomb it back to the Stone Age, employ a slow squeeze, or add a carrot to the stick was the only concern of official Washington. Covert activity had reached its saturation point. It no longer held the attention of the war managers. They needed a bigger game, increased risk, larger stakes. North Vietnam, that little Communist paradise situated in the middle of the Manichean world, and ruled by the avuncular and wily Ho, would get the full treatment. Game theory from Harvard, systems analysis from Detroit, politics from Texas, and stern morality from the cotton fields of Georgia would teach Hanoi the lesson of American toughness that Russia had already learned in Cuba.

The military and the civilian leadership, the patriots and the gamesters, had various motives for widening the war. Surprisingly, however, different motives led to substantially similar recommendations. Both groups approved of the bombing of the North and the dispatch of U.S. ground forces to Vietnam. Both dismissed any talk of withdrawal. Their only disagreement was with respect to the pace of the bombing. And since Hanoi furnished so little support to the war effort in the South, this amounted to a minor disagreement over a minor matter.

By and large, the military view of the world, as exemplified by the Taylor memorandum, reflected rather crude reasoning. The reality of Communist pluralism had replaced the specter of a Communist monolith. Sweeping statements unsupported by the barest evidence were no longer necessary to seduce the civilian leadership. The game spirit was adequate justification for the civilians. They recognized a contest. They talked in terms of averting defeat, improving their position in order to strike a better bargain. They viewed themselves as players whose purpose was to outmaneuver the other side with a more convincing strategy. They went out of their way to keep Russia and China out of the picture, to keep the game between two contestants. Ho was opposing U.S. interests, and that was enough to make the game. The strategy was to use just enough force to beat him. The emphasis was on a slower pace, flexibility, a multiplicity of signals. Don't overwhelm the opponent; that is too much like war. But don't pull out either; don't quit the game.

Most important in the game spirit is a fixed resolve, a test, a battle of wills. It is this trait that serves to unify the strategy and goals of the gamesters with those of the patriots. The name of the game is "national war of liberation," and the winner is the one who proves his mettle, who demonstrates he is serious. The victor need not use all of his reserves or all of his strength—only enough to convince the other side that it can't win. In the gamester's mind there is no war, just a series of strategic moves. Bombing is simply another signal, another play. Hence, you do it slowly. You measure your own response by giving the other side a chance to respond. The game is controlled; the very playing of the game is rational, unlike the crude and vulgar reasoning of the JCS. The game is fun, especially when one is planning the strategy, and just after the game has begun. Once the opponent plays, he may use dirty tactics; he may even inflict pain. But in a way that is all right too, for it is part of the game—the part where you prove your masculinity, your capacity to fight back. More bombing, more troops, more signals, you up the ante, until the coach, the public, tells you that it costs too much, that it will no longer foot the bill for your play. Then you have to back down. The game is over; no more energy, no more fun. Then the reality. The dead are brought home. The people hiss. You have committed the worst sin: You have lost.

In December 1963, Johnson had set up a Vietnam Working Group under the direction of William H. Sullivan to plan the new strategy for the war. Sullivan had been selected "to ease Roger Hilsman out of the picture." The JCS considered Hilsman too abrasive, and Johnson needed someone who could work well with each of the national security agencies. Sullivan was sponsored by

McGeorge Bundy and Averell Harriman, who considered Sullivan's politics to be quite dovish. He earned the respect of each of the agencies, and the hard work they did in return yielded him handsome dividends. He brought together the patriots and the gamesters. Together they developed the strategy of Rolling Thunder, the direct bombing of the North. Sullivan's politics proved to be adaptive.

Those represented on the Sullivan Task Force included McNaughton, Forrestal, Anthis, Clay, Colby, Mendenhall, Stoneman, and Jordan. The respective agencies represented were Defense, the White House, SACSA, the Air Force, CIA, State, and AID.

After ninety days of hard work, the Committee, according to Chairman Sullivan, made three judgments that bore directly on the utility of Operation Rolling Thunder. The first was that North Vietnam could take much punishment before it would capitulate or enter into negotiations on terms favorable to the United States. The North was not an industrialized state. It did not have enough targets to make it vulnerable to a systematic bombing campaign; one target was as valueless as another. But the theory of graduated response and the strategy of a slow squeeze depend upon a hierarchy of targets. Only if this hierarchy exists will the other side understand that the first bombing is just an indication of more significant devastation to come unless it too begins to bargain. If there is no hierarchy, the concept of graduated response becomes self-defeating; it becomes, in fact, double or nothing. The last bombing is as informational as the first. This conclusion was contested by Curtis LeMay, who engaged in a continuous dispute with McGeorge Bundy on whether the lack of a hierarchy foredoomed the efficacy of an air war. LeMay thought it did not.

The Committee's second judgment was that the United States would assume a "bully" image which would attenuate its international image, especially if the bombing were sustained for a protracted period of time. Such an image did not militate against bombing the North; it simply necessitated the participation of other nations in the bombing. This was the origin of Johnson's decision to get more flags.

Third, if the United States were to widen the war without international support, it would be necessary to obtain Congressional approval. The Bundy resolution calling for such Congressional support was drawn up under the auspices of the Sullivan Committee three months prior to Tonkin, at which time it was introduced and passed, almost verbatim. One needs political contingency plans as well as military ones.

In spite of its grave misgivings over the potential effectiveness of a campaign to bomb the North, the Sullivan Committee rationalized the move on the basis of "exploiting DRV concern over its loss of industry." Although the doctrine of graduated response was designed to break the will of an industrialized state, it could also be utilized against a primitive, Communist state, on the assumption that its leadership was proud of its industrial gain and would have a stake in protecting it. Rostow said to Rusk at the time: "Ho has an industrial complex to protect; he is no longer a guerrilla fighter with nothing to lose." Nevertheless, there were shortcomings in Rolling Thunder and, to compensate for these, it was also necessary to offer the North some "carrots." If the United States held out the possibility of economic gain at the same time that it bombed industrial plants, perhaps some positive results could be expected.

But what sort of results?

On March 1, just prior to his next trip to Vietnam, McNamara received from the Sullivan Committee an interim report that the North would want to protect its industrial base and could only defend it at the risk of

Chinese control. Since the North did not want to lose its recent economic gains and since it would not want to place itself under Chinese tutelage, the combined strategy of bombing and possible economic assistance would demonstrate to the world the power, determination, and restraint of the United States, and perhaps improve its negotiating position. But would an overt war against the North end the insurgency in the South?

McNamara was told that "unilateral U.S. actions would not compel Hanoi to call off the Viet Cong." The report noted pessimistically that even if the bombing did succeed in persuading the North of the rectitude of the U.S. position, it was "doubtful that Hanoi could call off the insurgency." If the United States started the bombing, the North would be unable or unwilling to call off the insurgency: unable because the insurgency was Southern, unwilling because the North, once it was attacked by the United States, would, in fact, positively support the insurgency. Since the bombing was expected to produce no results in terms of ending the war, and would most likely lead to further escalation, would this have an adverse effect on U.S. determination to remain? If the United States started the bombing, the report concluded, "it would imply a commitment to go all the way." Rolling Thunder was viewed as escalating and irreversible. The implicit judgment of the Sullivan Committee was that the bombing campaign would result in an indefinite war, continuously escalating, with both sides embroiled in a perpetual stalemate.

While the Sullivan Task Force was examining the possibility of bombing North Vietnam, the actual bombing campaign was being played out at the Pentagon by high-level officials. Drawing upon the use of computers, game theory, and systems analysis, interagency representatives were divided into two groups: North Vietnam and the United States, referred to as the red and blue teams, respectively. The first set of war games was played in the winter of 1963, the second in the spring of 1964. Each set ran for several sessions. The red team was headed by Marshall Green, Assistant Secretary of State for East Asian Affairs, and Robert Myers from the CIA. The blue team included McGeorge and William Bundy, and Generals Wheeler and LeMay. The purpose of the Sigma games, as they were called, was to bring together decision-makers from each of the national security agencies to exchange thinking and strategy, and implicitly to tear down any self-constraints against bombing the North. The results of the Sigma games supported the analysis of the Sullivan Committee. The North would be able to withstand American aerial punishment and expand in the South.

Some of the participants of the Sigma games later recalled with nostalgia how well they were able to anticipate each of the moves that Hanoi ultimately made in the war. Others remembered their expertise at countering U.S. strategy by inventing ingenious moves of their own. Marshall Green, for example, employed a strategem which located North Vietnamese civilians on the runway of a major airfield to show that the United States would not know how to respond. If we bombed the airfield, Hanoi would be able to rally its people for greater dedication and sacrifice.

Although the Sigma games and the Sullivan Committee both documented the case against strategic bombing of the North, they whetted the enthusiasm of the managers to make war, and rationalized the utility of bombing on other grounds. "We must prove to the world U.S. determination to oppose Communist expansion," the Sullivan report declared. USIA was commissioned to measure world and Congressional opinion. Conspicuously absent from these surveys was any study of American public opinion; the war-makers were not interested in the views of the nation. The results of the studies suggested that

111

the North Vietnamese people would rally behind their leadership, the world would charge the United States with the image of a bully, and Congress would support the campaign if its approval were gained in advance.

During the first three months of 1964, everyone seemed to be calling for the bombing of the North, but no one was able to furnish a justification for such a move. It was becoming rapidly apparent that the only reason for bombing the North was that it had not yet been tried. There was nothing else to do. With the basic research completed by the middle-echelon bureaucracy, attention shifted to the highest level of the state apparatus, where the decisions now were to be made. In March, McNamara returned from an inspection trip to South Vietnam and submitted his report to President Johnson. Together with the information gathered by the Sigma games and the Sullivan Committee, which had by this time filtered upward, this report served as the basis for an extensive policy review by the Administration.

JOHNSON SELECTS THE GOAL

The policy review, in brief, led President Johnson to adopt McNamara's conclusions as the official policy of the state. On March 17, the President issued NSAM 288 which, quoting from McNamara's report, declared that the U.S. goal was to achieve an independent, non-Communist government in South Vietnam. To underscore the significance of this goal, President Johnson called Ambassador Lodge on March 20 that "your mission is precisely for the purpose of knocking down the idea of neutralization wherever it rears its ugly head, and on this point I think that nothing is more important than to stop neutralist talk wherever we can by whatever means we can."

112

Having determined the goal, the Administration was then confronted with selecting the means. On McNamara's recommendation, the Administration decided not to begin bombing the North "at this time." McNamara supported his case against Rolling Thunder with three arguments: (1) The United States lacked adequate justification to bomb the North. The Sullivan Committee had stated that the only reason that could serve as a public justification for Rolling Thunder was "to have the North cease support of the insurgency." But the report also stated that the North would be unwilling and unable to do that. Moreover, the minimum support that the North was giving could not justify the maximum response envisioned by Rolling Thunder. (2) If we started bombing the North, the war would escalate, and the United States was unprepared militarily and politically to respond in kind. (3) There would be "pressures for premature negotiations." Johnson, as shown in his cable to Lodge, was afraid that a coalition government would emerge in Saigon.

In the above-mentioned cable of March 20, the President described some of his reasons for "reserving judgment on overt U.S. measures against North Vietnam." First, the Administration accepted General Kahn's judgment that "the immediate and essential task is to strengthen the southern base." That is to say, Khanh had not yet secured his rule in the South sufficiently to support an overt war against the North. As Johnson stated to Lodge, the "immediate problem in this area is to develop the strongest possible military base for possible later action." Second, "there is additional international reason," Johnson explained, "for avoiding immediate overt action in that we expect a showdown between the Chinese and Soviet Communist parties soon, and action against the North will be more practicable after than before a showdown." The goal of an independent, non-Communist South Vietnam had been adopted as official state policy, but aerial bombing against the North, according to Johnson, was placed "on a contingency basis at present."

Given the international climate, the limited resources of the Khanh government, and the low level of expectations attached to Rolling Thunder, the Johnson Administration decided to stay with the Southern strategy. Policy was directed toward building up the counterinsurgency campaign in the South and expanding the program of covert activities in Laos. McNamara had recommended and Johnson agreed that the United States would "stress numerous internal actions in support of the GVN's program to combat the VC insurgency." Authority was further granted for "continued high-level U.S. overflights of South Vietnam's borders, hot pursuit, and GVN ground operations into Laos for purposes of border control."

Although McNamara and Johnson opposed going North in the spring of 1964, both envisioned a value for it at some point in the future. McNamara and Johnson agreed that a distinction had to be made between forcing the North to call off the insurgency and lifting GVN morale to fight the insurgency. McNamara told Johnson that the bombing of the North could achieve the latter objective, but not the former. The final order in NSAM 288 thus called for the preparation of a capability to "mount new and significant pressures against North Vietnam, to include retaliatory actions against the North and a capability to initiate graduate overt military pressure within thirty days of notification." William Bundy was appointed coordinating executive to put together the thirty-day scenario for exercising direct pressure on the North. This work was not completed until May 23.

TIT-FOR-TAT

With Rolling Thunder temporarily shelved, at least until Bundy completed the details for the scenario, attention shifted to the possibility of going beyond covert acts short of a continuous bombing policy. Lodge, for one, believed it was necessary to anchor the covert program to an immediate set of higher policy considerations. Anything short of overt attacks, he maintained, would place all lesser acts into an informational vacuum. The concept of graduated pressures, especially when plans for bombing the North had not yet been approved, seemed too trivial and vague to justify spasmodic raids and incursions. If the action in the field didn't make any sense to Lodge, how could North Vietnam be expected to discern clear messages of U.S. intent out of these random activities?

Moreover, a series of recommendations had already been drawn up by the Sullivan Committee which could lend some badly needed coherence to the erratic military moves. Graduated pressures against the North, after all, were designed to inform the North that it would be punished unless it called off the insurgency. If this was the official explanation for Rolling Thunder, couldn't it also be used to construct a policy short of Rolling Thunder? Why not punish the North directly every time the GVN was hurt in the South? GVN morale would be raised and the North would be put on notice that it was being held responsible and would have to suffer for its responsibility. Perhaps the United States could achieve with a tit-for-tat policy what it expected to achieve with a continuous aerial assault. Moreover, retaliatory raids could serve as a trial run for Rolling Thunder. If Rolling Thunder could get us into serious trouble, in that it seemed to be irreversible, then perhaps we should try Flaming Dart (the eventual code word for retaliatory raids), a cheaper option which was obviously reversible. Punishment, furthermore, was predicated on the assumption that the North would want to protect its new industrial plant. If the United States believed in the operational value of this assumption, then it should mix some rewards with the punishment. Add the carrot to the stick and see if the assumption behind the stick is a valid one.

On February 20, Lodge told McGeorge Bundy that the United States should offer the North some rice to persuade it to call off the insurgency; if the North refused, a continuous bombing policy should be instituted. On March 15, Lodge told Johnson that Rolling Thunder should be shelved in favor of retaliatory raids. On March 17, Johnson authorized Lodge "to prepare contingency recommendation for specific tit-for-tat actions in the event attacks on Americans are renewed." On April 18, William Bundy, Rusk, and Wheeler held a meeting with Lodge in Saigon to compare the relative merits of Rolling Thunder and consider an increase in the size of the carrot. Lodge suggested that, as part of the carrot, some U.S. personnel should be withdrawn from South Vietnam. Rusk agreed, underscoring the lack of preparation for Rolling Thunder.

Before the United States embarked on a continuous bombing campaign, Rusk said, it must "prove Northern support both to the U.S. public and to the governments of Asia." Johnson did not want to engage the North directly until "we get more flags." Once the case against the North had been documented and some badly needed allies had been secured, it would still be necessary to devise a way to keep China out of the conflict. This could be accomplished, Rusk speculated, "by pressuring China through economic sanctions by our allies." In the meantime, the United States would go ahead with Lodge's suggestion and begin a tit-for-tat campaign. To further convey America's fixed resolve to the North, "we shall send a carrier task force to Cam Rhan Bay," thus establishing "a permanent U.S. presence." Rusk concluded by calling on SEATO support "to cut off North Vietnam from economic and cultural relations with the Free World."

Lodge submitted a more detailed plan to Rusk. J. Blair Seaborn, the Canadian ICC Commissioner, was to be called upon "to convey to Hanoi the seriousness of U.S. purpose and the limited nature of U.S. objectives." On April 30, Rusk went to Ottawa and obtained Seaborn's concurrence. It was agreed that Seaborn would go to Hanoi in mid-June. On May 15, Lodge told Johnson how he favored using the Seaborn mission: Seaborn should inform Hanoi that the United States would give it some badly needed economic assistance; if Hanoi declined the offer, it should be made to understand that bombs would follow.

To drive home the reality of the threat, Lodge urged bombing the North immediately before Seaborn arrived in Hanoi. "If there has been a terroristic act of the proper magnitude," Lodge recommended to Johnson, "a specific target in North Vietnam should be struck as a prelude to his arrival."

After the tit-for-tat approach had been adopted as official policy, the situation in Laos began to erupt. Throughout 1964, the JCS had been unsuccessful in trying to persuade the Administration to treat Laos and South Vietnam as a single military problem. To the JCS, the challenge confronting U.S. foreign policy covered all of Southeast Asia, not just South Vietnam. Moreover, the JCS argued, Hanoi was the cause of the entire problem. Given the broad scope of the problem and the identification of the single enemy in Hanoi, the JCS favored aerial bombing of the North, low-level reconnaissance flights into Laos, and the build-up of counterinsurgency forces in South Vietnam.

The State Department and ISA had advanced a different military strategy based on a different reading of the political situation. The civilian leadership assumed that each country was unique and must be treated as a separate entity. There was a long-term problem in Southeast Asia, and American success would turn on our capacity "to meet unique political demands." The State Department and ISA argued that, since we were working through Souvanna Phouma, U.S. military moves into Laos should be limited so as not to upset Souvanna's government. The United States should prohibit armed reconnaissance and ground probes in Laos, and concentrate on the infiltration corridor. Military moves into Laos should be justified only in i... :ms of their direct relationship to the military problem in South Vietnam.

In the early months of 1964, President Johnson favored the approach advanced by State and ISA. On March 17, for example, the President cabled Lodge that with respect to Laos he was reluctant to start overt acts without Souvanna's support. To initiate overt moves into all of Laos could trigger wider Communist action in Laos, which Johnson wished to avoid—especially while he was unsure that Souvanna would favor such a wider war. Thus, while Johnson had chosen to keep the lid on Rolling Thunder, he also manifested restraint toward Laos. Restraint in both instances was primarily attributable to the lack of political strength within the respective client states. Once that political strength surfaced or, in the alternative, once the military situation began to collapse, Johnson would change his mind. Neither factor came into play until May of 1964.

On May 17, the Pathet Lao seized the Plain of Jars. Four days later, Johnson put the JSC policy into effect. The United States began armed reconnaissance flights into Laos. The same day Rusk notified Lodge that the United States would have to build up solidarity in the South to support larger U.S. moves. "Provide a solid base of determination," Lodge was told, "from which far-reaching decisions can proceed."

The military situation had begun to deteriorate, and the political decision to widen the war had been made. Thereafter, South Vietnam and Laos would be treated as one, and the United States, in spite of the low probability of vindicating itself, would go for broke.

THE NEED FOR A CONGRESSIONAL RESOLUTION

During the rest of 1964, the problem in the field was to build up the Southern political base sufficiently to support whatever military moves the United States might make. Just as the political support of the client was considered an indispensable prerequisite to a wider war, Congressional support at home was deemed essential by the Administration. Congress was placed in the same class as the GVN.

On May 23, a draft Presidential memo specifically called for a Congressional resolution as a prelude to a continuous aerial assault on North Vietnam. The memo further stated that aerial strikes would continue until armed resistance in the South stopped and until Northern radio communications were conducted in an uncoded form. These two points were identified as the U.S. negotiating position.

On the same day, Assistant Secretary of State William Bundy presented to the members of the Executive Committee the thirty-day scenario for exerting graduated military and political pressure on North Vietnam. The scenario called for a planned sequence of diplomatic moves and public statements from both Saigon and Washington, culminating in GVN and U.S. air strikes against Northern war-supporting targets. Following the series of aerial attacks, the United States would call for an international conference on Vietnam. The first step in the scenario was a Joint Congressional Resolution affirming the President's right to use force, if necessary, in protecting the security of Southeast Asia.

After two days of discussion, the Executive Committee decided not to recommend the thirty-day scenario to the President because of the estimated high probability of escalation and the negative diplomatic image that such escalation would create. Rolling Thunder would cause Hanoi to doubt the limited nature of U.S. aims, and Russia or China might be invited to confront U.S. power directly. Escalation in Southeast Asia simply incurred too much danger of a world-wide confrontation with a major Communist power. The Executive Committee did not believe that the stakes in Southeast Asia were high enough to justify such a level of risk. Instead of gradual escalation, the Committee recommended that the United States pursue a policy of threats of gradual escalation. "A decision to use force if necessary," the Committee argued, "backed by resolute and extensive deployment, and conveyed by every possible means to our adversaries, gives the best present chance of avoiding the actual use of such force."

The Executive Committee wanted to win in Southeast Asia, yet it gave equal weight to avoiding a direct challenge by Russia or China. But what if the signals failed? What if Hanoi refused to bend to American threats? Most officials doubted that Hanoi would respond to the use of force, much less the wielding of threats. The Committee recommended the use of force if, and only if, the threats failed to achieve the U.S. objective. The fear of a world war was little more than a mask to delay the actual use of force. The real reason for delay was that the Administration was militarily unprepared in terms of force deployments and politically unprepared in terms of Congressional support for moving to the next level of violence.

On the same day that the Executive Committee recommended the use of threats instead of actual force, the CIA issued a short-term national intelligence estimate, analyzing Northern responses to Rolling Thunder and the international consequences of American defeat in Southeast

Asia. If the United States bombed the North, the Agency estimated, there was a significant danger that the North would fight. Hanoi would intensify the insurgency because, on the one hand, it did not believe that the United States would put in ground troops, and, on the other hand, it thought such troops could be defeated if they were deployed. Moreover, if the North did fight, the situation would probably get out of hand. Both sides would escalate further. In the language of the Agency:

> Retaliatory measures which North might take in Laos and South Vietnam might make it increasingly difficult for U.S. to regard its objectives as attainable by limited means. Thus, difficulties of comprehension might increase on both sides as scale of action mounted.

If Rolling Thunder would lead to a wider and indefinite war, what would happen to the U.S. position in the world if, instead of escalating, the decision were made to let South Vietnam go? What if the United States pulled out? How valid was the Domino Theory? The CIA determined that the United States would "retain considerable leverage in Southeast Asia even if Laos and South Vietnam came under North Vietnam control." The choice was posed: a wider war with an indefinite outcome or no war with the United States retaining considerable leverage. It would seem that the Agency had made the case against a war policy.

Five days later, the JCS again endorsed Rolling Thunder. The Chiefs furnished a report detailing U.S. capacity to destroy the entire Northern industrial base.

On June 1, another major policy review was conducted in Honolulu. Immediately before the conference, Secretary Rusk met in Saigon with Premier Khanh, who told him that South Vietnam could not win against the VC without the help of military actions taken outside its borders. Rusk replied that "we are purposely giving the Sino-

Soviet bloc many indicators that we are about to react to recent aggressions." The Secretary added that he could say nothing about specific American intentions in the immediate future because he simply did not know. The Honolulu meeting would produce some firm recommendations to the President and some plans, but ultimately only the President could decide. His decision would be influenced by consideration of all implications of escalation.

In Honolulu, the need for escalation and the proposed preparatory steps were put to the top officials. There was no dissent from the need to escalate. The major concerns were the extent of escalation and the amount of preparation. Lodge raised the question of a Congressional resolution supporting a wider war. McNamara, Rusk, and McCone agreed emphatically that such a resolution would be a necessary element in any preparation for more intensive U.S. activity against the North. The heads of Defense, State, and the CIA examined the specific levels of escalation that would require "specific confirmation of Presidential authority." The United States would have to deploy "as many as seven divisions, call up reserves, and protect the South from possible Northern and CHICOM [Chinese Communist] reprisals. Since escalation would bite deeply, the preparation would have to be extensive. The conference cited six specific steps to be taken before escalation: (1) force build-up; (2) more precise targeting studies; (3) a larger ARVN reserve; (4) a stronger GVN base; (5) the need to prepare allied governments and U.S. public opinion; (6) the need for a Congressional resolution.

The phrase "wider U.S. actions" was used several times at the conference as a shorthand term for U.S. escalation. The conference members believed there was a need to define "wider." It was stated for the record that "wider could mean committing up to seven U.S. divisions and calling up the reserves as action unfolds."

Following the Honolulu conference, Washington devoted its time and energy to preparations for a wider war which were broken down into two phases, one military, the other political. In mid-June, McNamara ordered immediate improvement in effectiveness and readiness and some expansion of prepositioned stocks in Thailand and Okinawa. The JCS refined the targeting objectives for North Vietnam. The Defense Department studied the requirements for a build-up in forces.

The Bundy brothers worked on the political preparations. On June 12, William Bundy recommended a prompt Congressional resolution to demonstrate U.S. resolve and to provide flexibility for Executive action. On June 15, McGeorge Bundy submitted a memo on the question, "What can we do without a Congressional resolution?" He argued that in Laos the United States could perform armed reconnaissance flights and deploy T-28's without such a resolution. Actions against North Vietnam without formal Congressional approval, he suggested, would have to be limited to responses to provocative acts, and even this class of action would have to be circumscribed. He said the United States could resort to "small scale reconnaissance strikes after appropriate provocation in North Vietnam." Congressional support was not deemed necessary for limited increases in air, sea, and ground troops assigned to South Vietnam. Bundy concluded his analysis, however, with the observation that major ground troop deployments in the South seemed more questionable "without a decision to go North in some form."

By June 15, political and military planning had been completed. The national security agencies now waited upon the President's decision to widen the war. But the President by this time had only one eye on Vietnam; the other was directed to the national political conventions and the fall election. The White House thus discouraged further work, emphasizing that actions involving no increased commitment would serve U.S. interests "during the next six months." The President wished to conduct his election campaign with clean hands. Thereafter, "December" would be the code word to identify the timing for a wider war.

Was Congress deceived by the Executive when it passed the Gulf of Tonkin Resolution? The Tonkin incident, discussed previously in this chapter, was not stage-managed by the Executive. The 34a operation and the DeSoto patrol were not intentionally associated with each other; if anything, they were intentionally dissociated from each other. Yet, both McNamara and Rusk misled the Congress when they claimed that 34a was a GVN program. Both knew it was a U.S. program under the jurisdiction of MACV. They lied because each covert program was designed, in part, to provoke the North so that the Executive could inaugurate its tit-for-tat retaliation policy and obtain a Congressional resolution for a continuous bombing campaign. It was unclear whether the North could be provoked, but it was obvious that the Administration had viewed a Congressional resolution as the indispensable prerequisite to widening the war.

Members of Congress regarded the resolution as a contingent grant of war-making power to the President. During the debate in the Senate, for example, the following dialogue took place between Senators Cooper and Fulbright:

Mr. Cooper: . . . Are we now giving the President advance authority to take whatever actions he may deem necessary respecting South Vietnam and its defense, or with respect to the defense of any other country included in the [SEATO] treaty?

Mr. Fulbright: I think that is correct.

Mr. Cooper: Then, looking ahead, if the President decided that it was necessary to use such force as could lead into war, we will give that authority by this resolution?

Mr. Fulbright: That is the way I would interpret it. If a situation later developed in which we thought that the approval should be withdrawn it could be withdrawn by concurrent resolution.

Congress was led to believe that the war powers might have to be invoked in the future, but that such a decision, authorized by Congress, would depend on the unfolding of events yet unknown. Congress had not been informed that the Administration had decided to go to war prior to Tonkin but had deferred the go-ahead signal until after the election. Congress was not advised of the extensive preparation for war, or appraised of the Administration's view that once it obtained a joint resolution, the light would shift from amber to green. Congress was simply told that the Executive needed the power to be flexible. Flexibility—that magical word used to describe Executive need to respond to events—really meant the right of the Executive to select the date of the war.

The resolution was not contingent upon some future event. The possibility of the North calling off the insurgency (since they were unable or unwilling) was so remote as to be nonexistent. War, as the necessary event to take place in the future, was contingent upon the issuance of the resolution. Congress was seduced into supporting the preordained decision of the Executive to wage an aggressive war against North Vietnam. Indeed, the Executive needed a Congressional resolution precisely because it was planning to wage an aggressive war. The Executive wanted Congress in its hip pocket to lend an aura of legitimacy to that aggressive war. In sum, the Executive deceived the Congress into believing that the

Administration had done nothing to incur the attack and that the resolution might or might not be employed in the future.

THE PRESIDENTIAL ELECTION VS. D-DAY

On August 7, the joint resolution was passed. On August 10, Ambassador Taylor submitted his initial report from South Vietnam to the President. At the close of the report, Taylor cited the major objectives of the U.S. mission, including this: "Be prepared to implement contingency plans against North Vietnam with optimum readiness by January 1, 1965." January 1 was thereafter referred to as D-Day.

The U.S. retaliatory raids against the North had lifted the morale of the GVN, but the Saigon government was still weak. Taylor estimated that "Khanh has a 50/50 chance of lasting out the year," and he called upon the U.S. mission to "do everything possible to bolster the Khanh government." The Premier himself was making public announcements to go North, though Washington had decided to avoid a major escalation until December. Having bombed the North once and having decided not to bomb it again until after the election, there was little that Washington could do to preserve the temporary euphoria following Tonkin, or to support Khanh's public posture. The GVN and Washington seemed to be bound on a collision course. Khanh interpreted Tonkin to mean that he could put the nation on a war-footing preparatory to an invasion into the North. Washington's interpretation was that it now had the necessary authority to bomb the North, but would not invoke that authority until the election results were tabulated. The GVN's need to attack and Washington's wish to wait raised concern in official Washington: If Khanh was not supported, it was conceivable that his regime would fall and a deal would be made between the North and South. The nature of that deal would be a coalition government; its first decree would be to expel the United States from Vietnam. As Taylor put it:

> We may face mounting pressure from the GVN to win the war by direct attack on Hanoi which if resisted will cause local politicians to seriously consider negotiation or local soldiers to consider a military adventure without U.S. consent.

Any negotiations at this point would have played directly into the Viet Cong strategy. "The Communist strategy as defined by North Vietnam and the puppet National Liberation Front," according to Taylor, "is to seek a political settlement favorable to the Communists." Taylor believed that the political objective of the Communists was "to be achieved by stages, passing first through 'neutralism,' using the National Liberation Front machinery, and then the technique of a coalition government." Such negotiations would commence if the South could be pushed "into a state of demoralization." Such demoralization would no doubt occur, the report went on, if the United States refused to support the Khanh regime in its militaristic adventures, or find some suitable means to maintain Southern morale. Did Washington have any advice?

In a reply to Taylor's report, the State Department outlined the essential elements of U.S. policy. It recommended actions of "minimum risks [that] get maximum results." Taylor was told emphatically to "oppose any Vietnam conference." The United States should hurt the North through covert activities and communicate its fixed resolve to the North, letting the GVN take credit for all covert acts. It should, in addition, engage in joint planning with the GVN for direct attacks on the North. Such planning "can be used in itself to maintain morale of GVN leadership, as well as to control and inhibit any unilateral GVN moves." This would further bolster the Saigon government's image with the people, and any leaks of such planning exercises would add to U.S. credibility with Hanoi. The Department estimated that the "above actions are in general limited and controllable." Nonetheless such acts would be

> foreshadowing systematic military action against DRV, and we might at some point conclude such action was required either because of incidents arising from such actions or because of deterioration in SVN situation, particularly if there were to be clear evidence of greatly increased infiltration from the North.

The United States might be forced to go to war sooner than it had expected. "However," the Department added, "in absence of such major new developments, we should be thinking of a contingency date for planning purposes, as suggested by Ambassador Taylor, of 1 January 1965."

Thus the U.S. policy during the election campaign was to use every conceivable device, short of engaging the North in an overt war, to bolster the Khanh regime in its militaristic posture. Two months after the election, the policy called for the commencement of the war, on the basis of either infiltration by the North or U.S. provocation. The timing was qualified with an injunction to go for broke before the election if the situation deteriorated to the point that a new regime took power and was about to negotiate directly with the North or the National Liberation Front.

Taylor formalized the State Department's position by outlining alternative courses of action. Action "A" called upon the U.S. Mission to do everything in its power to strengthen the Khanh government, and presumed that these efforts would be successful. This option encompassed the conventional steps that could be taken short of overt war: planning, covert acts, and retaliatory raids. If these measures bolstered the GVN forces sufficiently, the United States could begin the war on January 1 and "avoid the possible requirement for a major U.S. ground force commitment." Action "B" operated on the assumption that any measures taken would not stabilize the GVN, and that the United States must, as a result, start the war immediately. The difficulty with action "B" was that "it increased the likelihood of U.S. involvement in ground action since Khanh will have almost no available ground forces which can be released from pacification." Taylor hesitated to claim that the Khanh regime could be strengthened through any means short of overt war: "It is far from clear at the present moment that the Khanh government can last until January 1, 1965," he wrote. But the obvious advantage in avoiding the uses of U.S. ground forces was so great that the United States should embrace action "A" and bend every effort behind Khanh. "However," Taylor cautioned, "we should always bear in mind the fragility of the Khanh government and be prepared to shift quickly to Course of Action B if the situation requires." By mid-August, the question had boiled down to whether the United States would be able to rely exclusively on air war in Vietnam, or would also have to make a major troop commitment. These were the only options seriously considered from August 1964 to June 1965.

The Joint Chiefs of Staff dissented from Taylor's recommendation. They preferred adoption of his Course of Action B "to prevent a complete collapse of the U.S. position in Southeast Asia." Taylor had claimed that the United States should avoid the immediate path of war until "we have a better feel for the quality of our ally." In reply, the JCS pointed out that the United States is already deeply involved." If Taylor were really determined to bolster the Khanh government, the United

States should eschew any reluctance to administer "significantly stronger military pressures on the DRV." Moreover, the United States should not divert its attention from the leadership of the DRV while watching the GVN. If it failed to follow up the Tonkin episode, it "could signal a lack of resolve." The JCS provided McNamara with a list of ninety-four targets and called for a "sharp sudden blow." The wish to avoid the use of U.S. ground forces, as the underlying reason for delaying Rolling Thunder, received absolutely no attention from the JCS.

On September 3, McNaughton submitted his plan of action for South Vietnam. He concurred with the JCS view that follow-up action to Tonkin was needed because "the situation in South Vietnam is deteriorating." But McNaughton believed this could best be done by provoking the North into again attacking the United States. McNaughton, as has been noted, was concerned with the legitimacy of the U.S. enterprise and viewed provocation as a means of lending the aura of such legitimacy. He was equally concerned with orchestrating the U.S. appeal to the competing audiences which it had to satisfy: the Communists, "who must feel strong pressures"; the South Vietnamese, "whose morale must be buoyed"; the allies, "who must trust us as underwriters"; and the U.S. public, "which must support our risk-taking with U.S. lives and prestige." During the election campaign, however, it was important to signal "to the DRV that initiatives are being taken, to the GVN that we are behaving energetically despite the restraints of our political season, and to the U.S. public that we are behaving with good purpose and restraint."

However, if the situation were to deteriorate during the political season to the point of disintegration in Saigon, the United States would have to forgo its task as orchestra leader and become, instead, a "good doctor"—one who would punish the enemy and then gracefully exit from the scene. South Vietnam would be left with the image of "a patient who died despite the extraordinary efforts of a good doctor."

A month later, McNaughton gave further definition to what it meant for the United States to assume the role of the "good doctor":

> It is essential—however badly SEA may go over the next 2–4 years—that U.S. emerge as a "good doctor." We must have kept promises, been tough, taken risks, gotten bloodied, and hurt the enemy very badly.

He suggested that the opinion in which other nations hold the United States is the prime determinant of U.S. foreign policy:

> We must avoid appearances which will affect judgments by, and provide pretexts to, other nations regarding U.S. power, resolve and competence, and regarding how the U.S. will behave in future cases of particular interest to those nations.

Other nations might ask this question about U.S. foreign policy: "Is the U.S. hobbled by restraints which might be relevant in future cases (fear of illegality, of U.N. or neutral reaction, of domestic pressures, of U.S. losses, of deploying U.S. ground forces in Asia, of war with China or Russia, of use of nuclear weapons, etc.)?" America, in other words, would have to prove to the world that it was not deterred by any of these fears. It would have to do all the things that it was not expected to do in order to prove its power to the world. One should not assume, however, that these bizarre views were McNaughton's alone. William Bundy, in an interview, described how he and McNaughton held strikingly similar positions on strategy for Vietnam.

McNaughton concluded his account of U.S. foreign policy with a two-phase scenario, delineating specific moves against the North. The first phase, to be conducted in November and December, conformed to the pattern of activities proposed or endorsed by most officials. Phase two, on the other hand, placed McNaughton alongside Curtis LeMay and other hawks. It called for strikes inside the North, to begin in January. Specifically, the United States should "mine DRV harbors, strike infiltration routes, working in from border, strike other military targets, strike industrial targets." McNaughton argued at one point that the United States should hit and get out; at the next moment, he urged the President to bomb the North back to the Stone Age. The civilian leadership, as exemplified by McNaughton, did not want to be pinned down; it wanted to have it both ways. Primarily, it wanted the power to exercise power.

At the close of the first week of September, a high-level review of Vietnam policy was conducted by Taylor, Rusk, McNamara, and Wheeler on behalf of the President. They estimated that Khanh would stay in power for at least the next two to three months, and discounted the significance of Khanh's "go North" campaign with the observation that the "GVN leaders are temporarily too exhausted to be thinking much about moves against the North." The usual array of covert activities, cross-border operations, and retaliatory raids was recommended. The four high officials said the purpose of actions external to South Vietnam was "to assist morale in SVN and show the Communists we still mean business, while at the same time seeking to keep the risks low and under our control at each stage."

The JCS again reviewed the situation, but on this occasion found themselves divided on whether to attack the North directly. "The Chief of Staff Air Force and Commandant of the Marine Corps believe time is against us and military action against the DRV should be taken now." During the election campaign, the Air Force had lined up in favor of Barry Goldwater for President and continually exerted pressure on Johnson. It was the Air

Force view that "the American public should support any action taken by the United States government against the DRV," and that Johnson should, therefore, put his political fears aside. The majority view in the JCS was presented by the Chairman of the JCS, the Army Chief of Staff, and the Chief of Naval Operations, who approved of Taylor's recommendations calling for a tit-for-tat policy. They described the minority view as "purposely embarking upon a program to create an incident immediately."

Johnson had succeeded in selling his " 'keep cool' election strategy" to the JCS as well as to his senior advisers. Two days later, he issued a NSAM stating the official policy of the White House. DeSoto patrols would be resumed immediately, but must be "clearly dissociated from 34a maritime operations." The United States should obtain Souvanna's support for "limited GVN air and ground operations into the corridor areas of Laos, together with Laos air strikes and possible use of U.S. armed aerial reconnaissance." Tit-for-tat would govern U.S. air attacks against the North. McGeorge Bundy summed up the President's views:

> These decisions are governed by a prevailing judgment that the first order of business is to take actions which will help to strengthen the fabric of the Government of South Vietnam; to the extent that the situation permits, such action should precede larger decisions. If such larger decisions are required at any time by a change in the situation, they will be taken.

In September and October, Johnson personally authorized two probes along the Northern mainland: one to capture an enemy junk, the other involving ship-to-shore bombardment of radar sites. But when, the day before the election, an occasion arose to employ a retaliatory raid against the North in response to a VC attack on a U.S. base at Bien Hoa, he declined to do so.

The retaliatory principle, originally put forward by Lodge in December 1963 and employed at the Gulf of Tonkin, was urged upon the President on at least two other occasions. On the day before the election and on Christmas Eve, incidents occurred which fit directly into the tit-for-tat policy, but the President refused to apply it. Having been used to obtain the Congressional resolution, the President then went ahead with the planning for Rolling Thunder. In February 1965, when the prerequisites for an overt war had been completed to his satisfaction, he seized upon the incident at Pleiku to shift from the retaliatory principle to continuous bombing. In sum, tit-for-tat was used to obtain the Congressional resolution, and the Congressional resolution was then used to unleash Rolling Thunder.

THE BUNDY WORKING GROUP

On November 1, instead of retaliating for the incident at Bien Hoa, the President convened the National Security Council Working Group to determine the initial course of the overt war. Under the leadership of Assistant Secretary of State William Bundy, the group included McNaughton from ISA, Admiral Mustin from the JCS, George Carver and a Mr. Ford from the CIA, Michael Forrestal from the White House, and Robert Johnson and Jonathan Moore from the State Department. The group's mission was to determine the pace of the bombing, the necessity for troops, and the relationship between military strategy and the political objectives of the U.S. government. The group completed its work by the end of November, and on December 1 the President approved its findings. These called for two phases of pressure, the first ending early in 1965 and the second, consisting of direct aerial attacks on the North, to begin thereafter and to continue for two to six months. The recommendations of the NSC group, in brief, determined the direction of the war right up to July 1965, at which point the President would make the decision for an open-ended troop commitment. The combination of Rolling Thunder in the North and the troop commitment in the South has accounted for the American presence in Vietnam up to the present time.

It is useful at this juncture to examine the original purpose of the military strategy and the way it related to political objectives. Much of the work that was done by the NSC Working Group simply represented a duplication of the points of view already established. What remains of interest is how those previous thoughts came together in a unified way to develop a particular course of action.

The group's final summary, written by Bundy and McNaughton, consisted of three sections: an intelligence assessment of the situation in South Vietnam, representing the inputs of INR at the State Department, the CIA, and the Defense Intelligence Agency; U.S. objectives and stakes in South Vietnam and Southeast Asia, again drawing heavily on the intelligence community; and broad options, representing the work of the NSC group.

The final draft, drawn up on November 26, described the situation in the South as "critical and extremely fragile." Further deterioration was expected. How would this affect the prosecution of an overt war? "GVN determination and authority could virtually give way suddenly in the near future, though the chances seem better than even that the new GVN can hang on for this period and thus afford a platform upon which its armed forces, with U.S. assistance, can prosecute the war and attempt to turn the tide." The expectation was that the GVN was adequate to retain power during the next few months and could provide the United States with the "platform" necessary to begin a wider war.

The paper discussed the relationship between the VC and the DRV as a basis for estimating what could be expected if sanctions were applied directly against the North. "The basic elements of Communist strength in South Vietnam remain indigenous,[2] but the North Vietnamese (DRV) contribution is substantial and may be growing. There appears to be a rising rate of infiltration." Although the movement was acknowledged to be Southern, Bundy and McNaughton were optimistic in assessing Northern capacity to call off the insurgency. "We believe any orders from Hanoi would in large measure be obeyed by Communist forces in South Vietnam." Others, as previously indicated, thought the North was unable to control the Southern cadre to the point of calling off the insurgency, even if the North should want to do so. Thus, the capacity of the North to stop the insurgency was seen as a contingency. Another contingency was the capacity of

---

2/In an earlier draft, this point was given further elaboration: "The basic elements of Communist strength in South Vietnam remain indigenous: South Vietnamese grievances, war-weariness, defeatism, and political disarray; VC terror, arms capture, disciplined organization, highly developed intelligence systems, and ability to recruit locally; and the fact that the VC enjoys some status as a nationalist movement. The high VC morale is sustained by successes to date and by the receipt of outside guidance and support."

Summing up the strength of the VC, Maxwell Taylor put the point thus: "Not only do the Viet Cong units have the recuperative powers of the phoenix, but they have an amazing ability to maintain morale. Only in rare cases have we found evidences of bad morale among Viet Cong prisoners or recorded in captured Viet Cong documents." He ascribed this strength partly to the "increased direction and support of their campaign by the government of North Vietnam." But this "increased direction" from the North did not detract from the status of the VC "as a nationalist movement." If anything, it fed directly into it. Victory in the South, according to William Bundy, "would mark the completion of their [DRV] revolution." It would seem then that Hanoi, the VC, and Southern discontent had coalesced into a national movement which was challenged by the antinationalistic policies of the United States government. The imperium was fighting nationalism. This would seem to be a fuller explanation for the "recuperative powers of the phoenix."

the GVN to defeat the VC, after the North succeeded in ordering its cadre to lay down their arms. "If the DRV did in fact remove wholly its direction and support to the VC, the South Vietnamese could in time probably reduce the VC threat to manageable proportions." Why would the war continue at all if the Southern cadre would obey the North? This point was not discussed, but there was an apparent recognition that the insurgency in the South extended beyond the membership of the cadre that had infiltrated from the North. Southern discontent was not restricted to the trained cadre who had returned home. Moreover, no estimate was given as to the length of time the war might continue if the trained cadre did lay down their arms. In light of the wholesale opposition to the GVN that extended beyond the ranks of the trained cadre, and the earlier gloomy estimate that the GVN might not survive long enough to support a massive American presence, it could be concluded that the war would be a rather long one, even if the North were not involved.

The success of the overt war was thus seen as contingent on three factors: the ability of the GVN to remain in power while the United States prosecuted the war; the capacity of the DRV to call off the insurgency; and the capacity of the GVN to defeat the insurgency, even if the North called it off. The chances of all three contingencies coming together were not very high. If an overt war did not stand much chance of succeeding in Vietnam, why begin one? Precisely because the United States was not fighting for Vietnam, but rather to maintain our position in the world.

In the section of the report entitled "U.S. stakes in South Vietnam," Bundy and McNaughton summed up the NSC justification for fighting what could well become an inconclusive war in Vietnam: "Essentially, the loss of South Vietnam to Communist control, in any form, would be a major blow to our basic policies. U.S. prestige is heavily committed to the maintenance of a non-Communist South Vietnam, and only less heavily so to a neutralized Laos." America might not win, McGeorge Bundy concluded, but it must avert defeat. According to the NSC paper, we "must take forceful enough measures in the situation so that we emerge from it, even in the worst case, with our standing as the principal helper against Communist expansion as little impaired as possible."

But what is Communist expansion? Does a civil war in South Vietnam—undirected by Moscow or Peking and barely directed by Hanoi, a traditional rival of Peking—constitute Communist expansion? Although monolithic Communism was clearly perceived as an anachronism, the United States had to avert defeat in South Vietnam to "reassure" the rest of Asia—specifically, Nationalist China, South Korea, Japan, Thailand, Indonesia, Malaysia, the Philippines, India, and Iran. It should be willing to fight an inconclusive struggle in Vietnam to defend the stable governments of Asia:

> A U.S. defeat could lead to serious repercussions in these countries. There is a great deal we could still do to reassure these countries, but the picture of a defense line clearly breached could have serious effects and could easily, *over time,* tend to unravel the whole Pacific and South Asian defense structures.

How long would it be before the rest of Asia was threatened if the United States did not fight in South Vietnam? The phrase "over time" was estimated by the CIA to mean a generation. None of these countries was expected to fall immediately, nor was any of them even perceived to be under immediate threat. American economic strength and physical capacity would remain unimpaired, and each country would be assured of greater help, especially if the United States pulled out of Vietnam and explained its decision on the grounds that the problem there was not international Communism but local dictatorship, imprudent and unwise in its political rule. Indeed, Bundy and McNaughton underscored how the peculiar characteristics of South Vietnam could be seized upon as an adequate explanation if the United States decided to withdraw. We should "make clear to the world, and to nations in Asia particularly, that failure in South Vietnam, if it comes, was due to special local factors—such as a bad colonial heritage and a lack of will to defend itself—that do not apply to other nations." In other words, we could make a reasonable argument based upon the objective reality, then back up our commitment to other lands through word and deed. Our prestige need not be tarnished. There was little need to fight in Vietnam.

But withdrawal, William Bundy declared, would increase the likelihood of nuclear war. A pull-out from Vietnam, he said, would whet the appetite of China, which would then move with alacrity to threaten another Asian country, probably Thailand. This would make it incumbent on the United States to engage the Chinese in nuclear war. In the NSC paper, he put the point thus:

> There are enough "ifs" in the above analysis so that it cannot be concluded that the loss of South Vietnam would soon have the totally crippling effect in Southeast Asia and Asia generally that the loss of Berlin would have in Europe; but it could be that bad, driving us to the progressive loss of other areas or to taking a stand at some point so that there would almost certainly be major conflict and perhaps the great risk of nuclear war.

The Asians, Bundy believed, expected America to fight, and it would be far better to fight in Vietnam at a level of 300,000 U.S. troops (his estimate as of mid-1965) than to be forced to fight a nuclear war.

The consequences of pulling out were manageable. But what of the consequences of staying in and fighting an inconclusive war? Surely the effect would be negative in Europe and the neutral parts of the world. "Our key European allies," the managers observed, "could become seriously concerned if we get ourselves in a major conflict that degraded our ability to defend Europe and produced anything less than an early and completely satisfactory outcome." Similarly, the nonaligned nations "would by and large be opposed to support any course of action we follow in South Vietnam and Laos." In sum, Asia and Europe would admire a quick victory. No one, however, would be heartened by a long, drawn-out, inconclusive struggle. But the chances of a quick victory were deemed narrow, whereas the probability of a lengthy stalemate was considerable. There was little need to fight this type of war in the context of America's worldwide position. Only in the eyes of official Washington was the situation in Vietnam a license for war. The most rational explanation that emerged from the NSC working papers for the expansion of the war effort in Vietnam was that it suited the bureaucratic drive for power and the Presidential myth of not being a "loser."

Having cited the "major blow to our policies" as the justification for launching the war, the Working Group got on with the main business at hand: the planning of the broad options for playing the game. Bundy had stacked the options in advance so that the one he favored would be adopted. He assigned Robert Johnson the task of working out Option A, the do-nothing option. He informed the JCS that they should combine all of the recommendations they had heretofore presented into one package. This would guarantee its rejection. He assigned himself the middle-of-the-road position, the option that could play one off against the other, ensuring its approval. The final draft gave this description of Option A:

Option A would be to continue present policies indefinitely: Maximum assistance within South Vietnam, limited external

140

actions in Laos and by the GVN covertly against North Vietnam, specific individual reprisal actions not only against such incidents as the Gulf of Tonkin attack but also against any recurrence of VC 'spectaculars' such as Bien Hoa. Basic to this option is the continued rejection of negotiations.

Option B, composed by the JCS,

would add to present actions a systematic program of military pressures against the north, with increasing pressure actions to be continued at a fairly rapid pace and without interruption until we achieve our present stated objectives. The actions would mesh at some point with negotiation, but we would approach any discussions or negotiations with absolutely inflexible insistence on our present objectives.

Option C appeared in its final form as follows:

Option C would add to present actions an orchestration of (1) communications with Hanoi and/or Peiping, and (2) additional graduated military moves against infiltration targets, first in Laos and then in the DRV, and then against other targets in North Vietnam. The military scenario should give the U.S. the option at any time to proceed or not, to escalate or not, and to quicken the pace or not. These decisions would be made from time to time in view of all relevant factors. The negotiating part of this course of action would have to be played largely by ear, but in essence we would be indicating from the outset a willingness to negotiate in an affirmative sense, accepting the possibility that we might not achieve our full objectives.

The history of Option C deserves comment as a case study in bureaucratic maneuvering. William Bundy and John McNaughton both wavered in their own recommendations as to the proper strategy toward Vietnam. At one time or another they argued the case for withdrawal on the basis of their respective insights that the situation in Vietnam was simply too difficult for the United States to manage. McNaughton began with the premise that the GVN was steadily deteriorating, then drew two disjunctive conclusions from that premise. In October, he urged the adoption of the JCS list for provocative actions against the North to provide legitimate cover for escalating the war. A month later, he reversed himself and stated: "Should SVN disintegrate completely beneath us, we should try to hold it together long enough to permit us to try to evacuate our forces and to convince the world to accept the uniqueness and congenital impossibility of the South Vietnamese case." He was torn between committing "unbridled acts" of the most egregious sort, and detaching the United States from an untenable situation. It would seem that his reason compelled him to urge a pull-out, but his fear of being too weak to employ massive violence and his positive desire to wield power swayed him to betray his own reason.

William Bundy—perhaps the most experienced of the Asian hands, having worked for ten years at the CIA, four years at the Pentagon, and six years at the State Department—was all too familiar with the French example to believe that America could march through Indochina without suffering enormous losses in manpower, prestige, and domestic tranquillity. His arguments for pulling out, or cutting losses, were supposed by historic precedent and reasoned analysis. When he shifted gears to justify a wider war, he had to seek out the most remote contingencies to back up his recommendations; he, too, had to betray his own reason.

In the original Option C, Bundy recommended an initial sharp blow against the North, followed by a U.S. move to preempt negotiations by taking the conflict to the United Nations. There, we would indicate our willingness to make concessions and call for a cease-fire. The sharp blow would prove to the world that we were bold and had a capacity for risk-taking. The negotiated settlement, "accepting the possibility that we might not achieve our full objectives," would display moderation and willingness to settle a difficult situation. Thus, the original Option C, as conceived by Bundy, would have satisfied both of his urges, the one based on reason, the other on power. He wanted to have it both ways. McNaughton himself described the Bundy position as "hit and get out."

Lloyd Mustin, the JCS representative on the NSC Working Group, put up a fierce battle against the Bundy paper. Responding to this in-house opposition, Bundy sent Jonathan Moore, the State Department representative who assisted Robert Johnson on Option A, to the Pentagon with orders to destroy all copies of Option C. That option was then redefined by McNaughton, after a series of consultations with McNamara. The Secretary of Defense introduced the concept of flexibility and instructed McNaughton to employ language to that effect, apparently reasoning that if the option had the language of flexibility written into it, it would receive the full support of the managers. Accordingly, McNaughton penned in the sentence: "The military scenario should give the U.S. the option at any time to proceed or not, to escalate or not, and to quicken the pace or not." McNaughton referred to Option C as "the slow squeeze," to contrast it with the JCS option, identified as "the fast squeeze."

In analyzing the options, "A" was ruled out because it called for strengthening the pacification programs throughout South Vietnam, which in turn depended upon a stable GVN. Moreover, the actions envisioned under "A" were "common to all three options, and would be pursued with equal force under Option B or Option C." Option A should be adopted only in the event of U.S. withdrawal from Vietnam; that is, if America were willing to accept defeat. By adhering to the present course of action, a "defeat would be clearly due to GVN failure, and we ourselves would be less implicated than if we tried Option B or Option C and failed." Such a defeat would no doubt

143

occur in the absence of escalation. It would take the form of a "Vietnamese-negotiated deal, under which an eventually unified Communist Vietnam would reassert its traditional hostility to Communist China and limit its own ambitions to Laos and Cambodia." In the context of international politics, the United States could have encouraged the development of an independent Communist regime in Indochina, had it chosen to remove itself from that sphere. Escalation, on the other hand, would drive Hanoi into the arms of China. Peking's influence over Hanoi, which the United States could have abated but chose to enhance, was cited in the public rhetoric as the reason for the U.S. commitment to South Vietnam; the results of American policies were declared to be the causes of those policies.

Option B, "the fast squeeze," would open with "major air attacks on key targets in the DRV, starting with the major Phuc Yen airfield." Hanoi would be expected "to hold firm, doing its utmost to stimulate condemnation of our actions, but possibly trying to pretend that it had reduced its activity in the South."

If Hanoi held firm as expected, even when assailed with a rapid burst of bombing, the South would remain in "a continuing danger that the situation would resume its present deteriorating course." Deterioration of Southern morale was by this time considered to be an irreversible phenomenon no matter what the United States did, because "the Vietnamese people are clearly war-weary." Since Hanoi would be expected to infiltrate forces and the morale in the South would continue to decline, the United States "would be driven to up the ante militarily." Greater escalation would render the U.S. international position "very difficult." Moreover, it would encourage "some chance of a Communist military response against the South." This would make it necessary to deploy massive ground troops, and perhaps even nuclear weapons if Communist China joined the DRV. Was it worth it?

Would Hanoi yield, or would the South collapse? Bundy and McNaughton estimated that at best Hanoi would negotiate, while at worst the South would collapse. In the latter alternative, the United States "would be in the posiion of having got into an almost irreversible sequence of military actions, but finding ourselves fighting on behalf of a country that no longer wished to continue the struggle itself." Given this reality, it would have to choose between "an amphibious landing in the DRV"—proposed as a potential course of action—and negotiations on terms that would be "relatively but not necessarily wholly favorable to the attainment of our full objectives."

Option B ran the risk of nuclear war and international embarrassment. Option C, predicated on the principle of the slow squeeze, would allow the United States to control the level of violence and probably avert a showdown with a major Communist power. It would avert the specter of defeat as entailed by Option A, and at least defer the possibility of nuclear war implied by Option B. Thus, Option C was clearly preferable. But to avert nuclear war or imminent defeat, the United States would have to accept the probability of an indefinite and inconclusive struggle. Option C increased the chances that "the struggle would continue indecisively for a considerable period." The slow squeeze could not cut off infiltration, and if the North was willing to accept the pain of bombing, it could match any level of escalation within the bounds of the slow squeeze. Would a protracted war end up squeezing Hanoi or the United States? This matter was not discussed. It was simply assumed that the United States could bear the costs of an inconclusive struggle, one that did not necessarily end in victory or defeat. Yet, the historic example of the French militated against such a course of action.

The United States would begin the bombing of the North on the basis of either infiltration or "another Bien

Hoa." Under Option C, troops were not envisioned as a "military requirement, at least until or unless the DRV threatened a ground move to the south." Use of ground forces at the outset of battle did hold out a possible political advantage: "It would demonstrate resolve and also give us a major bargaining counter in negotiations."

The American negotiating position during the early stages of Option C would be to "resist any formal Geneva conference on Vietnam, since the mere convening of such a conference would have serious morale effects." Only after Hanoi had been hurt would the United States be interested in convening talks. It would insist on three fundamentals:

> (a) that the DRV cease its assistance to and direction of the VC; (b) that an independent and secure GVN be reestablished; and (c) that there be adequate international supervising and verification machinery. (These fundamentals would not be fully spelled out; in practice they leave room for minor concessions at later stages.)

In other words, the U.S. negotiating position under Option C was to accept nothing less than a clear-cut victory.

In conclusion, the NSC paper recommended a decision "to stick with Option A at least for the next few months," and then switch to Option C. "Congress and our major allies would have to be consulted at an early stage. Our basic rationale would be that the increasing DRV infiltration required this degree of action."

On November 27, at a meeting of the NSC principals with Ambassador Taylor, a consensus was reached that it would be difficult for the United States to continue its policies in Southeast Asia "if the GVN collapsed or told us to get out." Westmoreland recommended a six-month delay in wider actions, but this advice was rejected on the grounds that the situation might not hold together that long. The principals recommended "that over the next two months we adopt a program of Option A plus the first stages of Option C."

THE PRESIDENT DECIDES

On December 1, 1964, President Johnson approved the recommendation of the NSC. The President conceived that the first phase of pressures against the DVR would continue for thirty days or more. If the GVN made some progress during this period, the United States would shift to Option C, consisting of "progressively more serious air strikes, possibly running from two to six months."

Following the Viet Cong attack at Pleiku in February 1965, the President put Option C into effect. Continuous aerial bombardment, progressively moving northward in a slow but determined fashion, was set in motion. The purpose of the slow-squeeze policy was to achieve the goal set forth in NSAM 288, "an independent non-Communist South Vietnam." Was the strategy of the slow squeeze adequate to achieve the goal of a non-Communist South? The slow squeeze was adopted as the official strategy because it was governed by the concept of flexibility: "The military scenario should give the U.S. the option at any time to proceed or not, to escalate or not, and to quicken the pace or not." The slow squeeze was conceived as an astute political track for negotiations. But the goal of a non-Communist South was non-negotiable. To combine that strategy with that goal was a prescription for permanent warfare.

Moreover, the problem confounding the managers was how to convince Hanoi that the United States was serious in its commitment to the South and in its determination to see the battle through. Yet, at the same time, President Johnson had decided to do everything in his power to dampen the war psychology of the American public. He refused to impose wage and price controls; he refused to mobilize the reserves. How could Hanoi believe in America's fixed resolve to see the matter through if the American public did not fully accept the possibility of indefinite war? Hanoi's experience with the West had grown out of its protracted struggle against the French. Hanoi had succeeded in that war by wearing down the national will of the French people to persist in an inconclusive conflict. Undoubtedly, Hanoi would bend every effort to enervate the will of the American public as well. It would break the life-line between Washington and Saigon by proving to the American public that it was not committed to see the matter through. The government would then become isolated from the nation. Either the goal of a non-Communist South would have to be sacrificed, or the will of the American public would have to be ignored. Hanoi bet on the likelihood that Washington would eventually respond to the will of its own constituency.

Why didn't Johnson put the public on a war-footing? In the main, because he had to play Hanoi off against China and the Soviet Union. Drumming up the war fever at home might have produced two disastrous consequences: First, neither Hanoi nor Peking would have believed that U.S. intentions were limited to the South. If the regime in the North felt it was directly threatened, this could have triggered a preemptive response by the DRV and the Chinese. Such a response would have compelled the United States to resort, perhaps, to nuclear weapons. Second, war fever at home would have incited the right wing to demand stronger measures by Washington. A non-Communist South was not worth a nuclear war or land war with China.

To sum up, a slow squeeze would have placed Johnson under pressure from the left and the center to give up the battle. War fever at home, on the other hand, would have placed Johnson under mounting pressure from the right to respond to any Chinese move (which itself well might have been triggered by that very war fever) with nuclear weapons or U.S. forces. He selected the slow squeeze and hoped that he could achieve his aim of a non-Communist South within the three remaining years of his term. He lost the gamble.

5 /

FROM ESCALATION
TO STALEMATE

After the United States had retaliated for the Tonkin
incident, the JCS instructed CINCPAC to draw up a
prepackaged set of reprisal targets and to maintain forces
in a high state of readiness to carry out a detailed strike
plan that provided for a range of retaliatory options.
Orders were issued by CINCPAC on September 18, 1964,
and October 28, 1964, the latter entitled "Punitive and
Crippling Reprisal Actions on Targets in North Vietnam."
The orders provided that strikes against the North would
be launched within one hour of the receipt of an operational command. The reprisals were to take place in the
event that another DeSoto patrol was attacked by the
North. A list of ninety-four targets was drawn up by
CINCPAC and submitted to McNamara in the early fall.

In January, immediately after Johnson had approved
the recommendation of the NSC working group to begin
"progressively more serious air attacks possibly running
from two to six months," he authorized a DeSoto patrol
for February 3, 1965. On February 4, in response to JCS

instructions, CINCPAC issued an operational order for a retaliatory raid in the event that the patrol was hit or the VC staged a spectacular raid in the South.

The United States now had forces in position and a generalized, preplanned reprisal target package offering a wide spectrum of choices. Having decided to strike the North, the United States would either manufacture an incident through the provocative use of a DeSoto patrol or wait for the VC to stage an incident in the South on their own initiative.

Later in the day on February 4, however, Wheeler, as Chairman of the JCS, informed CINCPAC and other interested parties to cancel the DeSoto patrol because Soviet Premier Kosygin had announced a four-day visit to Hanoi beginning February 6. The Administration was divided as to the meaning of Kosygin's visit; some held that it signified an intention to defend Hanoi after years of flagging interest, while others believed that Moscow was about to exercise a benign influence upon Hanoi— one which would be consistent with U.S. objectives in the South. The latter possibility persuaded the Administration to cancel the DeSoto patrol.

The day after Kosygin arrived in Hanoi, the Viet Cong attacked U.S. military installations at Pleiku, killing eight Americans and wounding more than a hundred. At the same time assaults were launched against Camp Hollo- way, the air base at Pleiku, and two other installations on the coast. Washington believed the attacks had been organized by the hard-liners in Hanoi to abort any peace initiative by Kosygin. This was a dubious line of reasoning, since the Viet Cong had no assurance that the United States would retaliate; similar incidents had occurred over the past months without eliciting a U.S. response.

In any event, preparations for war received a higher priority than speculations on Kosygin's moderating influ- ence. After a seventy-five-minute meeting of the National

Security Council in the White House Cabinet Room, President Johnson, in the presence of Senate Majority Leader Mansfield and House Speaker McCormack, ordered a U.S. air strike at Donghoi, just beyond the seventeenth parallel in North Vietnam. McGeorge Bundy, along with Taylor and Westmoreland in Saigon, had recommended prompt retaliation. Shortly thereafter, Johnson sent a cable to Moscow assuring the Russians that Kosygin's presence in Hanoi during the U.S. reprisal was an unfortunate coincidence and that "no affront to the Soviet Union was intended."

While Kosygin was in Hanoi, McGeorge Bundy was visiting Saigon to review with the U.S. Mission the complex issue of future U.S. pressures on the North. As early as May 1964, Bundy had been an original and enthusiastic supporter of Operation Rolling Thunder. Indeed, his position had been so unyielding that McNamara had specifically told him to "cool it" until the President had been elected. As a result, his attitude toward the bombing policy in the intervening months had not been conspicuous. Some officials have even stated that Bundy was dispatched to Vietnam precisely because he was the only high-ranking policy-maker not yet committed to the decision to begin the bombing. According to this interpretation, Johnson, anxious to have everyone aboard the ship of state, set out to mousetrap Bundy into lending his support. This reading of Johnson's motives and Bundy's views is far too tortured. Johnson, of course, wanted a consensus, but he did not have to go out of his way to attain it; Bundy's initial burst of enthusiasm, although contained by the strictures of a Presidential campaign, never wavered. This is borne out by his wholehearted endorsement of replying to Pleiku, and the missionary zeal he invoked to back up his recommendations for a continuous reprisal policy.

Immediately after the reprisal decision of February 7

had been made, McGeorge Bundy and his group, consisting of McNaughton, White House Aide Chester Cooper, and Chairman of the Vietnam Coordinating Group Leonard Unger returned to Washington on Air Force One. En route a memorandum to the President was drafted, setting forth a detailed rationale for the Rolling Thunder policy. The memorandum is highly significant, since it reflects the thinking of the President's chief adviser on Vietnam policy, summarizes the views of some members of the U.S. Mission in Saigon, draws upon some of Bundy's impressions while in Vietnam, and, most importantly, recapitulates Administration doctrine at the very moment when the President was shifting away from a tit-for-tat policy and embracing a generalized bombing campaign.

The memorandum opened with a set of summary conclusions, followed by a more detailed elaboration of those ideas, including an annex which recommended precise actions to be undertaken forthwith. In the first two paragraphs, Bundy explained why the United States must act now:

> The situation in Vietnam is deteriorating, and without new U.S. action defeat appears inevitable—probably not in a matter of weeks or perhaps even months, but within the next year or so. There is still time to turn it around, but not much.

> The stakes in Vietnam are extremely high. The American investment is very large, and American responsibility is a fact of life which is palpable in the atmosphere of Asia, and even elsewhere. The international prestige of the United States and a substantial part of our influence, are directly at risk in Vietnam.

The memorandum suggested that only if the United States avoided a defeat in Vietnam would it be able to maintain its prestige around the globe. The United States was not, in Bundy's language, engaged in an anti-Communist crusade or, for that matter, even in defending its national security in any ordinary meaning of that term. Rather, it was displaying its prestige as the Number One Nation in the world; hence, it had to be committed to a posture of invincibility. And as if he were pointing to some tangible evidence which would de-mystify the elusive will-o'-the-wisp of being Number One, Bundy repeatedly referred to the unalloyed quality of the personnel in the field:

> But I want to stress one important general conclusion which again is shared by all members of my party: the U.S. mission is composed of outstanding men, and U.S. policy within Vietnam is mainly right and well directed. None of the special solutions or criticisms put forward with zeal by individual reformers in government or in the press is of major importance, and many of them are flatly wrong. No man is perfect, and not every tactical step of recent months has been perfectly chosen, but when you described the Americans in Vietnam as your first team, you were right.

The Number One Nation, having sent its first team abroad to defend its number one position, was unequivocally obliged to support that team in the face of any threat to it. Such tautological reasoning lies at the foundation of the imperial role. The mother country must first and foremost go to war to support its client states. This is quite different from the situation of a nation forced to go to war to protect the survival of its home front. The powerful are more committed to defending attacks on their own prestige than they are to protecting the survival of their own constituencies.

Accepting the overriding need to defend the prestige of the state and assert its influence, McGeorge Bundy advocated a policy of "sustained reprisal." He defined this policy as one "in which air and naval action against the North was justified by and related to the Viet Cong campaign of violence and terror in the South." A reprisal policy should be managed according to game stratagems of attack and counterattack, in which the manager evaluates the strength of the attack and, if he judges that the opponent scored sufficient points, then calls his play in the form of a counterattack designed to outscore the opponent. Bundy explained how the game would be played:

> We may wish at the outset to relate our reprisals to those acts of relatively high visibility such as the Pleiku incident. Later, we might retaliate against the assassination of a province chief, but not necessarily the murder of a hamlet official; we might retaliate against a grenade thrown into a crowded cafe in Saigon, but not necessarily to a shot fired into a small shop in the countryside.

Eventually, the playing of the game would no longer be dependent on particular acts and responses, but would fall into a "more generalized pattern." Again in Bundy's language:

> Once a program of reprisals is clearly under way, it should not be necessary to connect each specific act against North Vietnam to a particular outrage in the South. It should be possible, for example, to publish weekly lists of outrages in the South and to have it clearly understood that these outrages are the cause of such action against the North as may be occurring in the current period. Such a more generalized pattern of reprisal would remove much of the difficulty in finding precisely matching targets in response to specific atrocities.

The change in the rules from a particular to a generalized response, or from a tit-for-tat policy to one of continuous bombing, was not agreed to by the two parties; rather, it was invoked unilaterally by the United States. In fact, the rules were continually changed at the discretion of the United States. Bundy described the need to move from a generalized response related to a list of weekly outrages to one that would simply meet the need for reprisals in the first place. He stated:

> At the same time, it should be recognized that in order to maintain the power of reprisal without risk of excessive loss, an "air war" may in fact be necessary. We should therefore be ready to develop a separate justification for energetic flak suppression and if necessary for the destruction of Communist air power. The essence of such an explanation should be that these actions are intended solely to insure the effectiveness of a policy of reprisal, and in no sense represent any intent to wage offensive war against the North. These distinctions should not be difficult to develop.

Even if bombing were to fail to meet American objectives, Bundy argued, "the policy will be worth it":

> At a minimum it will damp down the charge that we did not do all we could have done, and this charge will be important in many countries, including our own.

> Beyond that, a reprisal policy—to the extent that it demonstrates U.S. willingness to employ this new norm in counter-insurgency—will set a higher price for the future upon all adventures of guerilla warfare and it should therefore somewhat increase our ability to deter such adventures. We must recognize, however, that that ability will be gravely weakened if there is failure for any reason in Vietnam.

The imperial player thrives on a global playing field. The way he plays the game becomes as important to him as the result of the game. If he loses in a way that nonetheless intimidates other players from engaging him in contest, he has plucked the fruits of victory from the jaws of defeat. Such intimidation cannot be achieved in just a brief flurry of violence. To McGeorge Bundy, the prospects for an early resolution to the contest were slim.

"One final word," he cautioned the President. "At its very best the struggle in Vietnam will be long."

William Bundy advanced an argument similar to his brother's, but as part of a milder prescription. He admonished the President that if the United States accepted defeat and decided to withdraw, it would be necessary to bomb the North and inflict some pain upon them as part of our act of withdrawal.

The policy of the "slow squeeze"—language selected by McNaughton and approved by McNamara—was little more than a recipe cooked up by an imperial chef. Part of the slow squeeze was the wielding of threats, not the application of force, but the very choice of language used in further refining the ingredients of the slow squeeze places it squarely within the imperial context. McGeorge Bundy elaborated on the slow-squeeze policy with an observation to the President that "we also need to conduct the application of the force so that there is always a prospect of worse to come."

McGeorge Bundy projected the game traits on an imperial screen. Ultimately, the strictures of imperialism held his attention more than the stratagems of the game. He made this abundantly clear when he offered the judgment that the rewards he expected from a policy of continuous reprisals would be far greater with the client in the South than with the putative enemy in the North. "We emphasize," he said, "that our primary target in advocating a reprisal policy is the improvement of the situation in South Vietnam." That improvement would come about once the United States took over direction of the government in the South. Explaining the larger meaning of a reprisal policy, Bundy told Johnson:

Joint reprisals would imply military planning in which the American role would necessarily be controlling, and this new relation should add to our bargaining power in other

157

military efforts—and conceivably on a wider plane as well if a more stable government is formed. We have a whip hand in reprisals as we do not in other fields.

The imperial power should go to war to use a "whip hand" over its client and a slow squeeze against its enemy.

McGeorge Bundy was the chief architect of the empire. He argued, summarily, that the United States should wage an aggressive war against the North—a war that would last a long time, that would not necessarily result in defeat of the North but rather would have to be fought to defend the prestige and influence of the United States abroad, that would allow the United States to take over the government of its client, that would inflict visible damage on the North as a reminder to them, and to others, that those who oppose the will of the United States would suffer accordingly.

While Bundy was advocating a policy of continuous bombing of the North to improve the situation in the South, Maxwell Taylor was pressing the President to pursue the same course but for another end: to give Hanoi "serious doubts as to their chances for ultimate success." In a cable to Johnson dated February 12, Taylor called for a properly-managed air campaign against the North— one which, in his words, "should present to the DRV leaders a vision of inevitable, ultimate destruction if they do not change their ways."

Although Taylor differed from Bundy on the prime purpose of aerial attacks, the process of the campaign would match Bundy's definition of the wielding of imperial power. Indeed, Taylor's selection of language moved beyond the realm of imperialism, reaching out to the concept of deification. "Inevitable, ultimate destruction" reflected a perception of American power that can only be described as godlike. The United States should apply its godlike power to "change the ways" of the enemy.

While McGeorge Bundy acted like a gamester to bring about an imperial goal, Taylor became a god who descended upon the enemy with his imperial stick.

Taylor exhibited his imperial drive toward the client in the South in an even more obvious way than he suggested toward the enemy in the North. In an extraordinary example of imperial language, Taylor, reprimanding the Young Turks in Saigon—Ky, Thieu, Thi, and Cang—for having attempted a coup against the government in December 1964, told them:

> Do all of you understand English? [Vietnamese officers indicating they did, although the understanding of General Thi was known to be weak.] I told you all clearly at General Westmoreland's dinner we Americans were tired of coups. Apparently I wasted my words. Maybe this is because something is wrong with my French because you evidently didn't understand. I made it clear that all the military plans which I know you would like to carry out are dependent on governmental stability. Now you have made a real mess. We cannot carry you forever if you do things like this. Who speaks for this group? Do you have a spokesman?

JOHNSON DECIDES ON ROLLING THUNDER

In addition to the Bundy memorandum and the Taylor cable calling for general and graduated reprisal programs, the JCS, on February 11, submitted to McNamara an eight-week program for bombing the North. McNamara had previously instructed the JCS to confine the targets to areas along Route 7 in Laos and south of the nineteenth parallel in North Vietnam.

The JCS program called for four strikes a week for eight weeks. In addition, the JCS requested that 325 aircraft be deployed immediately to cope with any escalation that might result. This deployment should include thirty B-52's to be sent to Guam, nine more USAF tactical fighter squadrons, and a fourth aircraft carrier. Marine and army units were to be dispatched to Thailand, and other units were to be alerted.

Rolling Thunder, in the eyes of the JCS, would be a success. "If the U.S. persevered in the face of threats and international pressures, and as the degree of damage inflicted on North Vietnam increased, the chances of a reduction in Vietcong activity would rise." On the other hand, "if the insurgency continues with active DRV support, strikes against the DRV will be extended with intensified efforts against targets north of the 19th parallel."

The Air Chief of Staff, McConnell, disagreed with the other members of the JCS, for he thought the JCS program was too mild. Wheeler, as Chairman of the JCS, added the suggestion that the bombing campaign should be directed against the Northern transportation system, especially the railroads. Along with Harold Johnson, the Army Chief of Staff, Wheeler believed that three U.S. ground divisions might have to be sent to Southeast Asia. He directed the JCS to examine the possibility of putting two of these divisions into northeast Thailand and the third, augmented by allies, south of the DMZ. The JCS, it should be noted, was the only agency in Washington that felt a ground commitment would be necessary while Washington was issuing the go signal on bombing.

The formal Presidential decision to inaugurate Operation Rolling Thunder was made on Sunday, February 13. A cable was drafted in the White House and transmitted to Taylor in Saigon late that afternoon. It informed Taylor that the President

today approved the following program for immediate future actions:

1. Intensify pacification program in South.

2. We will execute a program of measured and limited air action jointly with GVN against selected military targets in DRV remaining south of 19th parallel until further notice.

FYI. Our current expectation is that these attacks might come about once or twice a week and involve two or three targets on each day of operations.

Johnson further stated that the United States must be fully prepared to go to the United Nations "to make clear case that aggressor is Hanoi." But the United Nations would not be used simply as a propaganda forum to disseminate U.S. accusations against the North. Johnson instructed Taylor that we must "make it plain that we are ready and eager for 'talks' to bring aggression to an end." Pursuant thereto, Taylor was authorized to inform the GVN that "announcement of readiness to talk is stronger diplomatic position than awaiting inevitable summons to Security Council by third parties."

Were talks at the UN to be conducted in a serious manner with a view to entering into a realistic settlement with the DRV, or were the talks to be a cover to mask the preconceived wish to continue Rolling Thunder in an unabated form until the DRV capitulated to U.S. demands? Were the talks the goal of Rolling Thunder, or was Rolling Thunder to be the goal of the talks?

Taylor was told he could tell the GVN that "we are determined to continue with military actions regardless of Security Council deliberations and any 'talks' or negotiations. . . ." The Johnson formula was talk talk fight fight. "With or without Hanoi," Johnson said of the relationship between Rolling Thunder and the United Nations,

. . . we have every expectation that any talks that may result from our Security Council initiative would in fact go on for many weeks or perhaps months and would above all focus constantly on the cessation of Hanoi's aggression as the precondition to any cessation of military action against the DRV. We further anticipate that any detailed discussions about any possible eventual form of agreement returning to the essentials of the 1954 accords would be postponed and would be subordinated to the central issue.

Johnson, in other words, would be willing to talk about the conditions for stopping the bombing, but the condition for stopping military action would be surrender.

The first Rolling Thunder strike was set for February 20. A cable to that effect was sent from Washington at eight P.M. on February 18, and Taylor was directed to obtain GVN clearance. Five hours later, at one P.M. Saigon time, Colonel Pham Ngoc Thao attempted to oust General Khanh in a semi-coup. Until the coup was defeated and Khanh's resignation submitted some forty hours later, pandemonium reigned in Saigon. Taylor immediately urged cancellation of the air strike, and Washington agreed. The strike was rescheduled for February 26 but bad weather intervened, forcing another postponement until March 2.

The attack of March 2 involved 104 USAF planes. B-52's on Guam were alerted, but did not participate. Consistent with Johnson's orders, the strikes during the first two· weeks of March remained below the nineteenth parallel, occurred twice a week, and were directed at only a few fixed targets, especially storage depots, radar installations, and bridges.

McNamara had already expressed strong concern over the lack of bomb damage. As early as February 17, in a memorandum to Wheeler referring to the results of the February 7 raid which had put 267 sorties into the air to attack 491 buildings but had only destroyed 47 and damaged 22 others, McNamara had complained that "the four missions left the operations at the targets relatively unimpaired." He noted some satisfaction, however, because "our primary objective, of course, was to communicate our political resolve." But he warned that this would prove "hollow" in the future unless more military damage was done.

While McNamara was fretting over the lack of military damage to the North, Taylor was expressing sharp annoyance over what he considered to be an unnecessarily timid and ambivalent U.S. air-strike pattern. He felt that long delays between strikes and marginal weight of attacks rendered the current level of air strikes "meaningless," and recommended a dynamic program which scheduled several strikes per week, marching North in a relentless fashion to break the will of the DRV. He told Rusk in a message on March 8 that he wanted:

> a rational pattern which will convince the leaders in Hanoi that we are on a dynamic schedule which will not remain static in a narrow zone far removed from them and their sources of power but which is a moving growing threat which cannot be ignored.

Taylor objected to the proposed JCS eight-week program because it remained too long south of the nineteenth parallel. He cited Seaborn's opinion that Hanoi was under the impression that the limited nature of the air strikes signified little more than an attempt by the United States to improve its bargaining position. Taylor proposed that the bombing move beyond the nineteenth parallel immediately, "in order to avoid a build up of international pressures to negotiate."

General Westmoreland concurred in Taylor's message to Rusk. He also forwarded his own analysis of the situation to Johnson at this time. If the present pattern of the war continued, Westmoreland foresaw the GVN retiring to a few provincial district capitals, clogged with refugees and neutralists clamoring to end the war. The Viet Cong

163

would occupy everything else. It was essential for the United States to buy time. Three army helicopter companies for close air support were needed, and the United States would have to change its policy on the use of combat troops. This represented the first official request for U.S. ground forces, reflecting Westmoreland's thinking that the war had to be won in the South. Johnson had hoped that pacification could turn the trick in the South, but he now began to respond to Westmoreland's despair, not so much to shift the site of battle from North to South, but rather in order to continue the battle in the North. Johnson feared that an expanded effort in the air campaign, then being urged upon him by his senior advisers and about to be put into effect, would go for naught if the situation in the South collapsed. He did not want to be placed in the position of accelerating the bombing of the North while the Viet Cong were in the process of conquering the South. Thus, he dispatched General Harold Johnson to Vietnam with a high-ranking fact-finding team. On March 14, Harold Johnson reported his findings to the President: The United States would need ground troops in the South, as well as a greatly expanded bombing program in the North; otherwise, it would face defeat. On March 19, the President ordered the air campaign expanded beyond the nineteenth parallel, but shelved the request for U.S. troops.

THE AIR WAR EXPANDS

Target selection in late February and early March had been completely dominated by such political and psychological considerations as boosting GVN morale, altering the will of the DRV, and demonstrating to the world the determination of the United States. Relatively little weight was given to the more direct military and economic implications of whatever target destruction might be achieved. When Johnson ordered an expansion of the air war on March 19, he called for more raids, going beyond the nineteenth parallel, and finally, but most importantly, a movement away from fixed targets to what can be referred to as targets of opportunity, or interdiction bombing. The thinking behind the decision to go after targets of opportunity paved the way for Washington to adopt a new strategy for prosecuting the war—one which held untoward consequences for the future.

Interdiction bombing, according to Wheeler, "would hamper and delay the movement of DRV CHI/COM forces to the South and, likewise, would place a stricture on the quantities of material and personnel which can be infiltrated through Laos and South Vietnam."

McNamara responded to Wheeler's recommendation by requesting that the JCS develop an integrated attack plan on the railway system as set forth in the Wheeler memo. The JCS, in conjunction with CINCPAC, came up with a twelve-week bombing program essentially built around the destruction of lines of communications (LOC).

In a cable sent in mid-March by Westmoreland and Taylor to Sharp and Wheeler, the interdiction rationale received a strong endorsement. Westmoreland, in fact, discovered another value in hitting LOC. Aside from affecting infiltration to the South, the United States would be able to put the squeeze on the Northern population by reducing the flow of available consumer goods. Strongly reflecting an ethnocentric point of view, Westmoreland told the JCS:

> Moreover, these attacks by interrupting the flow of consumer goods to southern DRV would carry to NVN man in the street, with minimum loss of civilian life, the message of U.S. determination.

Air Chief McConnell again went far beyond his military colleagues in recommending a twenty-eight-day program, climbing up the list of ninety-four targets, culminating in a direct attack on Hanoi. McConnell and the other Chiefs reached a compromise, agreeing on a twelve-week program which would initially reduce the flow of consumer goods to the North and cut infiltration into the South, then move into the last phase of striking industrial targets outside of population areas, until the enemy would realize that "the Hanoi and Haiphong areas will be the next logical targets in our continued air campaign."

The civilian leadership, led by McNamara, refused to approve that part of the JCS program which called for attacks on Hanoi and Haiphong, as well as the request to permit the JCS to make target selection on a twelve-week basis. Both McNamara and Johnson preferred to retain personal control over attack concepts and individual target selection. The number of sorties per week was increased and interdiction bombing received high-level approval.

The decision to begin interdiction bombing signified a major switch in strategy. Instead of trying to alter the *will* of the enemy, bombing would now be designed to destroy the *capacity* of the enemy to conduct the war. Instead of an immediate capitulation based on fear of more damage to come, bombing would now inflict heavy damage on the enemy's logistics, wear him down physically, and thus prove to him that he could not win the war. In embracing the thinking behind interdiction bombing, Washington also moved toward the realization that in order to prove to Hanoi that it could not win the war, it would have to frustrate the insurgency in the South. This, of course, would compel Washington to switch its attention to the troop issue, and reduce the significance heretofore attached to the air war.

THE FIRST DECISION TO COMMIT
U.S. TROOPS

The first civilian official to raise the troop issue was John T. McNaughton. In a lengthy memorandum dated March 24, submitted five days after Johnson agreed to expand the air war in the North, McNaughton addressed himself to the overall situation in Vietnam, including specific proposals for victory. The opening question of the memo set the ominous tone of what was to follow. McNaughton asked rhetorically, could the situation in South Vietnam "be bottomed out" without extreme measures against the DRV or deployment "of large numbers of U.S. (and other) combat troops inside SVN? The answer is perhaps, but probably no." The situation in the South was turning from bad to worse, McNaughton said, with GVN control shrinking to the enclaves. Given the imminence of an American defeat, he offered a cold, rather cynical statement of U.S. aims:

> 70 percent—to avoid a humiliating U.S. defeat (to our reputation as a guarantor).
>
> 20 percent—to keep SVN (and the adjacent) territory from Chinese hands.
>
> 10 percent—to permit the people of SVN to enjoy a better, freer way of life.
>
> Also—to emerge from crisis without unacceptable taint from methods used.
>
> Not to "help a friend" although it would be hard to stay in if asked out.

He noted that the air war was not sufficient for the United States to achieve its objectives. With respect to the JCS proposal calling for will-breaking strikes against the North, McNaughton doubted that "DRV will cave," and that, even if they did, the VC would "obey a caving DRV." Parenthetically, he noted that what that left for Rolling Thunder was "only a political and anti-infiltration nuisance." One might ask, then, why did the United States start the bombing, except perhaps to legitimize the introduction of U.S. ground troops into the South?

Having minimized any potential that could be gained from an expanded air war, McNaughton rejected exit by negotiations because it was "tainted by the humiliation likely to follow." Having dismissed the alternatives of a much stronger air war and exit by negotiations, McNaughton recommended that to achieve our objectives, we must make our initial deployment of about three U.S. divisions and two Korean divisions. Their purpose would be to defeat the VC on the ground, improve GVN/VC morale, enhance the bargaining power of the United States in any negotiations, and show the world the lengths to which the United States would go to fulfill commitments.

However, he also listed eight risks that would attend the use of American ground forces in Vietnam:

(1) Deployment will suck Chicom troops into DRV.

(2) Deployment will suck counterbalancing DRV/Chinese troops into SVN.

(3) Announcement of deployment will cause massive DRV/Chicom effort.

(4) U.S. losses will increase.

(5) Friction with GVN (and Koreans?) over command will arise.

(6) GVN will tend increasingly to "let the U.S. do it."

(7) Anti-U.S. "colonialist" mood may increase in and outside SVN.

(8) U.S. forces may be surrounded and trapped.

"Once U.S. troops are in," McNaughton cautioned, "it

will be difficult to withdraw them or to move them, say to Thailand, without admitting defeat." But he added, "it will take massive deployments (many divisions) to improve the US/GVN:VC ratio to the optimum ten-to-one." Clearly, then, McNaughton was talking about many divisions to win the war, not just three as some kind of bargaining counter.

General Harold Johnson, according to a high official at the Defense Department, had held a series of discussions with McNaughton, and had impressed upon him the need to deploy U.S. troops in a combat role if South Vietnam were not to be cut in half. The McNaughton memo excited the President's interest, and he asked Taylor to return to Washington from Saigon and attend a high-level Presidential review to determine the next courses of action.

Meetings at the White House on April 1 and 2 culminated in NSAM 328, which promulgated the significant decision to change the role of the Marine battalions stationed in Vietnam from one of advice and static defense to one of active combat operations against VC guerrillas. The President, committed to an air policy that implied the war had to be won in the South, now took the momentous step of using U.S. troops in the South for offensive purposes. The next logical step, foreshadowed by this decision, would be a massive build-up of forces. The President was determined that the change in the role of the Marine battalions be given as little prominence as possible.

John McCone, the Director of the CIA, disagreed with the President's position. McCone understood that the decision to use the Marines in an offensive role would lead to a much larger troop commitment in the near future. He agreed that this was necessary, but felt the President should deploy troops only in an offensive role if he was willing to intensify the bombing beyond the limits that had been set on March 19. McCone warned the President that a "slowly ascending tempo" of bombing meant "time will run against us in this operation and I think that the North Vietnamese are counting on this." The DRV, he warned, would respond to a "modest scale of bombing" by building up Viet Cong capabilities through "covert infiltration of North Vietnamese and, possibly, Chinese cadres and thus bring an ever increasing pressure on our forces." How would this affect the use of U.S. ground forces in the South? "In effect," McCone argued, "we will find ourselves mired down in combat in the jungle in a military effort that we cannot win, and from which we will have extreme difficulty in extracting ourselves." To avoid a perpetual stalemate, "it is my judgment that if we are to change the mission of the ground forces we must also change the ground rules of the strikes against North Vietnam." McCone was so certain of this that he told the President that "if we are unwilling to take this kind of a decision [massive bombing] now, we must not take the actions concerning the mission of our ground forces."

The President shrugged off McCone's advice. A greatly expanded air war in the North, perhaps culminating in direct attacks on the population and strategic centers of Hanoi and Haiphong, simply incurred too great a risk of intervention by one of the Communist super-powers. The President, who referred to Operation Rolling Thunder throughout this period as "that bombing bull-shit," had firmly decided to increase the U.S. enterprise in the South instead of in the North. The bombing, in retrospect, was the ticket for U.S. soldiers to enter the South and become a sideshow to the main theater of battle, conducted below the seventeenth parallel.

Six days after he authorized the Marines to engage in offensive operations, Johnson began to bombard Taylor with messages and instructions to speed up the introduction of U.S. and third-country ground forces into the operational theater of battle in the South. Taylor, whose preferred strategy was an increased tempo of bombing, with the ARVN playing an exclusive ground role in the South, became quite critical of the measures that had been adopted by the President since the April 2 meeting at the White House. The President, according to Taylor, was not bombing enough, but was all too eager to deploy U.S. troops in a combat role. To Taylor, the air war in the North was a visible substitute for U.S. involvement in an uncertain future in the South. By the middle of April, communications between Washington and Saigon were becoming increasingly strained. Taylor's ill-concealed annoyance at mounting pressures burst on April 18, when he received another instruction from "highest authority," proposing seven complicated new measures having to do with ground force deployments. The White House justified these new measures on the grounds that "something new must be added in the South to achieve victory." Taylor forwarded an exasperated response to McGeorge Bundy the same day, expressing resentment over Washington's excessive eagerness to introduce U.S. combat forces into South Vietnam. This cable made it clear that meaningful communications between Washington and Saigon had all but broken down. McNamara immediately called for a Honolulu conference to clear up the difficulties and restore the consensus. Those who took part in this conference on April 20 were Taylor, McNamara, Wheeler, Westmoreland, Sharp, William Bundy, and McNaughton.

The conferees quickly agreed that DRV/VC would not "capitulate, or come to a position acceptable to us, in less than six months." According to a memorandum by McNaughton and McNamara which contained references to the minutes of the conference, "this is because settlement will come as much or more from VC failure in the South as from DRV pain in the North, and that it will take more than six months, perhaps a year or two, to demonstrate VC failure in the South."

This landmark position contradicted the entire range of thinking that had prevailed in Washington up to this time. At first, the goal had been to break the will of the DRV. When that hope was shattered, the aim was changed to that of breaking the capacity of the DRV to conduct the war by reducing the level of infiltration into the South. At Honolulu, the national security managers rejected the possibility of breaking either the will or the capability of the DRV. North Vietnam was no longer the key to victory, according to the highest level of official thinking; victory could only come about through actually frustrating the VC in the South. It had taken the Johnson Administration six weeks of actual war to verify what all intelligence had disclosed over the previous eleven years: There was a civil war in the South, and the Viet Cong were an independent factor, only partially aided and abetted by Hanoi.

Nevertheless, it was agreed that the futile air war would have to continue. "All of them," according to the minutes, "envisioned a strike program continuing at least six months, perhaps a year or more, avoiding the Hanoi–Haiphong–Phuc Yen areas during that period." The conferees added that "it is important not to kill the hostage by destroying the North Vietnamese assets inside the Hanoi Donut." Since the air war was no longer recognized as carrying any material advantage, it was important not to incur any unnecessary disadvantages by its continuation. Hence, the conferees further agreed that "tasks within South Vietnam should have first call on air assets."

Consistent with their assumption that the VC would have to be frustrated in the South, the conference recommended the deployment of seventeen battalions, bringing the troop level up to a figure of 77,250. It was further stipulated that these forces might have to be supplemented at some future date by an entire U.S. air mobile division of 15,800, with some Korean and Marine support. By April 20, 1965, only fifty days after the start of Operation Rolling Thunder, the United States was committing itself to a troop level of 100,000.

THE BOMBING PAUSE: PRELUDE
TO ESCALATING TROOP LEVELS

Following the Honolulu conference, pressure for some kind of bombing halt began to mount. The pressure originated with McNaughton, who had also been the first civilian leader to recommend a massive troop deployment. Although the President did not believe that a bombing halt would evoke any response from Hanoi, he did order a brief pause effective May 13, "to begin," as he expressed it, "to clear a path either toward restoration of peace or toward increased military action, depending on the reaction of the Communists." The bombing pause was designed to offer Hanoi the final opportunity for capitulation, before the United States escalated the troop level to ensure victory.

The project was given the code name "Mayflower," and its political purpose was made known to only a few officials. On the evening of May 10, Johnson sent a personal message to Taylor informing him that a decision had been made to call a brief halt in air strikes. "Buddha's birthday," Johnson cabled Taylor, "seems to me to provide an excellent opportunity for a pause in air strikes which might go into next week and which I could use to good effect with world opinion." Johnson cautioned Taylor to keep this information strictly private. "My plan," Johnson went on, "is not to announce this brief pause but simply to call it privately to the attention of Moscow and Hanoi as soon as possible and tell them that we shall be watching closely to see whether they respond in any way. My current plan is to report publicly after the pause on what we have done."

The next day McNamara sent a message to Sharp and Westmoreland ordering a halt in all strike operations against North Vietnam. He instructed Sharp to redirect all sorties that would have gone against North Vietnam to "appropriate targets in South Vietnam."

On the evening of May 11, Rusk cabled Ambassador Foy Kohler in Moscow, ordering him to make urgent contact with the DRV Ambassador to the Soviet Union and tell him that the United States was fully prepared to stop the bombing of the North in exchange for a DRV order to halt VC activity in the South. The pause would permit the United States to see whether the DRV would abide by this agreement. That same evening, Rusk summoned Dobrynin, the Soviet Ambassador to the United States, to his State Department office and repeated the same message. Dobrynin was relieved that the Soviets were merely being informed, rather than being asked to act as intermediary between Washington and Hanoi. Rusk told Dobrynin that "Hanoi appears to have the impression they may succeed, but the U.S. will not get tired or be affected by very small domestic opposition or by international pressures."

Meanwhile, Kohler tried to make contact with the DRV Ambassador in Moscow, but the Hanoi Embassy refused to see him on the grounds that there were no diplomatic relations between the two countries. State then advised Kohler to transmit the message by letter and to seek an appointment with Soviet Acting Foreign Minister Kuznetsov, requesting him to act as intermediary in behalf of the United States. The letter to the DRV Embassy was hand-delivered, and was returned the following morning in a plain envelope, addressed "Embassy of U.S. of A."

Since Kuznetsov was out of town, Kohler conferred with Deputy Foreign Minister Firyubin. In a lengthy cable to Rusk, Kohler reported that Firyubin had flatly refused to act as intermediary and had launched into a tirade against U.S. policy in Vietnam, interpreting the proposed pause as a veiled threat of "renewed and expanded aggression." Firyubin advised Kohler that instead of instituting pauses, the United States should be withdrawing from Vietnam. Kohler shrugged off this advice and repeated his request to deliver the message to the Hanoi Embassy. Firyubin replied: "I am not a postman." Interpreting this to the State Department, Kohler said that although he was annoyed at the Soviet refusal, "I could undersand if not sympathize with Soviet sensitivity, given CHICOM eagerness to adduce proof of their charges of collusion against the Soviets and, frankly, given rather strenuous nature of document they were being asked to transmit to DRV."

How did this exchange affect U.S.–Soviet relations? "We lose nothing," Kohler told the State Department, "assuming Soviets have not completely forgotten lesson Cuba and there is some flexibility in Soviet position which we should seek to exploit."

Kohler was obviously unwilling to face up to the fact that the Soviet Union had flatly rejected the U.S. request on the grounds that it opposed the expansion of the war into the North. Instead, he had convinced himself that were it not for the fear of being charged with collusion by China, the Soviet Union would have closed ranks with the United States to admonish its own "client" to mend its ways. The American Ambassador projected his own imperial role toward South Vietnam upon the Soviet Union, feeling that since the United States controlled the destiny of its own clients, the Soviet Union must be able to do likewise. He was convinced that the situation in Vietnam could be properly settled in private by the great powers.

When Rusk learned of Kohler's failure with Firyubin, he decided that a touch of personal diplomacy might do the trick. On May 15 he met with Gromyko for a kaffee klatsch at the Austrian Chancellor's residence in Vienna, and again suggested that the Soviet Union act as intermediary to work out a settlement. Gromyko, according to Rusk, "commented with considerable seriousness that the Soviets will not negotiate about Vietnam." Rusk continued:

> He said there were other parties involved in that situation and that the United States would have to find ways of establishing contact with them, and he specifically mentioned the DRV. He said they will continue to support North Vietnam and will do so decisively. He then made reference to a fellow Socialist country under attack.

Gromyko characterized the temporary suspension of bombing as "insulting."

Rusk, unlike Kohler, understood the message conveyed by Gromyko. Summarizing his impressions of the discussion with Gromyko, Rusk wrote:

> It is quite clear, however, that Gromyko wanted me to believe that they were not prepared to work toward a settlement in Hanoi and Peiping and that, indeed, unless we abandon our effort in South Vietnam there will be very serious consequences ahead.

The bombing halt fizzled. On the morning of May 18, bombing was resumed. Hanoi issued a public statement denouncing the pause as a "deceitful maneuver designed to pave the way for new U.S. acts of war."

The refusal of the DRV to capitulate did, in fact, irrevocably commit the Johnson Administration to the strategy of trying to defeat the VC on the ground in the South. Throughout the month of June, it was the debate on the size of the troop commitment, not the strategy itself, that preoccupied Johnson, his senior advisers, and a committee of "wise men."

THE RESULTS OF THE AIR WAR

In a memorandum dated June 30, McNamara submitted to Johnson an extensive review of the results of the bombing from February through June 1965.

At the outset, McNamara presented the purposes behind the decision to bomb. He listed these as follows:

  (a) to promote the settlement. The program was designed
      (1) to influence the DRV to negotiate (explicitly or otherwise) and
      (2) to provide us with a bargaining counter within negotiations
  (b) to interdict infiltrations. The program was calculated to reduce the flow of men and supplies from the North to the South—at least, to put a ceiling on the size of the war that the enemy could wage in the South.

McNamara added a supplemental list of purposes which included demonstrating U.S. commitment, raising the morale of the GVN, and reducing criticism of the Administration from advocates of a bombing program.

The Defense Secretary then evaluated the achievement of these major purposes. Promoting a settlement "has not been attained," but, McNamara claimed, the Administration at the very beginning recognized there could be no settlement "until the North Vietnamese had been disappointed in their hopes for a quick military success in the South." This was a misstatement of fact: The Administration had been motivated to *expand,* not begin, the air war in order to diminish the Northern capability in the South. Indeed, interdiction bombing itself, which Mc-Namara identified as one of the explicit reasons for commencing Rolling Thunder, was neither discussed nor authorized prior to the inception of the bombing. Interdiction bombing was the motivating force behind the decision to expand, not initiate, the air war. That decision took place more than a month after Rolling Thunder was authorized and seventeen days after it began.

McNamara's evaluation of the bombing campaign was further distorted when he described the success it had achieved as a bargaining counter. "There is no doubt," the Secretary stated, "that the bombing program has become an important counter in the current tacit and explicit bargaining process and will be an important counter in any future bargaining." The five-day pause in May shattered any hopes the Administration *might* have entertained about using Rolling Thunder as an effective bargaining chip in attaining the promise of the DRV to cease activity in the South.

According to the report, interdiction bombing had been unsuccessful in cutting off supplies coming into the North: "Substantially uninterrupted supply continues from China by rail into Hanoi and by sea into Haiphong to meet major North Vietnamese military, industrial and civilian needs." McNamara claimed some success, however, in using interdiction bombing to retard the operations of DRV main force units in the South, though he could not uncover any evidence that the bombing had put a damper upon VC activity in the South, which he estimated could be sustained with eight tons of supplies per day—an amount that could clearly be furnished by the rural peasant. The bombing, then, served to cut down somewhat the activity of the main force units, which had been infiltrated only after the bombing began, but which did not impinge upon the needs of the VC. The conclusion was inescapable: The bombing campaign had proved that the VC were not dependent upon Hanoi. Moreover, it had the negative effect of creating additional enemy strength in the South, which was only marginally affected by the bombing. Thus the bombing was not only ineffective; it was counterproductive. McNamara, however, ignored his own figures and analysis and told the President, "The program may have caused the VC summer offensive to be less intense, aggressive and unrelenting than it would otherwise have been." In later years, Walt Rostow was characterized as one who would go to any length, including the biased selection and doctoring of data, to persuade Johnson to continue the struggle. Did McNamara set that precedent for Rostow?

The Defense Secretary relied on this rather meager and greatly distorted evaluation of the bombing program to commend its past results and advocate its future use: "Even with hindsight, I believe the decision to bomb the DRV was wise and I believe the program should be continued." The future program, he wrote, should first and foremost "emphasize the threat." Harking back to the thinking of 1964 which viewed Rolling Thunder as an effective means to alter the will of the DRV—thinking which already had been dramatically discredited by the events of the previous five months—McNamara described the nature of the threat in almost the exact terms that McGeorge Bundy had used on the eve of the beginning of Rolling Thunder:

> It should be structured to capitalize on fear of future attacks. At any time, "pressure" on the DRV depends not upon the current level of bombing but rather upon the credible threat of future destruction which can be avoided by agreeing to negotiate or agreeing to some settlement in the negotiations.

WASHINGTON'S MANAGEMENT
OF THE AIR WAR

In the air war against the North, two types of targets accounted for all the bombing. These were classified as fixed targets and targets of opportunity, or interdiction bombing. McNamara and Johnson refused to relinquish control over the air war, as advocated by the JCS; they selected each of the fixed targets, but only set down guidelines for interdiction bombing. Since the latter accounted for 90 percent of the bombing, it is a myth that Washington actually retained control of Operation Rolling Thunder. On the other hand, Washington did select the criteria for interdiction bombing. Since this had a dramatic impact on the number of the strikes, it is fair to say that Washington greatly influenced the conduct of the entire air war. In sum, Washington selected the fixed strikes, determined the quantity of interdiction bombing, and finally established the restricted zones and limits to the air war. Whatever success or failure resulted from the air war was thus directly attributable to Washington, and especially to the President and his Secretary of Defense.

The chain of command for the selection of fixed targets had six links. The first link consisted of the 7th Air Force and the 7th Fleet. Relying on post-strike aerial reconnaissance photos, the commanding officer of the 7th Air Force, Major General Joseph H. Moore (succeeded by Lieutenant General William W. Momyer in July 1966), would collate the data and forward it to Admiral Ulysses S. Sharp, head of CINCPAC at Hawaii. At the same time, Rear Admiral Roger Mehle, who controlled the air strikes for Task Force 77, the carrier division of the 7th Fleet in charge of bombing operations, would perform a similar task on behalf of the Navy.

The second link in the chain was Admiral Sharp, who put together the data accumulated in the field and forwarded a list of recommended targets to the JCS in Washington.

The JCS would write up a formal memorandum and submit it, along with the list of recommended targets—which generally numbered about 525—to the Secretary of Defense, the Secretary of State, and the National Security Adviser to the President. At Defense, State, and the White House, the list would first be reviewed by assistants —Paul Warnke, Leonard Unger, and Chester Cooper.

At the White House, Cooper had authority to recommend vetoes on behalf of McGeorge Bundy. In an interview, Cooper described the three criteria he had applied in deciding whether a target should be approved. If the proposed target did not violate restrictions laid down by the President, if it would not cause civilian war casualties, and if it did not conflict with other events in the political world, Cooper would recommend approval. In arriving at a decision, he would first check with Warnke at Defense and Unger at State to determine what McNamara and Rusk thought about a particular target. If there was unanimity of opinion, Cooper would approve or veto as the case might be. If any disagreement was voiced, Cooper would notify Bundy, so that he would have time to prepare his case before the meeting of the final review board, where he could expect a challenge from Rusk or McNamara. Cooper said he found it easy to obtain Bundy's agreement to veto a target on the grounds that it might be too close to a populated village. Conversely, when the U.S. Embassy was bombed, Cooper recalled "how Bundy was overcome with a surge of anger and called for the bombing of a corresponding target in Hanoi or worse, but then he would quickly regain his composure."

McNamara played a far more active role than Bundy or Rusk in reviewing the proposed targets with his assistants. McNamara, Vance, McNaughton, and Warnke met regularly once a week. At Defense, according to an interview with Paul Warnke, four criteria were applied in determining whether a target should be added to the list: Did the target have military value, was there an undue risk to the pilots, would it lead to an escalation of the war, and would it avoid the risk of civilian war casualties? When McNamara could not attend these meetings, McNaughton and a Colonel Rogers would make the final judgment. Subsequently, when Warnke replaced McNaughton as the head of ISA, he and Charles Havens would work up the final list. According to Alvin Friedman, who was Deputy Assistant Secretary for the Far East and Latin America at ISA and who conducted the investigation of the incident at the Gulf of Tonkin, there was a marked difference between McNaughton and Warnke in exercising discretion for the approval of targets. Friedman said —and others have corroborated his statement—that McNaughton, while head of ISA, was quite uncritical in his recommendation of targets. McNaughton was known to have reservations about the bombing campaign, but would fashion his decisions consistent with the views of McNamara, one of the authors of the air war. When Warnke assumed his position as head of ISA, McNamara thought he, too, would carry out the policy regardless of personal reservations. This did not turn out to be the case. Warnke, according to Friedman, was "very tough, very much his own man, and opposed the bombing to the hilt." Richard Steadman and Les Gelb, both of ISA, have corroborated this point. Warnke himself said his disagreement with McNamara arose over the possibility that the bombing would draw the Communist superpowers into the war.

McNamara, an original exponent of the air war, had a stake in its success. Hence, he favored some fixed targeting and all of the interdiction bombing. He never wavered in his support of bombing targets of opportunity, even when he opposed fixed targeting before the Senate Armed Services Committee in 1967. Warnke, acting out of a total opposition to the air war, recommended vetoes for each and every target.

Warnke's example is instructive. It demonstrates that it is possible for a major bureaucratic figure to oppose vigorously the universally accepted bureaucratic strictures. To do so, however, requires a strong and determined character and powerful motivation to do what is right, regardless of the wishes of superiors, the momentum of the bureaucracy, or the policies of the state. These qualities of character, unfortunately, were extremely rare in the pantheon of power. Friedman summed it up by describing Warnke as "coming from a different geological age compared to the likes of McNaughton, M. Bundy, McNamara and Rusk.'

At the State Department, a small group would review the weekly target list each Monday morning. The group consisted of Leonard Unger, his military attaché, and a representative from INR. Upon reaching a consensus, William Bundy would summarize the views in a memo to Rusk. Again, if there happened to be disagreement, Rusk would confer with McNamara prior to the final review held the following day.

The last link in the chain of command was forged at the celebrated meetings known as the "Tuesday Lunch." Begun in the first half of 1964 and continuing to the end of Johnson's tenure, these sessions would bring together the five highest officials making policy on the war to issue command decisions on new military moves. Those attending were Rusk, McNamara, McGeorge Bundy (later succeeded by Rostow), and Johnson. Wheeler, the Chairman of the JCS, was invited on a regular basis starting only in 1966. Each session lasted one to three hours. Maps, charts, photos, statistics, and memos were the mediating devices relied on to influence the decision-makers. In addition to selecting the fixed targets, the participants furnished guidelines for interdiction bombing and gave the green light on major search-and-destroy operations in the South. The Tuesday Lunch was the institutional device for retaining civilian control over the conduct of the war.

The meetings would open with a discussion of the JCS list of proposed strikes. Each proposal would represent a package of targets to be added or to be retained on the list. Authority to repeat strikes was generally granted, but authority to add strikes was sharply circumscribed. Each week, the Chiefs presented a half-dozen proposals for striking restricted areas in violation of the original guidelines that Johnson had laid down for the total bombing campaign. The guidelines, or rules of engagement as they were called, provided that the United States would not hit Cambodia and that it would spare Hanoi and Haiphong. The theory underlying these restrictions was to limit the war zone to Vietnam proper, so as not to excite the fear of the Communist superpowers, and also to maintain a credible threat of future devastation as an incentive to induce Hanoi to come to the bargaining table and comply with U.S. demands for a non-Communist South Vietnam. But time and again the JCS, acting under pressure from Admiral Sharp, would recommend strikes along the Chinese border and direct hits upon Haiphong.

The question of whether or not to bomb Haiphong would consume most of the discussion. According to Paul Warnke, staff members of the Senate Armed Services Committee worked behind the scenes with the staff of CINCPAC to devise arguments which would persuade the high command to explain how the bombing of Haiphong would bring the war to a close. Partly out of a desire to eliminate these pressures and partly to exercise greater personal control over the war, Johnson managed to ease CINCPAC out of the chain of command early in 1966. Thereafter, the pressure to bomb Haiphong came exclusively from the Armed Services Committee, but this occurred at the time when McNamara began to dominate the Tuesday Lunch with his pleas to end target bombing. Johnson compromised; he decided to eliminate McNamara from the chain instead of adding Haiphong to the target list. Johnson steadfastly held to the original guidelines, and resisted the pressure from the Armed Services Committee to increase the bombing as well as McNamara's pressure to diminish it. This middle-of-the-road position —refusing to expand the war outside of Vietnam and refusing to lessen the bombing inside Vietnam—had the net effect of turning Hanoi away from the conference table and turning Vietnam into a wasteland.

Interdiction bombing, in contrast to fixed bombing, had widespread support among all of the participants in the Tuesday Lunch, including McNamara. Washington controlled the quantity of interdiction bombings by granting the field authority for a fixed number of sorties. Requests for sorties came to Washington from the 7th Air Force and the 7th Fleet, and these requests were fully complied with: not once did Washington cut down the sortie rate. The field always flew the exact number of sorties that had been requested by it and authorized by Washington, because the following year's budget for the armed services was to a large extent determined by the number of sorties flown.

A consultant, who helped set up the computerized programming for targeting in North Vietnam, claimed that the effectiveness of the air war was gauged by Washington in terms of the utilization of the sortie quota. Responding to the need to maximize sorties, the pilots were forced to fly two per day. To accomplish this, they had to fly the shortest route to the target so they could get back to the base in time to refuel and fly another mission. Forced to take the shortest route, the planes departed at the same time each morning and were forced into what the pilots referred to as "milk runs"—fixed routes saturated with enemy antiaircraft guns and SAM missiles. While the shortest route is the most efficient from the point of view of maximizing sorties, it is also the most vulnerable to enemy countermeasures. The only maneuverability left to the pilots was to fly at high or low altitudes. If they flew over 6,000 feet, surface-to-air missiles would hit them; if they flew under 6,000, antiaircraft would get them. The results were disastrous; planes were shot out of the air at a brutally high rate.

Once this loss pattern developed, pilots decided to avoid their primary targets and proceed instead to secondary targets, where there was less chance of being shot out of the sky. Each pilot was assigned three targets: North Vietnam, Route Pack One (the Ho Chi Minh Trail along the Laotian border), and Laos proper. The pilots would continue to fly the milk run, but they would drop their bombs short of the primary target or in the sea, receive credit for a sortie, return to base for refueling, and head to Route Pack One. Hanoi, meanwhile, would observe the planes failing to enter their primary target zone, then time their return back to the base and their second mission to Route Pack One. Hanoi would then notify the trucks moving along the infiltration corridor; fifteen minutes before the planes arrived at their secondary target, the trucks would get off the road, wait in the bush, watch the bombs drop, then continue on their way. The net result of the air war against the North was an extremely high sortie rate, a waste of ordnance, an appallingly high percentage of U.S. planes lost, and few targets hit with any degree of accuracy.

The sortie rate was fed into the computers and the after-damage reports were doctored to make it appear as if the primary targets had been hit. The data from the computers in the field were then fed into the computers in Saigon, Hawaii, and Washington. It was a relatively easy matter to fabricate reports in the field and deceive Washington. It was said, "Computers lie all the way up the chain." Washington was led to believe that the air war was taking a heavy toll of the enemy.

Dr. George Rathjens, Jr., who was Deputy Director of Advanced Research Projects Agency (ARPA), confirmed the same analysis. "No matter what the criteria advanced by systems analysis in Washington," Rathjens said, "sorties length of time in the air, or number of bombs dropped, the data would have been fabricated in the field." Rathjens summed up Washington's mismanagement of the air war by observing that "the personnel in the field could meet any criteria advanced by systems analysis, and never, in fact, drop their bombs over the designated targets."

Admiral Laroque, Assistant Director of Strategic Plans, chaired a study conducted under the auspices of Paul Nitze in 1967 to determine the effectiveness of the air war. The results of the study were completely negative. It concluded that there was no way to stop the flow of material into the North, or to interdict it on the way to the South. Laroque was able to show that 95 percent of all supplies entered the North through Haiphong harbor, and Haiphong was one of the restricted zones. Yet, the results would have been no different if Washington had decided to bomb the harbor. Since the South did not need massive supplies to conduct the land war, and the North could have opened up an alternative supply route between Port Biurd in China and an overland railroad into the North, this new route would have been more than adequate to handle all of the supplies previously going through Haiphong. To remove the North from the Southern struggle, the United States would have had to engage China in a direct confrontation, without any assurance that it would materially alter the course of the war in the South.

To illustrate how the North had increased its output in the same period that the United States had escalated the bombing. Laroque cited the following statistics: The North started the war with 11,000 old trucks. After two-

and-a-half years of bombing, the North had 11,000 new trucks. Furthermore, the United States had knocked out 70 percent of the North's electrical generating capacity. Again, after two-and-a-half years of bombing, the North had more generating capacity than it did before the war began. Diesel generators were shipped into the North.

When asked what effect the target list drawn up at the Tuesday Lunch had upon the conduct of the air war, the Admiral replied, "Such a list may have existed, but I was never able to locate one." He said that no one in the Navy knew what targets were on the list. The Navy had been informed of one rule set down by the President: Do not bomb Hanoi or the dikes. Each of the services was assigned a designated area in the North, which had been selected by CINCPAC. The naval area was inland from Haiphong and the first two bomb zones above I Corps. The rest of North Vietnam was assigned to the Air Force, except for the lower half of the lowest bomb zone in the North, which was granted to the Marine Corps. Bombing lists were drawn up each week by the members of the Tuesday Lunch, but the lists were totally ignored by the services in the field, which simply bombed within their private domains and did not intentionally bomb within the restricted areas. If adverse weather or other factors made it impossible for a service to bomb in its own area, it would receive permission to bomb in another area. But joint raids, even when ordered by Washington, were ignored in the field.

The Air Force and the Navy were not inclined to carry out orders from Washington. They paid scant attention to the list of fixed targets, and avoided their primary targets. They refused to conduct joint attacks. The reality for the pilots and the services was the *criterion* established by Washington, but not the *objective* underlying the criterion. Washington measured the effectiveness of the air war by the quantity of sorties flown by the services, and believed that there would be a correlation between sorties flown and targets hit. There was no such correlation.

For the pilot, the number of sorties flown determined length of duty and rapidity of promotion. The more missions a pilot could run, the sooner he would leave Vietnam and the more quickly he would be promoted. But there was no incentive to hit the target, especially if it was surrounded by missiles. Hence, the pilot was solely interested in receiving credit for a sortie. His world of reality crossed that of Washington at the mouth of the computer, not at the targets in North Vietnam. For the services, the sortie rates determined their budgetary allocations for the following year. The reality for the services was to compete with each other to see who could fly the most sorties; thus, they had an incentive in backing up the needs and claims of their pilots. Such considerations swayed the pilots and the services to maximize the sortie rate and minimize the damage to the enemy. The field had concocted a conspiracy against Washington. Finally, the services wanted the war to continue so that they could try out their new weapons systems for experimental purposes.

In sum, there was every incentive in the field to fly sorties, continue the war, and to lie about the results. Sortie competition, steeped in the capitalistic ethic and confirmed by the advanced technology of computers, was no match for a coordinated but primitive enemy. The United States fought the war as if it were a war game. The North Vietnamese fought for their lives.

THE JULY DECISION: POINT OF NO RETURN

When Johnson had first assumed the Presidency in November 1963, 16,500 U.S. troops had been deployed in Vietnam. This level of forces was maintained until the incident at the Gulf of Tonkin in August 1964. Between Tonkin and Pleiku (February 1965), Johnson increased the number of troops to 25,000. After Rolling Thunder had begun, additional elements of the Marine Corps were dispatched to Danang to protect the air base, and the decision was made, as previously noted, to authorize the Marines to engage in offensive operations. The March decision further authorized an increase in the troop level to 77,250.

By the end of April, the air war had proven to be a failure. It had not affected the will or the capacity of the DRV. During the same period, however, the VC had been relatively inactive. The United States was making no progress in the North and the VC seemed to be marking time in the South. It was the lull before the storm.

On May 11, the VC attacked the capital of Phuoclong Province, employing more than a regiment of troops. According to the Pentagon historians, "the storm broke in earnest." The town was overrun; heavy casualties were inflicted upon U.S.–GVN forces, and the VC withdrew after holding the area for one day.

Later in May, two ARVN battalions were decimated in Quangngai Province, and early in June ARVN units near Bagia, according to the Pentagon study, were "devoured by the enemy." Immediately after this assault General Westmoreland cabled Admiral Sharp, requesting a force build-up to forty-four battalions totaling almost 200,000 men. Westmoreland noted the VC's capacity to launch battalion-size attacks and described ARVN as "experiencing difficulty in coping with this increased VC capability." ARVN desertion rates, Westmoreland added, "are inordinately high. Battalion losses have been higher than expected." To cope with this situation, Westmoreland called for reinforcements "as rapidly as is practical during the critical weeks ahead." This message, dated June 7, became known as the "forty-four battalion request."

William Bundy, in an interview, confirmed that the situation had been as depicted by Westmoreland. "It was between May 20 and June 10," Bundy recalled, "that a series of reports were sent from the field to Washington and these reports clearly indicated the worsening situation. The missing-in-action figures were eight times the known casualties. This sort of rate indicates entire outfits had broken and run."

It was not until June 17, however, that Ambassador Taylor joined Westmoreland in requesting a massive build-up. Up to that point, Taylor had made it his practice to forward Westmoreland's requests for troops with covering letters of his own advising Washington that he disagreed with Westmoreland's findings. Taylor had steadfastly held to his own strategic position, favoring a dynamic air campaign against the North rather than a ground war in the South. In his June 17 report, Taylor "confirmed the seriousness of the military situation as reported by General Westmoreland and also pointed up the very tenuous hold the new government had on the country." According to the Pentagon study, "this report apparently helped to remove the last obstacles to consideration of all of the forces mentioned in Westmoreland's request of June 7."

On June 22, Wheeler inquired of Westmoreland "if the forty-four battalions were enough to convince the enemy forces that they could not win." Westmoreland replied: "There was no evidence the VC/DRV would alter their plans regardless of what the United States did in the next six months. The forty-four battalion force should, however, establish a favorable balance of power by the end of the year. If the United States was to seize the initiative from the enemy, then further forces would be required into 1966 and beyond. . . ." On June 26, Westmoreland was authorized to commit U.S. forces to battle when he decided they were needed "to strengthen the relative position of GVN forces."

forces as General Westmoreland was likely to get," the Pentagon historians point out, concluding that by June 26 "the strategy was finished, and the debate from then on centered on how much force and to what end."

Once the reports from the field had indicated the need for forty-four battalions and Westmoreland had been given a free hand with respect to deployment, President Johnson called in an outside group of corporate, academic, scientific, and military leaders to discuss the need for reinforcements up to 200,000 and beyond "as rapidly as is practical during the critical weeks ahead." On July 8, a representative group of about twenty members of the national power elite, including Paul Hoffman, George Kistakowsky, John McCloy, Omar Bradley, and Clark Clifford, met at the White House to discuss the matter with the President. William Bundy referred to this meeting as "the President's rumination time." He recalled:

> Johnson was tough on everyone. He was very inclined to be negative in his approach. When anyone would argue in behalf of escalation, Johnson would invariably exclaim, "what makes you think it will do any good?"

Johnson apparently had not yet made up his own mind, Bundy indicated, and the decision to commit troops was contingent on the series of meetings then taking place.

However, Clark Clifford, one of the participants in the meetings, recalled that "the decision had already been made in reality before the meeting had been held." John McCloy commented immediately after the meeting that "it looks as if we're going to get our nose bloodied."

It would appear, therefore, that the July 8 meeting was not designed as an exercise in deception. Clifford, for one, clearly understood that the troop decision had already been made and he was merely being consulted, chiefly for the purpose of ratifying that decision.

The July 8 meeting stood in sharp contrast to the methods that had been used in obtaining the Gulf of Tonkin Resolution from Congress a year earlier. The President was willing to deceive Congress in order to obtain legitimacy for the air war, but he was forthright in his dealings with the national power elite when he deemed it necessary to legitimize the ground war. The issue, as defined by Johnson, was not one of deception but of ratification. When the magnitude of the conflict suggested that the United States was becoming immersed in an indefinite war at the edge of the empire, the President considered it essential to consult with America's most powerful men. The power elite, not the Congress, becomes the chosen instrument for ratifying executive wars that call upon the resources of the nation. The public has no voice whatever in determining its own fate, its own life and death. Instead of instituting a national referendum in which the public could determine whether it wished to undertake the sacrifice of war, the State submits its decision to a small group of oligarchs, not even bothering to include the duly elected representatives of the people.

The decision to commit forty-four battalions of troops was taken in mid-July. According to the Pentagon historians,

> the conflict was seen to be long, with further U.S. deployments to follow. The choice at that time was not whether or not to negotiate, it was not whether to hold on for a while or let go—the choice was viewed as winning or losing South Vietnam.

Over the course of the next three years, President Johnson was willing to commit 500,000 troops—but no more —to the Indochina theater of battle. He was willing to bomb Vietnam and Laos, but he resisted pleas from the military to invade Cambodia, Laos, and possibly North Vietnam. He gambled to win, but he held to his terms of the gamble.

Johnson was invariably viewed as an astute politician—one who was loyal to his friends, devious and destructive to his enemies. Men whose careers were closely identified with Johnson's rose and fell with him. Robert Baker, Walter Jenkins, Abe Fortas, and Hubert Humphrey, to name four in particular, were pushed by Johnson, were promised greater rewards and honor by Johnson, but stumbled and fell at the zenith of their own careers. Fortas was to become the Chief Justice of the Supreme Court, but was rejected by the Senate. Humphrey was to become President, but was rejected by the electorate. Baker was to be a tycoon, but ended up in jail. Jenkins was to be a private confidant, but was disgraced. Johnson, it may be said, could not deliver on his promises to his closest associates.

Similarly, he could not deliver on his promise in the case of the one issue that summed up his political career. He promised victory in Vietnam, but he failed. By the early months of 1968, he could not appear in public for fear of being ridiculed, insulted, or ignored. He was isolated in the White House—a powerless President. He could not deliver promises to his friends or to the people. The only thing he could still deliver was his own resignation. He did just that; politically speaking, Johnson purged himself.

But even this gesture, significant and magnanimous to Johnson, proved to seem trivial and futile to the people.

For years after Lydon Baines Johnson resigned, the war dragged on, claiming the lives of countless numbers of innocent people abroad and draining the Republic of its residual power at home.

The war is larger in scope than the tenure of any one President. It has not been the sole responsibility of the Chief Executive, but the disease of an entire ruling class. Long after the American people made it clear that they wanted the war stopped, a narrow circle of elitists continued to prosecute it. They toned it down in order to dress it up, so that it would be less repulsive at home.

Johnson's resignation demolished what had hitherto been regarded as an unshakable article of faith in the American form of government: that significant change could be wrought through the electoral process. The war continued outside the political structure. If the war is larger than the President, it is also larger than the constitutional form of the Republic.

PART II /

THE MEN WHO MADE THE WAR

Richard J. Barnet

Much of the critical energy and initiative that has gone into planning and executing the Vietnam war has been supplied by the National Security Managers. These men, the President's principal advisers, exercise their power chiefly by filtering the information that reaches the President and by interpreting the outside world for him. The President decides, and for that reason bears the ultimate responsibility, but the National Security Managers determine his choices.

The advisers who actually work in the White House, the McGeorge Bundys and the Henry Kissingers, see the President at the beginning of the day and at the end. They are his immediate link with a vast bureaucratic machine for collecting intelligence and evaluating it, for thinking up options and possibilities, for "staffing out" risks, and for defining the "threats" posed by the outside world. The heads of the Military Establishment—the Secretary of Defense and his principal advisers, and the Joint Chiefs of Staff—tell the President the limits and possibilities of using homicidal power to promote what they define as "national security." The Secretary of State shares responsibility for discovering "vital interests" across the world, sanctioning and legitimizing the use of force to protect them, and advising the President on the reaction of other governments to American moves.

The relationship between the President and the National Security Managers is truly symbiotic. They are engaged in a complex and continuous process of mutual persuasion. The President, as we shall see, is as concerned with how to move the bureaucracy as the advisers are concerned with how to convince the President. In the Vietnam war Lyndon Johnson and Richard Nixon pressed their advisers to formulate plans that would bring them the victory they could not renounce. The advisers, in turn, pressed the President to take the risks and to commit the homicidal power necessary to avoid defeat.

In one sense everyone in the national security bureaucracy is a decision-maker. This includes the B-52 pilot who decides where to unload his excess bombs after destroying his assigned target, for in a literal sense he has the power of life and death over hundreds, possibly thousands, of people on the ground below. The State Department desk officer who sends a routine cable to an embassy in a minor country on a "back-burner" issue is making policy for the United States. But on the great issues it is the President who decides. It is his to say "yes" or "no" or, as is often the case, "wait!" On the great issues of the Vietnam war the President made the final decisions, but he decided on the basis of advice offered by the National Security Managers.

It is in the nature of the President's job that most of his decisions are affirmations, or at most modifications, of proposals submitted by his advisers. "I am the responsible officer of the government," John F. Kennedy told reporters the day after the Bay of Pigs fiasco, but within a few weeks he had fired Allen Dulles, the head of the CIA and leading advocate and technician of the ill-fated invasion. President Johnson used to defend himself and his

Vietnam policy by pointing out that all his advisers were "unanimous" in approving his course. Eisenhower insisted that the Joint Chiefs of Staff bring him unanimous recommendations. No President, of course, will tolerate public disagreement among his advisers. Even private disagreement on the premises and goals of policy is very threatening, and for this reason advisers feel pressure to "get their ducks in order" before they face the President. So when policy bubbles up from the bureaucracy, to use Dean Acheson's phrase, there is a consistency to it.

There is also a certain predictability. The President probably exerts his greatest influence over his future foreign policy decisions when he recruits his leading advisers. It is difficult for the President not to take their advice, particularly when it is unanimous, but he can get a pretty good sense in advance of the kind of advice he is likely to get. For one thing, the pool of eligible National Security Managers is extremely narrow. When President Kennedy was putting together his cabinet, Robert A. Lovett, according to Arthur Schlesinger, "exerted a quiet influence on his tastes." The former Secretary of Defense, senior partner of Brown Brothers, Harriman, and key Truman adviser in the early, crucial days of the Cold War, was the man who suggested both Dean Rusk and Robert S. McNamara for the two top national security posts.

To become a National Security Manager, you must be known personally to the President, as McGeorge Bundy was, or you must be endorsed by another National Security Manager. "I'd like to have some new faces here, but all I get is the same old names," Kennedy complained to his biographer. But having asked Robert Lovett, he could hardly have expected the list to include Norman Thomas, Martin Luther King, or, for that matter, William Fulbright. A prospective appointee who has been certified as "responsible" by the man Schlesinger calls "the chief agent" of "the New York Establishment" is not likely to depart significantly from the national security wisdom of the past. One of the explanations for the remarkable consistency of U.S. national security policy is that the National Security Managers transact business with one another, give each other awards, belong to the same clubs, and review each other's memoirs. Most of the top 400 Presidential appointments since 1945 could be located in ten city blocks in five of America's largest cities.

The pool of eligibles is further narrowed by the security procedures. Unconventional associations, heretical views, or "derogatory information," which need be no more than an unfriendly remark by a reasonably credible "informant," are enough to eliminate potential National Security Managers from the list. Then appointments must also be checked against various Congressional lists, such as that compiled by the House Internal Security Committee. (In the early Kennedy Administration a Congressional committee had obtained "information" that Paul Nitze, investment banker, Truman adviser, and Cold War hardliner, was "soft" on the United Nations and disarmament, and he weathered some hostile questioning after he was appointed Assistant Secretary of Defense. A less certifiably "responsible," experienced, and conventionally valuable man would have been dropped from the list.)

Thus the range of advice a President will get is circumscribed from the start by the selection process. Within the narrow circle of top advisers there are, it is true, differences of outlook, and these differences translate themselves into predictably different policy recommendations. At an early crucial stage in the deliberations on Vietnam, President Kennedy sent General Maxwell Taylor to Saigon for a firsthand analysis and recommendation for action. Sending Taylor (along with Walt W. Rostow, whose views on the subject were almost as fixed) was a virtual guarantee that Kennedy would receive a recommendation for war. Had he entrusted the mission to John Kenneth Galbraith instead of asking him to "stop off in Saigon and forward his views," he would have received entirely different advice. But there were good political reasons why Taylor wrote the report while Galbraith commented from the bureaucratic sidelines.

The Taylor mission and the Presidential reaction to it offer an illuminating illustration of the workings of the national security bureaucracy. The decision on November 16, 1961, to send additional military advisers and equipment in violation of the limits agreed to at the Geneva Conference was a crucial watershed in American escalation of the war. It was Kennedy's first major decision on Vietnam and it set other forces in motion. One result of the Taylor–Rostow mission was the establishment of MACV (the Military Assistance Command, Vietnam) as a major theater headquarters in Saigon. Once this headquarters was staffed, it became a powerful advocate of increased military involvement. An organization whose mission was preserving Vietnam by military means was now a major factor in bureaucratic politics.

John F. Kennedy knew General Taylor's views on Vietnam because during the 1960 campaign the General had lectured the candidate on the need for a "flexible response" against all forms of "Communist aggression." Moreover, the General had resigned from the U.S. Army in the Eisenhower Administration because Ike was unwilling to give the Army money to fight just such "brush-fire wars." Kennedy came to the White House convinced that the great battle of his Administration would be the fate of the Third World and that that fate would be decided by the ordeal of guerrilla warfare. Shortly after his inauguration, he appointed Taylor a special White

House assistant and put him in charge of "Special Group Counter-Insurgency."

Supported by the ideological notions of Walt Rostow, who was coming to believe that the whole future of mankind hung on the outcome of jungle wars, and the energetic commitment of his brother Robert, Kennedy devoted much attention early in his Administration to the rehabilitation of the Army's Special Forces. The previous Administration had prepared a counterinsurgency plan for Vietnam. The new President vigorously backed those bureaucracies committed to unconventional warfare and personally restored the Green Beret, which, as the symbol of the new elite fighting force, had inspired the derision and jealousy of the regular Army. He was briefed on the euphoric literature on counter-guerrilla warfare then beginning to emerge from the CIA-sponsored research in leading universities, and turned his personal attention to improving the technology of such warfare. At his carved oak desk he pored over the design of a new sneaker for America's jungle warriors.

In a bureaucracy, contingency plans play a crucial role because they set the terms of the bureaucratic debate. If a plan is in existence, its bureaucratic advocates have an advantage over those who oppose it but have no plan of their own. "Well, what would you do?" is as effective a ploy in political debate inside the national security bureaucracy as it is anywhere else. It is most unlikely that President Nixon would have ordered the sudden invasion of Cambodia had the Joint Chiefs of Staff not already worked out detailed contingency plans. In a crisis, real or imagined, the President reaches for a plan. The second effect of contingency plans is to spread illusions of success. The military do not write "scenarios" that predict their own defeat. If they have "staffed out" a military operation and have indicated which units should move where, they have, in effect, certified victory.

Thus the planning at the beginning of the Kennedy Administration helped set the climate for future decisions. When Taylor, the chief planner, was sent to report on whether to implement his own plans, his recommendations were predictable: send in more advisers and a "military task force" of about 10,000 men. The risks of backing into a big war, he grandly assured the President, were "not impressive." Vietnam was not an unpleasant place to operate—much nicer than Korea. North Vietnam, he was pleased to report, was "extremely vulnerable to conventional bombing." The final paragraph of Taylor's report to the President was a brilliant piece of bureaucratic advocacy:

> It is my judgment and that of my colleagues that the United States must decide how it will cope with Khrushchev's "wars of liberation" which are really para-wars of guerrilla aggression. This is a new and dangerous Communist technique which bypasses our traditional political and military responses. While the final answer lies beyond the scope of this report, it is clear to me that the time may come in our relations to Southeast Asia when we must declare our intention to attack the source of guerrilla aggression in North Vietnam and impose on the Hanoi Government a price for participating in the current war which is commensurate with the damage being inflicted on its neighbors to the south.

Taylor here employed two time-honored techniques of the Presidential adviser, one directly and the other ever so subtly. No one advises the President without being an advocate for something. (There are, to be sure, always a certain number of sycophants, valets, raconteurs, even an occasional friend, who amuse the President, but if they are ever asked for "advice" they know that it is reassurance that is wanted, and they provide it.) Advisers represent bureaucratic constituencies, such as the Department of Defense, or if, like White House advisers, they have none, they are in the business of selling their own reputations. This means that even if they have no ideological bill of goods to sell, they must keep defending last week's advice.

The professional adviser must be a good judge of the Presidential character and have an understanding of the peculiar way the President—the only nationally elected official, the only man with the authority to push the button for nuclear war—looks at the world. Issues are framed for the President in such a way as to put maximum psychological pressure on him to make the "right"—that is, the adviser's—choice. This is often done in a deceptively neutral framework which creates the illusion that "all options have been presented" merely because they may have been stated.

In his report, Taylor placed the Vietnam conflict into the larger context of a world struggle against Communism. The still-small conflict in a tiny, remote country was not the issue. The conflict, as Taylor described it, assumed the proportions of an historic battle that could decide the political organization of the globe. It was the great test of America's power. To engage Presidential attention, much less Presidential commitment, it is necessary to exaggerate the importance of an issue and to paint all alternatives to the recommended course of action in hopeless black. No sane President will start a war over Berlin, Laos, Vietnam, or more obscure places. But "Berlin," "Vietnam," even "Quemoy and Matsu," once invested with the symbolic importance developed and rationalized in a hundred state papers, become causes worth dying for and killing for.

The sacrifice of American lives is a crucial step in the ritual of commitment. Thus William P. Bundy stressed in working papers the importance of "spilling American blood" not only to whip up the public to support a war that could touch their emotions in no other way, but also to trap the President. Just as the "symbolic" deaths of American soldiers in a war in Europe would, according to U.S. war plans, serve as a "tripwire" for a retaliatory attack on the U.S.S.R., leaving the President no option but to drop hydrogen bombs on Soviet cities, so sending Americans to face death in Indochina was designed to convince Ho Chi Minh that the United States also "meant business" in Southeast Asia.

The deliberate inflation and distortion of issues in the advocacy process leads to what I call the bureaucratic model of reality. It is a collective view of the world put together through the process of bureaucratic struggle, the final purpose of which is to induce the President to do something or to make him feel comfortable about something the bureaucracy has already done. The essence of the bureaucratic model of reality is conspiracy. The National Security Manager seldom uses Stalin's favorite expression, "it is not by accident," but the message is always there. Nobody does anything visible in the world unless there is an invisible agent pulling the strings.

Thus William C. Bullitt reported in 1947 that Ho Chi Minh's independence movement was designed "to add another finger to the hand that Stalin is closing around China." Mao Tse-tung, according to a speech delivered by Dean Rusk two years after the Chinese Revolution, was a Stalinist agent and his regime "a colonial Russian government." In the bureaucratic model of reality there is no way to deal with spontaneous political feeling or the phenomenon of national independence. That is why there has been such fundamental and pervasive misunderstanding of the politics of revolution. The model is the product of a bureaucratic need for an imperial design. It is a way of making sense out of and imposing order on the extraordinary political chaos which characterizes this era. For a country determined to act as a global power, seeking to exercise maximum possible control over the external world, chaos and indeterminacy are extremely threatening. A workable theory of causation to explain the outside whirl of events is, for the National Security Manager, both a psychological and a political necessity.

The bureaucratic model of reality has a second foundation stone—one which no one who likes to be driven to the office in an official limousine or have his desk banked with flags or thrill to a hurried summons to the White House Situation Room is disposed to cast aside. It is the official theory of human motivation. All killing in the national interest is carried out in strict accordance with certain scientific principles concerning human behavior. Those are the principles that persuade Presbyterian elders, Episcopalian wardens, liberal professors, and practitioners of game-theory rationalism alike, that killing and threatening to kill foreigners are rational, necessary, and effective instruments for building what President Nixon calls "a generation of peace" and what Dean Acheson twenty-five years ago called "situations of strength."

The official theory of human nature is a hopelessly oversimplified derivative of the rat psychology that many of the National Security Managers learned in college. If you want to motivate a rat, give him a carrot or beat him with a stick. In international politics it is dangerous to be overgenerous with carrots because that constitutes "appeasement" which, as the history of the prewar period showed, merely whets rat appetites. Unlike the well-stocked laboratory with its inexhaustible supply of carrots and sticks, a modern militarized nation such as the United States suffers from a shortage of positive inducements, since politicians feel they cannot make very many political concessions without losing the game. But the panoply of weapons to burn, blast, poison, or vaporize the rat is limitless. Such "negative reinforcement" will render him less dangerous and will set a good example to all other rats.

When the National Security Managers began in 1964 to plan the escalation of the Vietnam war, the strategic discussions were permeated by these traditional theories of human motivation, for the rat view of man was the rationale for the very existence of the national security establishment. Indeed, the goals pursued by the United States government were almost exclusively psychological. Neither territory nor economic advantage has been pursued in Vietnam. The entire purpose of the enormous and costly effort has been to create a specific state of mind in three different audiences. The war became a disaster because the National Security Managers misjudged each audience.

The first audience was the government of South Vietnam. As early as May 1961, the Joint Chiefs of Staff had recommended that "U.S. forces should be deployed immediately to South Vietnam" and had said the primary purpose was to "indicate the firmness of our intent." Throughout the Kennedy years the recommendations for increasing the number of U.S. military advisers and military aid in South Vietnam were to show that the United States "meant business." As General Taylor put it in his report to Kennedy, we need a "U.S. military presence capable of raising national morale and showing to Southeast Asia the seriousness of U.S. intent." In October 1963, Ambassador Henry Cabot Lodge, reflecting the views of his clients, the Vietnamese generals who had taken over after the assassination of Ngo Dinh Diem, urged John Kennedy to apply "various pressures" on North Vietnam and suggested that regular bombing of North Vietnam be commenced. Although the President's Special Assistant for National Security, McGeorge Bundy, also favored bombing at this time, the decision was postponed for almost a year.

Instead, the President appointed a working group under Assistant Secretary of State William Bundy, Mc-

George's brother, to propose a "thirty-day scenario" of actions to lift morale in Saigon and strike fear in Hanoi. The National Security Action Memorandum setting up the group (NSAM 288) specified the U.S. objective in Vietnam as an "independent non-Communist South Vietnam." Years later, in bureaucratic fights with civilians who were losing stomach for the war, the Joint Chiefs of Staff would cite this document, much as lawyers wave a Supreme Court decision under the nose of inferior court judges. Meeting in May 1964, the group conceived an elaborate series of "graduated" measures, a careful orchestration of covert actions, diplomatic warnings, and public statements. A Canadian diplomat would be dispatched to warn Hanoi. "Diplomatic preparations" for bombing the North (a euphemism for a propaganda campaign designed to convince the world that they deserved to be bombed) would be undertaken. A draft Joint Congressional Resolution, much like the text of the Tonkin Gulf Resolution actually submitted three months later, was prepared. The scenario culminated in air strikes against North Vietnam. The planners were attempting to concoct the right mixture of carrots and sticks, but, as one State Department participant at these meetings put it, "it was all stick."

The Executive Committee of the National Security Council (Rusk, McNamara, Bundy, JCS Chairman Wheeler) decided to postpone the opening of this drama until all less dangerous alternatives had been exhausted. In July, President Johnson directed all appropriate government agencies to "seek to identify actions which can be taken to improve the situation in Vietnam: action which would produce maximum effect with minimum escalation." Meanwhile, the planning of stepped-up covert actions against North Vietnam went on. General Khanh, Ambassador Taylor reported, needed "to be reassured that the U.S. continues to mean business." Assistant

Secretary of Defense John T. McNaughton, McNamara's leading thinker on the war, mused about "the extent to which we should add elements (in the scenario) . . . that would tend deliberately to provoke a DRV [North Vietnamese] reaction, and consequent retaliation by us." Such actions, he noted, would help boost morale in South Vietnam and show the Communists "we still mean business."

When the decision was finally made in February 1965 to initiate Operation Rolling Thunder, the daily bombardment of North Vietnam, the primary bureaucratic reason stated in the planning documents was to buoy up the rapidly failing morale of the South Vietnamese government. It worked for a while. "The happiest day of my life," Marshal Ky exclaimed when he heard that American bombs were falling on North Vietnam, where he had been born. "It's like taking a drink," President Kennedy had said of the policy of charging up weak governments by a display of military power. But the United States was now firmly committed to this form of intoxication in the "battle for men's minds" in Southeast Asia.

By the summer of 1964, the National Security Managers were concentrating more on Hanoi as the audience. Shortly before President Kennedy's death, one of his most trusted assistants had gone to Vietnam and concluded that there was no evidence of any weapons captured in the South, which had been infiltrated from the North since 1954. (The massive supplying from the North would not begin until after 1965 and the U.S. intervention.) He corroborated the view of the CIA and the State Department intelligence experts at the "working level" that the insurgency in the South grew out of local Southern issues, was led by Southerners although supported by the North, and could not be crushed by pressuring the North. Indeed, the "sigma" war games, the report of the interagency study group chaired by Robert Johnson of the

State Department Policy Planning Council that began meeting in February 1964, and studies of bombing effectiveness by McNamara's then prestigious systems analysts in the Defense Department all led to the conclusion that bombing could not win the war. The "will" that had to be "broken," to use a favorite JCS term, was of the Vietnamese in the South who would rather fight than live under the Saigon government. There was no cheap way to do that by breaking Hanoi's "will."

Nevertheless, the bureaucratic model had completely displaced reality; the hard and stubborn facts, which so many intelligence analysts were paid so much to collect, were ignored. Any view that tended to buttress the rat psychology premises of the National Security Managers, who in their frustration were straining to lash out at Hanoi, was welcomed. Thus when Bernard Fall, an expert on Indochina who had been critical of the French military effort, suggested after a visit to Hanoi that Ho Chi Minh might disavow the war in the South if some of his new industrial plants were made a target, his ill-considered speculation created something of a stir in the Pentagon. (In the succeeding three years, when he became one of the most informed and accurate critics of the U.S. war strategy, Fall was ignored, and as an alien was subjected to a certain amount of harassment.)

Since little could be done to arrest the deteriorating political and military situation in the South, the National Security Managers began to bank all their hopes on "squeezing" Hanoi. The planning alternatives soon divided into the JCS "option"—a recommendation for "a sharp, sudden blow" based on the blitz bombardment of ninety-four strategic targets in North Vietnam—and the civilian alternative, the "slow squeeze." The "moderates" prevailed and the slow squeeze—inflicting measured amounts of "pain" in greater increments by bombing increasingly sensitive targets—was adopted. The Pentagon planners used the language of the professional torturer and they shared the torturer's classic problem. How do you keep the victim alive long enough to surrender? "Too much" coercion is as bad as "too little," General Taylor warned, for "at some point we will need a relatively cooperative leadership in Hanoi."

As the war in the South appeared more and more hopeless in the second half of 1964, with dramatic rises in desertions from the ARVN, loss of control by the Saigon government of vast areas of the country, and mounting Viet Cong terrorist and military operations almost everywhere, the National Security Managers began to develop what could be described as the faucet theory of how to end the war. It was impossible to stop the torrent in the South except by turning off the faucet in the North. Once again the theory violated the best intelligence about the nature of the Viet Cong, their relationships with Hanoi, and the political dynamics of revolutionary movements. According to one analysis in October 1964, "the basic elements of Communist strength in South Vietnam remain indigenous South Vietnam grievances, war weariness, defection and political disarray, VC terror, arms capture, disciplined organization, highly developed intelligence systems and the ability to recruit locally. . . ." The faucet theory had only one thing to recommend it: It seemed to fit American technology. It was the only plausible strategy that could work at acceptable cost.

Under this theory Ho Chi Minh would eventually feel so much "pain" once the "screw" was "twisted" tight enough (the words were used in planning documents prepared by William P. Bundy) or suffer so much "economic strangulation" (Maxwell Taylor) that he would broadcast an order on the radio for the VC to give up and turn in their arms at the local police station. The guerrillas naïve enough to comply would be caught and the rest would "fade away" in the hills, just—as Walt

Rostow, Johnson's resident historian, would remind skeptics—as the Greek guerrillas had faded in 1949 when U.S. guns had brought an abrupt end to the Greek civil war.

This fantasy became the official goal of American escalation planning, despite the fact that the intelligence community, with the not surprising exception of Air Force Intelligence, was most skeptical. Moreover, a number of high officials of the administration—Deputy Secretary of Defense Paul Nitze, for one—had participated in the post-World War II Strategic Bombing Survey, which assembled in a remarkably thorough manner data from Nazi Germany demonstrating that strategic bombing would not compel surrender. (As it later developed, the bombing solved serious domestic political problems for Ho Chi Minh, uniting the country against the foreign invader and, once Roman Catholic churches were bombed in large numbers, effectively ending Catholic dissidence.)

Thus for twenty years every President and almost every key Presidential adviser has been impressed with the catastrophic consequences of an American pull-out from Vietnam, not because of any strategic or commercial importance of that real estate, but because of the over-riding symbolic importance that had already been attached to the commitment. (Once the commitment is made, however, military services, banks, oil companies, and insurance agencies quickly enlist in the continuing struggle against world Communism, and air-conditioned office buildings, drilling rigs, used car lots and super-markets follow the flag.)

The myth of monolithic Communism—that all activities of people everywhere who call themselves Communists or whom J. Edgar Hoover calls Communists are planned and controlled in the Kremlin—is essential to the ideology of the national security bureaucracy. Without it the President and his advisers would have a harder time identifying the enemy. They certainly could not find opponents worthy of the "defense" efforts of the mightiest military power in the history of the world. The effect of this bureaucratic model of reality is to perpetuate such concepts as the "Sino-Soviet bloc" in top-secret papers long after the two leading Communist powers have publicly been at each other's throats. This could be passed off as a bureaucratic foible if it did not happen that some of the secret papers are the War Plans. Until 1961, these plans called for an automatic full-scale nuclear attack on China in the event of war with the Soviet Union. (These plans were modified when General David Shoup, who had just become Commandant of the Marine Corps, discovered that the gratuitous slaughter of millions of Chinese would be an *inevitable* consequence of any major war with the Soviet Union and persuaded President Kennedy to change the plan.)

The second way in which Presidential advisers talk about war, an approach Taylor barely suggested in his Report, is to paint national conflict as a personal joust between leaders. It is "Khrushchev's new and dangerous technique" that is at stake in Vietnam. This egocentric view of the universe is closely related to the conspiratorial ideology we have just discussed. National leaders seldom have reasons of their own for their foreign policy moves. Their "national interest" is deemed to be trapping the President or embarrassing the State Department. According to the National Security Managers' view of reality, other countries largely exist to be America's sparring partners. This paranoid style in diplomacy is widely shared. A foreign service officer specializing in Chinese matters recalls his astonishment at listening to John Foster Dulles ascribe an obscure and inconsequential Chinese troop movement to Eisenhower's heart attack which had occurred a few days before.

President Kennedy was peculiarly susceptible to the

suggestion that foreign policy moves by other nations were principally designed to test him. He interpreted the Vienna meetings with Khrushchev in June 1961 as a personal combat. There is some reason to believe that he shared George Kennan's later published assessment that he had failed that test. He had clearly failed at the Bay of Pigs. During the Berlin crisis, he had been lectured by Dean Acheson, three weeks after the Vienna meeting, that Khrushchev's policy in Europe "had nothing to do with Berlin, Germany, or Europe" (just as "Vietnam is not really the issue" in Vietnam). Khrushchev's object, as Acheson saw it, "was not to rectify a local situation but to test the general American will to resist." Since the issue involved nuclear war, the National Will that such National Security Managers as Acheson used to talk about was really a euphemism for Kennedy's will. In the Cuban missile crisis, he told the American people, it was "our courage" that was being challenged.

Kennedy understood that his short-term political reputation and his longer-term historical reputation rested on his meeting and surmounting his crisis in Southeast Asia. "I can't take a 1954 defeat today," he told Walt Rostow in the spring of 1961, a few weeks after the Cuban disaster. His two successors held to the same refrain, using almost literally the same words: "*I* will not be defeated in Vietnam." In Johnson's case his two closest personal nonofficial advisers, Clark Clifford and Abe Fortas, kept feeding his personalized conception of the national interest, the latter reminding him almost nightly, "You do not want to be the first President to lose a war."

Presidential advisers are in the business of simplifying the world for their employer. Nuances, doubts, complications are eliminated in the effort to come up with a tough, lean analysis and a practical plan of action. When

216

McGeorge Bundy reflected on his role while still in office, he pictured the Presidential adviser as a "prism through which the President saw public problems." In the great game of making policy each adviser had his own "spin," but advisers have "got to do things his way." Loyalty to the President is the adviser's most important asset. The ambitious adviser quickly comes to see that the National Interest viewed from the President's desk is indistinguishable from the Presidential ego. Like monarchs in Shakespearian plays who call each other "England" or "France," Presidents quickly come to see themselves as personifications of the nation. For this reason there are dangers in world leaders getting to know each other better. "If Khrushchev wants to rub my nose in the dirt," Kennedy told a visiting newspaper editor after their Vienna meeting, "it's all over." The "it" was world civilization, for the President was talking about nuclear war. "What worried him," Arthur Schlesinger reports, "was that Khrushchev might interpret his reluctance to wage war as a symptom of an American loss of nerve. Some day, he said, the time might come when he would have to run the supreme risk to convince Khrushchev that conciliation did not mean humiliation."

The shrewd adviser tailors his advice to the President's prejudices as best he knows them. This is another example of the universal phenomenon of telling superiors what they want to hear, or "protecting" them from bad news and from discouraging predictions. Choleric kings of old used to have messengers who were indiscreet enough to bring the wrong answer executed on the spot. Presidential displeasure in Johnson's time took the form of tongue lashings. A glimpse of what regularly lay in store for advisers who stumbled was given in an interview with President Johnson by a visiting history professor. Dean Rusk, the President's most loyal counsellor, had inadvertently leaked some information. In "an unmodulated voice," the professor reported, the President went on about the "disloyalty" and "unpatriotic sentiments" in the State Department. "It's gotten so that you can't have intercourse with your wife without it being spread around by traitors," Johnson said. Any subordinate willing to put up with such a man will try very hard to please him.

Advisers must have sensitive antennae to what is salable advice and what is not. National Security Managers, in defending their recommendations or their failure to speak up, talk about preserving their "credit points" with the President. You cannot propose too many ideas that are unfamiliar or incompatible with Presidential beliefs. McGeorge Bundy used to tell his staff that an adviser has only so many swings at the ball. (In the Pentagon the vernacular is to have a "chop" at the "action," but it is the same game.) Opportunities for influencing policy are limited. Opportunities misused destroy "credibility" and "effectiveness."

The President, for his part, is deeply conscious of his dependence on the bureaucracy—not only on the senior advisers he has personally selected, but also on the thousands farther down the line. After all, they were discovering "vital interests" in some distant country long before he may have even heard of it, and they will remain long after he has gone home to write his memoirs and build his library. Every President has complained about the difficulty of moving the bureaucracies below him. Sometimes they see themselves fighting the government they are supposed to be leading. In an interview with Jean Daniel shortly before his death, John F. Kennedy hinted that he was ready to change American policy on Cuba, but he didn't know whether "the government" was.

Presidents are keenly aware that they will never know more than a fraction of what subordinate agents do every day in the name of their Administration. Indeed, even the most autocratic rulers face the same problem. Nicholas I, who ruled Russia with a terror not equaled until Stalin's day, used to complain that it was not the Czar of all the Russias, but 10,000 clerks who really ruled that vast domain. In his memoirs, Albert Speer notes that Hitler, who could have anyone within the Third Reich shot within hours, was unable at times to get the bureaucracy to carry out his orders.

As he was about to leave office, Harry Truman remarked of his successor, General Eisenhower, "he'll say 'do this' and 'do that,' and nothing will happen. Poor Ike —it won't be a bit like the army." Presidents have resorted to deep secrecy to avoid having their policies sabotaged by what they believed to be hostile bureaucracies. Throughout his memoirs Roosevelt's Secretary of State, Cordell Hull, complains about being left in the dark on the great issues. With the outbreak of war, communication between the White House and the State Department broke down almost entirely. "Don't tell anybody in the State Department about this," the President told Robert Murphy, then a junior foreign service officer about to leave on a Presidential mission to North Africa. "That place is a sieve." To insure against State Department interference in his foreign policy, Roosevelt carried on his most important correspondence in Navy Department Codes. When President Kennedy decided to introduce a wholly new rhetoric on U.S.–Soviet relations in his American University speech in June 1963, the text was prepared by his intimate advisers in the White House and the State Department learned about the new direction in foreign policy along with the public. The way "to get America moving again," Kennedy believed, was to circumvent the conventional bureaucracies and to take charge of America's most crucial foreign policy involvements through new, streamlined bureaucracies over which the President could hope to exercise some direct control.

Thus the relationship between the President and his chief advisers is one of mutual dependence which involves a certain tension. The character of that dependency, as we shall see, has the effect of reinforcing certain kinds of policies. Once again, it is useful to turn to the Vietnam war as the example, not only because it is typical in many ways of the bureaucratic process, but also because it was a conspicuous failure. At least one hundred bureaucratic accomplices in the tragedy have rushed into print with their own exculpatory versions of the story. One of them, John Roche, grandly declassified a secret memorandum written by Assistant Secretary of State Roger Hilsman in the pages of *The New York Times Magazine*, the better to impeach the historical testimony —and the character—of his bureaucratic rival. Anyone interested in understanding the phenomenon of bureaucratic homicide can only welcome such public display. In politics, as in medicine, the only way to gain insight into the way an organism works often is to wait for the pathologist's report.

The Presidential adviser assumes his boss's goals to be about as Henry Adams described them a hundred years ago in his novel, *Democracy*:

> He came to Washington determined to be the Father of his country; to gain a proud immortality—and re-election.

Presidential incapacity or ignorance provides opportunities to exert influence. In the closing months of the Roosevelt Administration, when FDR's strength was ebbing, and in the early months of the Truman Administration, when both the President and Secretary of State Byrnes lacked background and understanding of crucial foreign policy issues, the professional bureaucrats had unusual flexibility in making decisions. Usually, however,

advisers are bound by the fundamental beliefs and prejudices the President brings with him to the White House.
In the case of the Vietnam war, for example, both Kennedy and Johnson were publicly committed to the
preservation of South Vietnam as a non-Communist state
and an American sphere of influence long before they sat
in the President's chair. As early as June 1956, Senator
John F. Kennedy had given a speech defining America's
vital interests in Southeast Asia:

> Vietnam represents the cornerstone of the Free World in
> Southeast Asia, the keystone to the arch, the finger in the
> dike. Burma, Thailand, India, Japan, the Philippines and,
> obviously, Laos and Cambodia are among those whose
> security would be threatened if the red tide of Communism
> overflowed into Vietnam. . . . Moreover, the independence
> of Free Vietnam is crucial to the free world in fields other
> than the military. Her economy is essential to the economy
> of all of Southeast Asia; and her political liberty is an in-
> spiration to those seeking to obtain or maintain their liberty
> in all parts of Asia—and indeed the world. The fundamental
> tenets of this nation's foreign policy, in short, depend in
> considerable measure upon a strong and free Vietnamese
> nation.

Lyndon Johnson came to the White House even more
of a committed partisan. Less fascinated than his predecessor with the technology of counterinsurgency and the
rhetoric of "wars of national liberation," he was more
committed than Kennedy, personally and psychologically,
to preserving the American role in Vietnam. In May 1961,
Kennedy had sent him to Southeast Asia on a fact-finding
mission. He came back talking about Diem as "the Winston Churchill of Southeast Asia." Ringing in his ears
were the warnings of the leaders of Thailand and the
Philippines that their pro-American regimes would be
imperiled if the United States were humiliated in Viet-

nam. Johnson privately recommended to Kennedy the dispatch of combat troops:

> Our mission arrested the decline of confidence in the United States. It did not—in my judgment—restore any confidence already lost. . . .

> I cannot stress too strongly the extreme importance of following up this mission with other measures, other actions, and other efforts. . . .

Thus Johnson was already on record within the Administration as a hard-liner on Vietnam. Two days after assuming the Presidency, he had a conversation with Kennedy's Ambassador to Vietnam, Henry Cabot Lodge, who told him that hard decisions were in the offing. Johnson replied, "I am not going to lose Vietnam. I am not going to be the President who saw Southeast Asia go the way China went."

For the generation of National Security Managers who lived through the early postwar era, the great political trap was "appeasement." Alger Hiss, the old China hands, the Poland losers, the Czechoslovakia losers, and other "vendors of compromise" in the State Department (as Senator John F. Kennedy would later call them) had become symbols of wrecked careers and warnings to the wise many months before Senator Joseph McCarthy went on the rampage. John Foster Dulles's security officer, a friend of McCarthy, had a sign on his desk: "An ounce of loyalty is worth a pound of brains." The point was not lost on the men who came to Washington in the 1960's to advise the President. Loyalty to the nation means loyalty to the President. Lyndon Johnson did not know much about the outside world, and nothing whatever about Southeast Asia. But he knew a lot about politics in the United States and he had powerful hunches about what motivated men everywhere else. "I grew up with Mexicans," he told some reporters shortly after he moved into the White House. "They'll come right into your yard and take it over if you let them. And the next day they'll be on your porch, barefoot and weighing 130 pounds, and they'll take that, too. But if you say to 'em right at the start, 'hold on, just wait a minute,' they'll know they're dealing with somebody who'll stand up. And after that you can get along fine." There is a whole world view in the story.

It is the same world view Johnson expressed before the troops in Vietnam when he told them to "nail the coonskin to the wall" because we are "outnumbered fifteen to one" and the poor of the world, if not put decisively in their place, will "sweep over the United States and take what we have." A President, particularly one with a powerful personality, who feels strongly and expresses himself strongly about such elemental fears, creates a climate for his subordinates. He is sure to have his prejudices packaged back in the form of neatly rationalized options.

A President who is strongly committed to a foreign policy objective that can only be achieved through force presents a problem for his advisers because no matter how zealous the President may be, he also exhibits the caution that comes with having ultimate responsibility. This ambivalence at the highest level of government—a mixture of dread of being branded a "loser" and terror at the prospect of being the man who started World War III—goes far to explain the pattern of escalation in Vietnam. As noted by Daniel Ellsberg and Leslie Gelb, both of whom were second-level advisers during the process, the President invariably accepted less military escalation than his advisers proposed. Maxwell Taylor presented his recommendations to President Kennedy for an initial task force of 8,000 men as an essential part of the effort. "I do not believe that our program to save South Vietnam will succeed without it," General Taylor flatly asserted. In so recommending he was backing up the Joint Chiefs of Staff, who had called for the sending of ground troops to Vietnam and Laos within four months of Kennedy's inauguration. Even Taylor pointed out that sending the task force would not necessarily avert defeat. It would show Diem and the Communists that the United States "meant business" and would shore up America's sagging "credibility" in Asia, but if Hanoi and "Peiping" were to intervene, the United States would have to be prepared to commit six divisions, or about 205,000 men.

Kennedy, in Sorenson's words, "in effect voted 'no'—and only his vote counted." He increased the established military advisers and set up a major headquarters in Vietnam. He did not send in the troops, but he set forces in motion that he knew would compel him to make further decisions. He told Schlesinger in November 1961:

> They want a force of American troops. . . . They say it's necessary to restore confidence and maintain morale. But it will be just like Berlin. The troops will march in; the bands will play; the crowds will cheer; and in four days everyone will have forgotten. Then we will be told we have to send in more troops. It's like taking a drink. The effect wears off, and you have to take another.

Like his successor, John Kennedy wanted to do the minimum necessary to avoid immediate defeat. As Ellsberg has pointed out, it was not that he had optimistic illusions that he had done enough; rather, he had made a judgment that for now he could postpone the politically unpalatable decision, just eight years after the Korean armistice, of ordering American boys into another land war in Asia.

The President and the National Security Manager have different perceptions of risk. Military officers in the Johnson Administration consistently argued that the risks of defeat and humiliation were greater than the risks of mining Haiphong, obliterating Hanoi, or bombing "selected targets" in China. Since they had responsibility for not losing the war and no responsibility for dealing with the diplomatic crisis that would follow the bombardment of Soviet ships in Haiphong Harbor or the wave of global outrage that would have greeted saturation bombing of Hanoi, they constantly pressed for escalation.

The civilian advisers, on the other hand, consistently favored slower and more subtle means of escalation. Though always respectful of military opinion in the presence of the generals, once back in their own offices they were openly contemptuous of their blunderbuss methods. They believed that they understood the management of violence in the modern "political" war better than the uniformed professionals. Yet the differences were principally on matters of timing and style. The military and the civilians did not differ on the objectives of the war or on the propriety of using such military force as was needed, but they did have conflicting views on the techniques of risk management. The civilians, it should be noted, were much more adept than the military in packaging military options for a President who wanted the fruits of victory without the costs of war.

In such a crossfire of advice, the President thinks of himself as a moderate. When he turns down unending requests of his senior military advisers to use new chemical agents or tactical nuclear weapons, or to increase the tonnage of bombs and authorized targets, he may privately congratulate himself on his courage. Yet each request denied is only the beginning of a negotiation. Thus the Joint Chiefs of Staff exacted a price from President Johnson for their agreement to support the cessation of bombing over North Vietnam. They insisted on taking the bombs they had counted on dropping in the North and dumping them on the South and Laos. Because the Joint Chiefs of Staff threatened to put the case for defoliation directly to Congress, President Kennedy authorized a limited test program for herbicides in Vietnam in the spring of 1961. So also in the area of arms control: In 1963 the White House agreed that the partial Nuclear Test Ban would not be allowed to inhibit weapons development, although that was one of the arms control purposes it was ostensibly to serve. And, indeed, more test weapons have been exploded underground in the seven years since the treaty than in the previous eighteen years.

Even when the President denies the request of the military, his decision is more of a postponement than an outright rejection. Thus Kennedy's rejection of General Taylor's recommendation for ground troops in Vietnam in 1961 was not definitive. In Roger Hilsman's words, "in an interesting example of one type of gambit, the President avoided a direct 'no' to the proposal for introducing troops." The Joint Chiefs of Staff continued to plan and recommend this course as the military situation in Vietnam deteriorated over the next four years. By playing this familiar Presidential gambit, the President has the illusion that he is "buying time," but he is really buying trouble. Military officers are no less adept than other bureaucrats at constructing myths to explain their failure. "The civilians made me go into battle with one hand tied behind my back" is a peculiarly dangerous myth not only because it has more than a germ of truth to it or because it can lead to its more serious version—the "stab in the back" myth—but also because it can be used as a powerful weapon of psychological warfare against the President. Having turned down one set of dangerous recommendations, he is in a much harder position to reject the second and the third.

How difficult it is for a President to turn down military advice is suggested by Lyndon Johnson's crucial decisions of March 1968. To back up his rejection of the Joint Chiefs' recommendations for a huge troop increase and invasion of North Vietnam he announced he would not run again, thus abandoning the office he had spent a lifetime seeking.

The fourteen-month period between the assassination of John F. Kennedy and the inauguration of Lyndon B. Johnson as President in his own right was the heyday of the National Security Managers. This was the era of "McNamara's war," when the crucial planning on the escalation of the Vietnam war took place. During the 1950's, when Vietnam was still a "back-burner" issue, bureaucrats "in the field"—such men as the CIA station chief, John Richardson—had great latitude to set American policy. By 1966, on the other hand, the President himself was the Vietnam desk officer, squadron commander, and sometimes even patrol leader. He would personally approve bombing targets and wait up through the early hours of the morning until the planes had returned from their missions. But in his first year of office he was engaged with other matters, passing the Kennedy legislative program, developing one of his own, emerging from the shadow of Camelot, and getting himself reelected. Since the events in Southeast Asia were moving too fast to be ignored, this meant that the handful of men who had already become "old Vietnam hands" had the action. Within broad limits, they were free to frame the issues and to propose the alternatives

For almost three years the Pentagon had been running the war. In 1961, according to Arthur Schlesinger, Kennedy had made a "conscious decision" to turn the Vietnam problem over to the Secretary of Defense. The Secretary of State did not object, writes Roger Hilsman, who at the time was the Assistant Secretary of State in charge of Asia, because Rusk always regarded Vietnam "as essentially a military problem." President Kennedy had approved a program of covert actions against North Vietnam which had been recommended by a Vietnam Task Force established in the early weeks of his Administration. These actions included the dispatch of agents into North Vietnam to set up "networks of resistance, covert bases and teams for sabotage and light harassment." Other proposals called for increased overflights of North Vietnam and for U.S.-supported South Vietnamese guerrilla operations in Laos, especially against Communist aerial resupply missions in the vicinity of Tchepone. During this period the State Department was particularly strong in pushing for military operations in Laos, and some of these President Kennedy rejected. On March 9, 1962, U.S. officials announced that American pilots were accompanying Vietnamese pilots on combat missions as part of a "combat training" program. By the fall of 1963, the Joint Chiefs of Staff had approved a plan developed by Admiral Ulysses Grant Sharp, the Commander of the Pacific Fleet, which called for amphibious raids using Vietnamese Rangers Airborne and Marine units against targets in North Vietnam.

A few days after he took office, Lyndon Johnson called for renewed planning for possible increased activity against North Vietnam. Within two weeks MACV, the military headquarters in Saigon, had obliged with plan 34a, which offered "a spectrum of capabilities" against North Vietnam including air attacks, all designed to "convince the DRV leadership" that they should stop supporting insurgent activities in South Vietnam and Laos. Thus, by posing essentially military questions to military bureaucrats, the President effectively guaranteed that the Vietnam drama would be a war story.

The principal goal of a President in office, more than even reelection or historical vindication, is to govern. In domestic affairs he barely governs: He presides. John Kennedy died without enacting any major piece of domestic legislation. During the years in which he was making life-and-death decisions affecting the fate of the Northern Hemisphere, he could not persuade Congress to enact a minimum wage bill or a federal education act. When he tried in 1962 to use the power of command of his office to halt inflation and publicly denounced steel company executives for raising their prices, he spent the rest of his term apologizing for his bitterly criticized "strong-arm methods." Harry Truman remarked, "I sit here all day trying to persuade people to do things they ought to have sense enough to do without persuading them. . . . That's all the powers of the President amount to."

Where the President resorts to command to solve problems at home, he usually ends up looking foolish. Truman was ordered by the Supreme Court to give back the steel mills he had ordered seized during the Korean War. His earlier attempt to draft striking railroad workers into the army was blocked by Congress. Because of a remarkable constellation of circumstances—his predecessor's assassination, mounting civil disturbance and a sense of crisis, and his own special skills and associations—Lyndon Johnson was able to enact much of John Kennedy's legislative program, but by the time the war escalated he, too, had run out of steam. As a wartime President, he lacked the power or leadership authority to curb crippling inflation. Richard Neustadt, in his book *Presidential Power,* has observed that command "is not a method suitable for everyday employment" in domestic affairs. In controversial issues of social reconstruction, the President's power is hobbled. Only when he acts in his capacity as Commander-in-Chief can the President command and count on a high probability that he will get obedience and sometimes even the desired results. Thus only in foreign and military affairs, insulated as they are from the political restraints of domestic conflict, can the President exercise the full scope of his enormous powers.

This does not mean that foreign problems are ultimately any more tractable than domestic problems, but it does mean that a President can have the illusion of success when he acts as Commander-in-Chief. A President who lacks the power to raise the price of postage stamps is peculiarly susceptible to the illusion that he can manage the world. In national security affairs, particularly in the twilight world of half-secret brush-fire wars, the President is in command of his own reputation in a way that he never can be in domestic affairs. If he claims to be winning the "war on inflation," it is possible to determine the accuracy of his claim at the local supermarket. But who can successfully challenge his claim to be winning the hearts and minds of Southeast Asia by improving the "kill ratio"? Only when a foreign war meets with obvious disaster does the President lose his firm (and exclusive) grip on the flag.

The bureaucratic structure of the national security establishment over which the President presides is built on the principles of hierarchy and command. The art of governing by persuasion, which is essential in domestic affairs, is a rare political skill. It is far easier to govern by command, and the only area where this is possible is beyond the shore. Whether there is to be "action" or not depends in large measure on the feelings, interests, fears, and hopes of unpredictable human beings. By contrast a military operation ignores such "soft" considerations and deals with the "hard" data. Where is the enemy? How many are there? How many men do we move from here to there in order to destroy them? When the President decides to order the movement of troops, he can have a high degree of confidence that his orders, in contrast to Presidential commands in many areas of domestic policy, will be carried out with dispatch and even a touch of virtuosity. Also, the possibilities for the experimental use of power beyond the frontiers of American society are tempting, while legal and political restraints still operate within our borders. Thus Kennedy could consider solving the "Cuban problem" by arranging for Castro's assassination or the Congo problem by bribing the entire parliament. However much he may be tempted, a President cannot solve his tax problems or inflation problems by using similar methods.

In Vietnam the President was presented with a seemingly limitless panoply of "options," all of which made use of homicidal technology organized under commandable bureaucratic structures. Although, as we have seen, the long-range intelligence prognoses on the war at the crucial stages of escalation were guarded or pessimistic, the President was offered a variety of tools to try. He could do something. He did not have to "sit in my rocking chair," to use Lyndon Johnson's words, and admit that he, the President of the United States, was as powerless to influence the dangerous outside world as he was to change America.

All through 1964 the tempo of contingency planning quickened. The idea men at the Pentagon worked overtime. Various proposals for demonstrating American displeasure—bombing, defoliating, conducting reconnaissance, infiltrating agents, even using the supersonic boom of B-52's to break windows in Hanoi—were forwarded up the bureaucratic ladder. McNamara insisted on managing the planning process himself, sharing his war primarily with his trusted lieutenant, Assistant Secretary John T. McNaughton. The planning process consisted of evaluating the risks and effectiveness of various combinations of military and paramilitary measures put forward by specialists in homicide in the military services and in the "intelligence community." Chester Cooper, an old CIA hand on Vietnam, has written, somewhat unfairly, that "serious thinking with respect to the choices available was desultory." (It was indeed highly imaginative: a dozen James Bond scripts could be written from a month's output of Joint Chiefs of Staff recommendations.) In noting the militarized nature of the planning process, Cooper observes:

> By and large the non-defense elements of the government were neither psychologically nor organizationally able to come to grips with an insurgency that was quickly getting out of hand. None of the courses at the Foreign Service Institute, and none of the experiences of AID specialists and Foreign Service officers elsewhere, seemed relevant to what was going on in Vietnam.

Why was it that, while the Pentagon bureaucracy churned out dozens of recommendations for making the life of the Vietnamese more miserable in imaginative new ways, no staff work of any consequence was devoted to the kind of peace settlement the United States wanted or had reason to expect, or how to get it? Why was the fear of negotiation so great that proposals for settlement from U Thant, the Soviet Union, and DeGaulle, as well as peace feelers from Hanoi, were turned aside? "We do not believe in conferences to ratify terror, so our policy is unchanged," the President announced. Meanwhile, Assistant Secretary of State William Bundy was exploring a Laos conference as a possible diplomatic "gambit" which could be used as a "plausible way of holding off Vietnam negotiations."

That the world's greatest power fears political negotiation and prefers to treat political disputes as tests of military strength has been a fact in our national biography since World War II. The principal thrust of U.S. policy in Europe has been to avoid the negotiation for a European settlement which the Soviets have been proposing. The United States has preferred to advance its security interests by preserving the confrontation of nuclear-armed NATO and Warsaw Pact forces in the heart of Europe. U.S. policy in Asia has been to resist negotiation with China, even on so uncontroversial a matter as recognizing its existence.

During the Cuban missile crisis (October 14 to 28, 1962), according to Adam Yarmolinsky, at the time a third-level but strategically placed National Security Manager, the Executive Committee of the National Security Council "spent at least 90 percent of its time studying alternative uses of troops, bombers, and warships." Although "the possibility of seeking withdrawal of the missiles by straightforward diplomatic negotiation received some attention within the State Department, it seems hardly to have been considered by the President." Nor was any significant attention given even to the use of economic leverage on the Soviet Union in preference to the confrontation and eventual ultimatum. Yarmolinsky finds it "curious" that nonmilitary agencies should have had so few expedients to put before the President.

There are profound reasons why it is not particularly "curious" that the United States government specializes in violence in its approach to national security. The basic characteristics of our institutional structures, the rewards and incentives that operate on men when they become National Security Managers, and the elaborate private language and ideology that has been developed to absolve men from personal responsibility for bureaucratic homicide all reinforce each other. The actors in the Vietnam tragedy by and large did what they were trained to do, were paid to do, and, under happier circumstances, would have been praised for doing.

One of the first lessons a National Security Manager learns after a day in the bureaucratic climate of the Pentagon, State Department, White House, or CIA is that toughness is the most highly prized virtue. Some of the National Security Managers of the Kennedy–Johnson era, looking back on their experience, talk about the "hairy chest syndrome." The man who is ready to recommend using violence against foreigners, even where he is overruled, does not damage his reputation for prudence, soundness, or imagination, but the man who recommends putting an issue to the UN, seeking negotiations, or—horror of horrors—"doing nothing" quickly becomes known as a "soft." To be "soft"—that is, unbelligerent, compassionate, willing to settle for less—or simply to be repelled by mass homicide, is to be "irresponsible." It means walking out of the club.

Bureaucratic *machismo* is cultivated in hundreds of little ways. There is the style of talking to a subordinate (the driving command masked by superficial informality) or to a superior (fact-loaded, quantitative, gutsy). The Kennedy operators, particularly, cultivated a machine-gun delivery. If a man could talk fast, loud, and often, he proved he was "on top of the job." Speed reading, too, became a kind of badge of prowess. To be an operator is to be active in "putting out fires," a free-wheeling generalist who is "in on the action" wherever it might be. The ambitious and successful bureaucrat reaches for the great issues. He specializes in the crisp, uncomplicated, usually mechanistic analysis of a problem because in a militarized bureaucracy that is the easiest view to sell. Those who specialize in the "long view" soon get a deadly reputation for writing "interesting think-pieces" which by definition have "no status." (A paper acquires "status" in the bureaucracy by being passed around from department to department for initialing by appropriate officials. The less the paper disturbs the prevailing bureaucratic climate, the faster the signatures are collected and the sooner the author of the paper is on his way to making history.)

The most important way bureaucratic *machismo* manifests itself is in attitude toward violence. Those who are in the business of defining the national interest are fascinated by lethal technology because in the national security bureaucracy weaponry, unlike politics, is revolutionary.

234

For years the only real movement in the national security bureaucracy was provided by the momentum of the arms race. On the political issues positions were frozen. Officials could handle problems of managing the NATO "crises" of 1967 by dredging up papers prepared ten years earlier. But the weapons revolutions which occurred every five years presented a new, dangerous, and exciting reality that had to be dealt with. To be a specialist in the new violence was to be on the frontier.

To demonstrate toughness a National Security Manager must accept the use of violence as routine. Proposals for the use of violence are inserted into the normal rush of bureaucratic business. Thus messages on the commencement of the bombing campaign in North Vietnam also included such routine matters as the procurement of PX supplies. Crises in which violence is to be used are treated in the national security bureaucracy as mere extensions of everyday life. When President Kennedy informed the country in 1961 that the Berlin crisis might result in imminent nuclear war, he took the occasion to lament the Post Office deficit. Even the language of the bureaucracy—the diminutive "nucs" for instruments that kill and mutilate millions of human beings, "surgical strike" for chasing and mowing down peasants from the air by spraying them with 8,000 bullets a minute—takes the mystery, awe, and pain out of violence. The socialization process is designed to accustom bankers, lawyers, and military technocrats with no more than normal homicidal inclinations to the idea of killing in the national interest, much as at lower levels recruits are trained to grunt and shout "kill!" as they thrust their bayonets into sawdust bags.

The best evidence that the "tough"—that is, specialists in violence—prevail in the bureaucracy is provided by looking at what "making it" means in the national security world. Those who recommend more killing than the President is willing to sanction do not seriously jeopardize their position. The generals who urged President Johnson to obliterate eleven Chinese targets or to mine Haiphong Harbor (along with any Soviet ships that happened to be there) neither lost their jobs nor were reprimanded when the President rejected their advice. Members of the Joint Chiefs of Staff during the Cuban missile crisis recommended solving the problem by bombing the Soviet missile sites, advice which the President rejected because he thought it risked a nuclear war and a minimum of 150,-000,000 fatalities. Once the crisis was over, the Chiefs resumed business as usual. General William Westmoreland, who was allowed to play out his own "scenario" in Vietnam to the point of disaster, was rewarded with an appointment as Army Chief of Staff. We are not suggesting that bad advice, or even good advice that is rejected, should necessarily result in dismissal. The point is that only certain kinds of bad advice or rejected advice are likely to have that result. This fact of life is not lost on carcerist bureaucrats. Certain kinds of advice are safe to give, even if rejected, and certain kinds involve immense personal risks. That reality sustains a bureaucratic atmosphere that supports permanent military involvement.

The obvious but fundamental fact is that for the Number One Nation, reliance on violence or the threat of violence to get its way is easier than all other methods of dealing with the outside world. There is a huge superfluity of force. If a foreign policy problem can be converted into a military operation, the responsible officer can count on getting action. The problem may not be solved—it may eventually be complicated, as in Vietnam —but the wheels of government will move. Managers are concerned with process, not results, because in the game view of international politics there is no end. John F. Kennedy called the State Department a "bowl of jelly," in part because foreign service officers are cautious and conservative, but, more important, because by nature diplomacy is slow business. "I don't feel I have an action group at my command as they do in other departments," Secretary of State William Rogers confessed to reporters a few months after taking office. In the age of well-developed lethal technology, to put it in the simplest terms, it takes much less time to kill a man than to change his mind or change your own. To solve a political problem nonviolently requires patience, understanding, and objectivity. The National Security Manager is lacking in all three by the very nature of his job.

The top managers of an institution which defines its mission as being the "locomotive of humanity," "the guardian at the gates," staying "number one," or exercising "world responsibility" are, clearly, very busy men. They hop from crisis to crisis, spending most of their time in meetings or reading reports of subordinates. In rapid succession the National Security Manager figuratively roams the globe, "putting out fires," as he likes to call it, with a telegram here, a strong statement there. He reacts to immediate events that are pressed upon him, and much of the time he literally does not know what he is doing. Not only has he no time to think, but he would be suspicious if someone tried to present him with the opportunity. Most of the proposals for reforming the State Department miss this point. The smartest, best-informed men, operating in the most streamlined bureaucracy, cannot run the world.

The National Security Manager operates under another handicap—one directly related to the predilection for violence in the bureaucracy: ignorance. James Thomson, Jr., who was an officer in the National Security Council during the Vietnam escalation, notes that the men who made the basic decisions about Vietnam knew nothing about the area. One reason Vietnam was so quickly elevated as a symbol in the world of national security is that people at the top knew virtually nothing about the reality. Walt Rostow liked to write learned memos about the "Southeast Asians," lumping people of a hundred cultures divided by ancient animosities into a single convenient target much as the statesmen of the Eisenhower era converted the rest of the world outside North America and Western Europe into a manageable unity by calling it the "gray areas."

There was of course no particular reason why investment bankers, generals, Texas politicians, or foreign service officers should have known anything about Vietnamese politics. Often they knew little about the political forces in their own immediate community. In addition, once they occupied their offices, they became willing victims of a social process that compounded their ignorance. In a bureaucracy there is a clear correlation between rank and credibility. Generals, ambassadors, and cabinet ministers can safely pronounce inanities which would end the careers of junior officers.

Top National Security Managers are forced by the circumstances of their job to be generalists. To serve the President and retain his confidence, which is the only source of their power, they must be prepared to commit themselves to any crisis wherever it appears. They must also try to relate the chaotic rush of events into some coherent pattern which the President can understand. This means that facts must be fitted into available theories, for there is neither the time nor the energy to change theories in which bureaucracies have huge investments. Obscure events must be immediately located in a familiar ideological landscape. It is for this reason that State Department planners were talking about the "Sino-Soviet bloc" four years after the split in the Communist world had exploded into public view. The global manager cannot afford to compromise his ideology with uncongenial facts, for his power rests on his reputation for being able to manipulate events in accordance with a theory.

The pervasive ignorance of the National Security Managers concerning the politics of Vietnam led them into the trap of collecting isolated facts and figures. Robert McNamara was the leading specimen in the national security bureaucracy of *homo mathematicus*, the man who believes other men behave primarily in response to "hard data," usually numbers (infiiltration rates, "kill ratios," bomb tonnage). Like the classic private eye on television, *homo mathematicus* always looks for "the facts." In the process, he misses reality, for he never gets close enough or related enough to another society to do more than count things in it.

If you relate to a country as a military target you do not need to know anything about it except such details as are easily supplied by reconnaissance satellites, spy ships, secret agents, etc. You need never know who the victims of your attack were. Your job is merely to count. Things that stay still long enough to be counted are either inanimate or dead. Living human beings, complex and changing political relationships, such intangibles as national pride, elude the best analysis. All foreigners who do not know a society are at an enormous disadvantage, but *homo mathematicus* is intellectually crippled in special ways. When Desmond Fitzgerald, top CIA specialist in covert intelligence operations, briefed McNamara and told him that he had a "feeling" for the events in Vietnam that contradicted the optimistic "hard data" which lower echelons were feeding Washington, the Secretary of Defense glared icily at him and never invited him to give another briefing.

Many of the National Security Managers prided themselves on taking a systems analysis approach to foreign relations—collect the facts, calculate the costs and the benefits, outline the possible options, and select the best course. The problem was that they did not know enough about the rest of the world to understand what system they were operating in. Chester Cooper gives an illuminating, if biased, picture of the meeting of East and West at a crucial point in the Vietnam war:

> Much more worrisome than the meetings with government officials were those with the dissident Buddhists and students. Bundy came out reeling from a two-hour session with a leading member of the Buddhist hierarchy. His razor-sharp mind just couldn't cut through the ooze of generalities. Two cultures and two educational backgrounds did not directly conflict but rather slid past one another.

(It would be interesting to get the Buddhists' impression of Bundy's "razor-sharp mind.")

This vignette illustrates the classic limitation on the power of imperialist nations to rule other societies effectively: lack of political understanding. This limitation goes far to explain why empires resort increasingly to violence to maintain their hold on weak countries and why the attempt to make violence a substitute for power ultimately destroys that hold.

Perhaps the most important quality in a man seeking nonviolent, political solutions rather than violent solutions to national security problems is objectivity, and this is the quality that is least in evidence. The man who tries to see the point of view of the adversary or explain his perspective has to defend himself against the charge that he is advocating the adversary's cause. The experience of the "old China hands" in the State Department in the late 1940's is a good example. Such men as Edmund Clubb and John Stewart Service attempted to argue that the Maoist regime in China had a more popular base than had Chiang Kai-shek and that the Chinese Communists were serious dedicated men who were neither bandits nor puppets as the anti-Communist ideologues liked to believe. For telling the truth as they saw it, their careers were broken and they were branded as "disloyal" or "lacking in judgment," depending upon how prescient they had actually been. For someone to have suggested in April 1961 that the Cuban people were not likely to revolt against Castro because he was a popular leader— far more popular than the émigrés whom the United States was supporting—was to sound pro-Castro. To suggest that the Soviet Union's moves in Eastern Europe after the war were a reflection of deep-seated security fears rather than the first step toward world conquest was to be a Soviet apologist.

In the game of international politics practitioners must be fiercely partisan. The United States is the client and the task of the manager is to increase her power and influence in the world, whatever the cost. *Raison d'état*, the historic principle asserted by sovereign nations that they are above all law, is a daily operating rule in the national security bureaucracy. In the jungle world of international politics the duty of the National Security Manager is to pursue every seeming advantage he can get away with, regardless of law.

Thus, the issue of war crimes in Vietnam only became a matter of concern in the national security bureaucracy after the public disclosures of My Lai. Indiscriminate bombing, free fire zones, torture of prisoners, wholesale crop destruction, and other acts which violate the letter and spirit of solemn treaties signed by the United States and should shock any civilized conscience, were common knowledge throughout the national security bureaucracy. The 1949 Geneva Conventions signed by the United States with respect to the treatment of civilian populations, treatment of prisoners, etc., are not regarded as problems, except to the extent that the State Department Legal Adviser is ordered to write a justification of American conduct.

Objectivity has never been a notable characteristic of political power-seekers. "The man of politics," Boccalini of Loreto wrote in the late seventeenth century, "gets firmly into his head the principle that everything else must give way before the absolute necessity of asserting and maintaining oneself in the State; he sets his foot on the neck of every other value in heaven and earth. The desire to govern is a daemon which even holy water will not drive out." The way to "maintain oneself in the State" is to promote the State. The politician who works for the aggrandizement of the State, for its glory and expansion, is a hero (until he fails); the man who counsels moderation and restraint is a nuisance. No politician has felt called to preside over the liquidation of an empire (although some have ended up reluctantly doing so). For rulers and their clerks personal satisfaction has always been achieved in the reflected glory of state power. This is especially true in the age of the organization man.

Like the manager of a soap company who paces himself by the bars of soap the corporation sells, the National Security Manager also measures his worth by how well his organization is doing. As John Kenneth Galbraith has pointed out, people in government, unlike poets, opera singers, and brain surgeons, are sustained by organizations. The defeated politician, retiring ambassador or general—one might add the ex-Cabinet officer—who fails to get a bank, foundation, or university to manage, "faces total obscurity." They are "sustained by an organization," Galbraith observes, and "on losing its support they pass permanently into the shadows." This being so, National Security Managers have a personal investment in the health and aggrandizement of their own bureaucratic organizations. They equate the national interest and their organization's interest as a matter of course. They will fight to maintain an obsolete air base, build redundant weapons systems, proliferate arms around the world by certifying that the nation's "vital interests" are at stake when it is merely their own budgets. Thus they demonstrate the same objectivity as an advocate for their own bureaucratic component as advocates for the nation display in dealing with the rights of other nations.

In the attempt to understand why the "brightest and the best" in American society—all "honorable gentlemen," as the severest critics among their own number always concede—defined the national interest as requiring the prosecution of an aggressive war as brutal as any in history, two principal theories are adduced: the "mistake" theory and the "conspiracy" theory. Under the "mistake" theory, the National Security Managers did not mean to do what they did. They were misled by history and their own misguided good intentions. Such a theory cannot stand up to either legal or moral scrutiny. The National Security Managers understood the homicidal nature of the policies they recommended although they were clearly "mistaken" as to their consequences, as indeed is every ruler who embarks on a war and fails to achieve victory. It was to achieve certain specific results and to protect specific values that the United States committed and recommitted itself to a war in Vietnam. To have avoided the war would have meant a major revision of the operational code of the National Security Managers.

But there are problems with the "conspiracy" model as well. Two questions arise: Did the National Security Managers have a conscious plan, an imperial design? Did they believe that they were transgressing the laws of civilized behavior? These questions are not particularly important for judging the legal guilt or innocence of individuals, for in a government under law officials should be held accountable for a pattern of conduct which violates the civilized conscience no matter what their intentions. (Whether or how they should be punished raises many separate questions, but whether they should be held accountable seems beyond argument if the "rule of law" is to be anything more than a slogan.) But the questions are important to any attempt to gain a deeper understanding of what goes on in the mysterious world of the national security bureaucracy.

Anyone willing to read the historical record will find it hard to deny that American policy-makers for a generation have had a rather clear design for expanding American power. Americans acquired their global empire in the same mythical fit of absent-mindedness in which Great Britain gathered hers. The maintenance of strategic territory occupied in World War II, the containment of the two great potential power rivals, Russia and China, the filling of "power vacuums" left by the collapse of French and British imperial power, the expansion of American influence into all open areas of the "developing world," and the maintenance of a world capitalist economic system dominated by the United States have been conscious policies. To accomplish any of them the United States has been prepared to use force.

The great documents of the Cold War that have come to public light bear out the existence of a reasonably coherent grand design. True, American officials often stumbled and faltered in carrying out the design. Sometimes their actions were self-defeating. But faulty execution does not negate the existence of a plan. It has been fashionable for critics of foreign policy to assert that America's troubles with the outside world stem from the lack of national security planning, that we have too many agencies going off in too many directions. A better founded criticism, it seems to me, is that there has always been a plan, but it was hopelessly obsolete from the very beginning. In the second half of the twentieth century no nation, however powerful or however enlightened, can play the imperial game without paying too high a price.

Yet the "conspiracy" concept does not fit the facts, because conspiracy, for the layman if not for the lawyer, implies some consciousness of guilt. Conspirators, according to popular understanding of the term, are men who plot to commit acts they know to be wrong. Here is the crux of the problem. The men who were ready in the Cuban missile crisis to risk civilization for prestige, for what Dean Acheson calls "the shadow of power," and to destroy Indochina to save America's reputation for toughness, to lie and kill on a grand scale, all believed that they were doing right—that, indeed, they were acting under duty. It is impossible to understand how dangerous the structures of the national security bureaucracy are without also understanding the systems of absolution that operate within those structures. These systems of absolution serve to stand ordinary principles of private morality on their head and to transform reasonably law-abiding professors and bankers into killers.

The official lie in its myriad forms is only one of the systems of absolution operating in the national security bureaucracy. Another, clearly related, is the "need not to know" phenomenon. In approving a stepped-up defoliation program in Vietnam in late 1965, Secretary of State Rusk observed to his staff assistant in charge of counter-insurgency that Vietnam was really an "empty jungle." The only people "who would get hurt by defoliation" would be the Viet Cong. The statement, absurd on its face, was clutched at by the Secretary to resolve inner moral doubts and to legitimize the ordering of a crime. Just as there is a "need to know" requirement which

245

restricts classified information to the fewest possible hands, there is a "need not to know" which makes it possible for conscientious men to authorize bureaucratic homicide. I came upon another example of the "need not to know" after I returned from a visit to North Vietnam and reported to a senior American statesman, by that time an opponent of the war, that the U.S. Air Force had systematically bombed churches and pagodas in the province I had toured. His immediate response was that these buildings had been used to hide trucks and were therefore legitimate targets. The reality which I saw was that the churches were for the most part in the middle of fields and could not have been used for military purposes. The bombings took place not because of specific orders to hit churches but because of a standing order to hit everything. In a primitive economy there is a shortage of good targets, and a pilot under orders not to come back with leftover bombs finds the biggest structure in the village irresistible. There is no easier way to deal with such typical examples of bureaucratic homicide than "not to know."

Official ignorance also provides a good defense against unanticipated and embarrassing facts. The crucial factor that upset all the calculations of the optimists in the national security bureaucracy was the willingness of the enemy to accept a staggering loss of life. From 1965 to 1968, the Pentagon more than once reported the destruction of the whole Viet Cong force. Even allowing for official U.S. exaggeration, the actual number of enemy deaths was enormous. But the implications of the fact that the Vietnamese were ready to die on a vast scale rather than give up were clouded in official ignorance. No one at the top knew or considered it important that the Vietnamese had been fighting foreign invaders for almost 2,000 years. No one understood the depth of their nationalist feeling. The official explanation inside the Pentagon was that Vietnamese value life cheaply and are accustomed to dying in droves. The implication of this racist analysis, with its connotations of human waves, yellow hordes, and Kamikazes, is that they are exceedingly dangerous people and deserve to be killed in even greater numbers.

The structure of bureaucratic language is itself an absolution system. For the National Security Managers the flavor and connotation of the words they use on the job reinforce the legitimacy of what they are doing and obscure the reality of bureaucratic homicide. On one level there are the obvious examples of verbal camouflage. The "surgical strike" to "take out" a "base" implies that the operation is therapeutic. No pictures of flaming children, torn limbs, or shattered bodies pinned under rubble come to mind. "Attack objectives" are easier to think about than the multilated, weeping, and dazed human beings who will be the actual target of the bombs. "Pacification" trips off the tongue far more easily in a Pentagon briefing and looks better on the page of a neat memorandum than phrases that would actually describe the death and suffering to which the antiseptic term refers. Emotional distance from the homicidal consequences of his planning is essential to the mental health of the planner, and bureaucratic language is rich in the terminology of obfuscation.

There are more subtle uses of language as well. The routine use of such words as "power vacuum" disguises a major policy premise and forecloses debate on what is actually a highly debatable proposition. The idea concealed by the term "power vacuum" is that a weak country must inevitably be dominated by a stronger one, that the power of one or the other of the Great Powers will "flow into" the country. The implication of those who use the term in the American bureaucracy is, of course, that it had better be U.S. power that flows in. Thus the idea of the impossibility of neutralism, national independence for weak countries, or avoiding the spread of American power is built into the working vocabulary of the National Security Manager.

Language is also useful for building in unconscious bias. When McNamara's assistants in the Pentagon were planning what by any legal standard was aggressive war against North Vietnam, they referred to their client, the United States, in memoranda as "the good doctor" whose military operations against the Vietnamese would presumably bring a cure. Once substantial numbers of U.S. military "advisers" began to accompany South Vietnamese units into battle in 1964 and the Viet Cong began to attack U.S. installations as at Pleiku, Pentagon planners used the language of reprisal to make their plans for carrying the war to North Vietnam appear defensive—not only to the outside world, but, at the emotional level, to themselves.

The same psychological pattern is even clear at lower levels of the bureaucratic ladder. In the air war in Vietnam, as Frank Harvey has pointed out, pilots of the Tactical Air Command "cruise around over the Delta like a vigilante posse, holding the power of life and death over the Vietnamese villagers living beneath." So convinced are the pilots of their right to spray Vietnam with bullets at will that they are genuinely outraged when "the little mothers" begin "shooting back." As Robert Crichton notes, Americans accustomed to 1,000-to-1 superiority in firepower over the enemy have come to feel that it is their inherent right to kill people without retaliation. Bureaucratic language of reprisal sustains this incredible assumption at the same time as it obscures its real meaning.

Perhaps the most striking characteristic of bureaucratic language is the recurrence of the imagery of manipulation.

"The timing and crescendo" of operations "should be under our control." "We should rev up Mr. —— to explore negotiations." "The United States Government might do better to carry forward the war on a purely unilateral basis." "How should we permit negotiations to develop?" Such random quotations from official documents all have one quality in common: They reinforce the myth of control—that is, the notion that the National Security Manager, with all the technological power at his command, can play upon the world like a giant console. Indeed, James C. Thomson, Jr., recalls that an Assistant Secretary of State in late 1964 proposed bombing and strafing patterns with these words: "It seems to me that our orchestration should be mainly violins, but with periodic touches of brass."

The most compelling absolution systems are the myths which exalt the significance of the targets of American military operations. These myths come in two principal varieties: The Myth of Monolithic Conspiracy and the Myth of the Inexorable Blueprint. The second had more of a vogue in the early days of the Cold War. The first played a crucial role in the Vietnam escalation. One of the principal problems in justifying the magnitude of the American commitment to keep South Vietnam from having an indigenous Communist government is that it is a very small country, very far away, with no record of having harmed any American interest. If it is to be the object of ten years of ferocious attention by the world's most powerful nation, it must be invested with sufficient importance. The myth of Monolithic Conspiracy was an ideal device for finding an enemy in Vietnam worthy of the U.S. effort. Who that enemy was changed from time to time. In 1961 when the Viet Cong insurgency was still at a relatively low level, a State Department White Paper conceded that the enemy were the "Vietnamese Communists" but they were using "the same methods" including "Mao Tse-tung's theories" which were used "in Malaya, in Greece, in the Philippines, in Cuba, and in Laos."

By 1965, before North Vietnamese regulars had crossed the seventeenth parallel, before Chinese and Soviet weapons had been found in any quantities in the South, and just before the United States itself sent an army to South Vietnam and began bombing North Vietnam around the clock, the State Department had changed the enemy. "In Viet-Nam a Communist government (North Vietnam) has set out deliberately to conquer a sovereign people in a neighboring state." By 1967, after the United States had committed more than a half-million men in South Vietnam and had dropped more bombs on Indochina than were dropped in five years of World War II, the enemy was again escalated. When asked at a press conference why he thought "our security is at stake in Vietnam," Secretary of State Rusk replied unhesitatingly:

> Within the next decade or two, there will be a billion Chinese on the mainland, armed with nuclear weapons, with no certainty about what their attitude toward the rest of Asia will be.

> Now the free nations of Asia will make up at least a billion people. They don't want China to overrun them on the basis of a doctrine of the world revolution.

The same confusion as to the real enemy was manifested in internal debates inside the bureaucracy because there never was a credible theory for making the war the principal international project of the United States. Unless one believed in some form of the Domino Theory, it was perfectly obvious that the costs of fighting the war far outweighed the gains. But, as in any human activity, acts bring with them their own explanations. The more aggressive the act, the more elaborate the explanation. Thus, for Rusk, Vietnam was a "test case" of "wars of liberation" supported by Moscow as well as Peiping. International Communism had a design to control all Asia, Africa and Latin America, "thus encircling and strangling the Atlantic world." If we do not defeat "them" in Vietnam, President Johnson warned, we will have to fight "them" in San Francisco. At last the cause in Vietnam had been made worthy of the destruction and the suffering being visited upon it.

The other myth, the Myth of the Inexorable Blueprint, is closely related. The basic idea is that the Communists are so unconnected to the rest of the world, so autistic, that nothing the "Free World" does, save credible military threats, influences their conduct. Inside the government, intelligence reports are sifted daily which contradict so inherently absurd a proposition. The Communist system is changing. The Soviet Union is changing. Soviet leaders clearly react to moves in the outside world, and not only to threats. Indeed, many of their proposed concessions—the test ban treaty, for example—have been a response to conciliatory initiatives by the United States. The National Security Managers know all these things. For years these have been familiar ideas in their daily work. Yet in making crucial decisions they cling to the myth of the blueprint. Put most simply, "the underlying crisis of our time," according to Secretary Rusk, "arises from this fundamental conflict: between those who would impose their blueprint on mankind and those who believe in self-determination."

The myth had been preserved almost intact since 1950 when Dean Acheson, speaking on the "Communist Menace," observed that the conflict with the Soviet Union transcended ordinary international disputes and declared that "there can be no greater disagreement than when someone wants to eliminate your existence altogether." The Soviet plan to "bury" America along with the capitalist system was inexorable. Indeed, as early as 1946 Harry Truman, dispatching an aircraft carrier, four cruisers, a destroyer flotilla and the battleship *Missouri* to the eastern Mediterranean to counter Soviet pressure on Turkey for a share in the control of the Straits, told Acheson that "we might as well find out whether the Russians were bent on world conquest now as in five or ten years."

The myth of the blueprint gives credibility to the idea of preventive war. If the Communist design to rule the world is implacable, it makes sense to fight them now in a small war when they are relatively weak than to wait for Armageddon. With the Nazi takeover of the Rhineland, Austria, and Czechoslovakia etched in their mind, the National Security Managers determined to treat any Communist advance anywhere as a harbinger of that final confrontation and as a justification for a final solution. A speech of Senator Lyndon B. Johnson in 1952 (when the Soviet Union had yet to develop a way of delivering the atomic bomb on the United States) typifies widely-held American attitudes on preventive nuclear war:

> We should announce, I believe, that any act of aggression, anywhere, by any Communist forces, will be regarded as an act of aggression by the Soviet Union. . . . If anywhere in the world—by any means, open or concealed—Communism trespasses upon the soil of the free world, we should unleash all the power at our command upon the vitals of the Soviet Union. That is the policy we should build toward.

A Soviet government, which can be dealt with only through ever-increasing military power rather than diplomacy, is the perfect adversary for an American government whose primary activity is war preparation. It is the indispensable partner. That Communists everywhere are guided by a fixed hostile ideology rather than limited and possibly flexible interests has been an essential part of American ideology, for it has absolved the National Security Managers of responsibility for waging a generation of war.

PART III /

FROM IMPERIAL WAR-MAKING TO A CODE OF PERSONAL RESPONSIBILITY

Marcus G. Raskin

1 /

THE EROSION OF CONGRESSIONAL POWER

America's war in Indochina has brought into focus the momentous events which led its government into an imperial pattern of behavior. As the United States became the dominant world power in the twentieth century, the American ruling elite found itself legitimizing military incursions while routinizing and rationalizing the Executive's usurped power of war-making. It whittled down the constitutional authority of Congress and systematically excluded the people from the process of making fundamental decisions on war and peace.

This series of events, which led to the militarization of the American government and a fundamental reliance on force in its relations abroad (and later at home) ran counter to a very different trend in American statecraft which developed after World War I—a trend toward viewing war itself and the making and planning of aggressive war as a *crime*. Such American statesmen as Secretary of State Frank Kellogg signed the Pact of Paris

(Kellogg–Briand Pact) on outlawing war. By World War II, American officials, including Presidents Roosevelt and Truman, were denouncing the German and Japanese leaders as war criminals for having made war. A major charge leveled against them was that they had militarized their societies. American leaders proclaimed that the primary peace aims of the United States were the development of the rule of law, the demilitarization of Germany and Japan, and the holding to account of war criminals. Indeed, government officials even said that American citizens in *future* times would be able to hold leaders personally accountable for their actions. To this end the United States proposed resolutions in the United Nations General Assembly and signed and initiated charters on war crimes, treaties (as yet unratified) on genocide, and stern measures against militarism and ultranationalism.

But the Cold War intruded and American leaders began justifying their militarism in the name of defending the "free world" against "aggression"—a process that culminated in the massive and tragic adventure in Indochina. Now that the dead end of such political behavior has become plain, people are beginning to rediscover the other impulse in American statecraft: that of holding leaders accountable to the people and the law for their plans and actions. This may be the major hope of avoiding the terrifying degeneration of American society and its governing processes. The rules and laws fashioned over several generations as the alternative to international terror politics, brush-fire wars, preemptive aggressive wars, and nuclear war are laws of personal responsibility which must be incorporated into the domestic law of nations. The irony of American history is that these two trends, that of imperial rule and that of holding leaders to personal account for war-making, principles applied in the flush of victory in 1945, must now stand in direct conflict with each other. The lesson of Vietnam could have been learned at Nuremberg, not Munich. The concept of rules of personal responsibility in public office or among "professionals" is not new. It poses a threat only to those who believe that power should remain untrammeled and that the populace should be held hostage to the wielders of such power. As Karl Jaspers has said, "For wherever power does not limit itself, there exists violence and terror, and in the end the destruction of life and soul."[1]

THE POWER TO WAGE WAR

Members of the Constitutional Convention understood that the power to declare and make war was not an abstraction. It meant the power to impress the young and destroy community, family, and commerce. For precisely these reasons the authority for undertaking war was not placed in the hands of the Executive. Alexander Hamilton, who on other matters favored wide latitude for the Executive, noted that the power to "embark" on war was something which the Constitutional Convention reserved for the Congress:

> In direct contrast to the power of the British sovereign to initiate war on his own prerogative, the clause was the result of a deliberate decision by the framers to vest the power to embark on war in the body most broadly representative of the people.[2]

Thomas Jefferson wrote to James Madison in 1789:

> We have already given in one example one effectual check to the Dog of War by transferring the power of letting him loose from the Executive to the Legislative body, from those who are to spend to those who are to pay.[3]

1/*The Question of German Guilt* (Dial Press, 1947), p. 34.

2/81 *Harvard Law Review*, June 1968, p. 1768.

3/*The Papers of Thomas Jefferson*, 15, ed. Julian Boyd (Princeton University Press, 1955), p. 397.

From its beginnings, the American form of government generated a built-in area of conflict. If the President had the power to determine foreign policy, suppose the foreign policy which he pursued should end in war, which fell within the power of Congress? In this debate the Hamiltonian view prevailed over the Madisonian: The day-to-day business of foreign policy was left in the hands of the President. However, the limits imposed on Presidential power in this regard were evident in the conduct of the early Presidents. As one recent Senate document has said, "The early Presidents carefully respected Congress's authority to initiate war." The Supreme Court, in an 1801 case, concluded that the "whole powers of war" were "vested in Congress." Historians have pointed out that Presidents Adams and Jefferson declined to act against France despite their conviction that France was invading and destroying American shipping. Hamilton told Adams in an official opinion, "In so delicate a case, in one which involves so important a consequence as that of war, my opinion is that no *doubtful* authority ought to be exercised by the President."[4]

Yet, according to Alexander Hamilton, the President, on his own authority, had the power to "repel sudden attacks." But what was a sudden attack? And on what? The question has never been fully resolved. Hornbook learning in constitutional law supported the idea that the President had the power to respond to a "sudden attack" without prior Congressional sanction. This power was broadened in the famous Prize cases during the American civil war when the Supreme Court ruled in a five-to-four decision that the President had the unlimited power to wage war when another nation waged war directly upon the United States:

4/In *The Viet-Nam War: The President Versus the Constitution* by Francis Wormuth, quoting a letter from Hamilton to James McHenry, Secretary of War, May 17, 1798.

If a war be made by invasion of a foreign nation, the President is not only authorized but bound to resist force by force. He does not initiate the war, but is bound to accept the challenge without waiting for any special legislative authority.[5]

More pertinent than the instance when the United States was under attack was the reverse. When could the United States do the attacking, and, consequently, when was the United States at war? The United States has been involved in military actions every few years since its beginning. Such actions have not been recognized by the Congress as "war," perhaps because Congress is abjured by the Constitution from making aggressive war. When the House of Representatives voted its appreciation of General Taylor at the end of the Mexican War, it declared that the United States had won "a war unnecessarily and unconstitutionally begun by the President of the United States."[6]

The Supreme Court interpreted the war power as one granted to Congress only for the purpose of national defense. The war power was not granted, according to this view, for aggressive purposes. In effect, Congress's war-making power was limited to defensive wars only. In *Fleming v. Page*,[7] Chief Justice Taney, speaking for the Supreme Court, argued that American wars cannot

. . . be presumed to be waged for the purpose of conquest or the acquisition of territory . . . [but] the genius and character of our institutions are peaceful, and the power to declare war was not conferred upon Congress for the purpose of aggression or aggrandizement, but to enable the

---

5/67 U.S. (92 Boack) 635 (1863).

6/*Documents Related to the War Power of Congress,* Committee on Foreign Relations, July 1970, GPO, p. 76.

7/Case #50 U.S. 602 (1850).

general government to vindicate by arms, if it should become necessary, its own rights and the rights of its citizens.[8]

If the Congress and the people were reluctant to exercise the power to make war, this was hardly the case with the Executive, which saw the use of the military, and the engagement of the military in hostilities, as essential components of foreign policy. Since the Administration of President Washington, the United States has used military force on 150 separate occasions outside the continental United States.[9] However, it was not until the twentieth century that the Executive used the military as a major and, ultimately, predominant tool of foreign policy.

The Congressional war-making power had significantly eroded by the end of the nineteenth century, and finally washed away with the bully actions of President Theodore Roosevelt in Panama in 1903,[10] when U.S. armed forces went beyond the traditional goals of protecting the status quo or punishing insurgents who might endanger American interests. Military force was used purely on Executive authority to establish a government that would serve American economic and military interests. The U.S. intervention in Panama did not pass through the legitimat-

---

8/While there is much evidence that American military actions were undertaken in Vietnam for the purpose of vindicating a clique in the American government who through their decisions and programs involved the United States more and more deeply, it can hardly be said that the rights of American citizens or of the general government of the United States were under attack by North Vietnam or the NLF.

9/Congressional Record, 1st Session, June 23, 1969, pp. S6955–6958.

10/I do not mean to overlook President Polk who, in his war with Mexico, usurped Congressional power. Abraham Lincoln, then a member of Congress, wrote to his law partner that Polk was setting a precedent for making war at the President's pleasure. The war-making power, according to Lincoln, was given to Congress because "Kings had always been involving and impoverishing their people in wars, pretending generally, if not always, that the good of the people was the object. This our convention understood to be the most oppressive of all kingly oppressions, and they resolved to so frame the Constitution that no men should hold the power of bringing this oppression upon us." (Feb. 15, 1848—Lincoln to Herndon—S10495, July 31, 1967).

ing procedures of Congress. It was during Theodore Roosevelt's Presidency that the Navy fleet was sent around the world to show that the U.S. was ready for any "eventualities." The fleet was sent over the objections of Congress and in derogation of Congressional power under Article 1, Section 8.

President Roosevelt also gave a broad new interpretation to the Monroe Doctrine.[11] During his administration, various European powers attempted to assert economic claims against Santo Domingo. Roosevelt objected, saying that the Europeans had no right to come to Latin America to collect debts. A popular concept at the time was that disputed debts should be submitted to arbitration before an international tribunal; indeed, in other situations arbitration had been proposed by the United States. But Roosevelt decreed that if Latin American countries could not keep order and pay debts, it fell to the United States to keep order and secure from the debtor nation resources to pay its creditors.

As the list of military interventions suggests, the United States did not shrink from such actions. Indeed, it would appear they were welcomed as a means of showing American interest and interests in the lands of others. No doubt all of them fell within the bounds of imperial propriety, since other nations aspiring to "greatness" carried on in similar ways. The conflict within China at the time of the Boxer Rebellion, and then later after the nationalist rebellion in 1912, involved the United States in a military intervention that spanned a generation. When, in the 1950's, the Republicans charged that the United States had "lost" China, they had in mind the halcyon days of the Ameri-

---

11/Even the Monroe Doctrine was limited in its application. According to a response by John Quincy Adams to an inquiry from Colombia as to the "manner" in which the United States would resist interference of the Holy Alliance, Adams replied that "the ultimate decision of this question belongs to the *Legislative* department of the Government."

can military constabulary in China which protected roads to the sea, missionaries, and trading companies.

The guard at Peking and along the route to the sea was maintained until 1941. In 1927, the United States had 5,670 troops ashore in China and forty-four vessels in its waters. In 1933 we had 3,027 armed men ashore. All this protective action was in general terms based on treaties with China ranging from 1858 to 1901.[12]

STRUCTURAL TRANSFORMATION FOR IMPERIAL PURPOSES

To cavort in the world in a grand way required a structural transformation of America's internal governing apparatus. It was during the Wilson Administration that major changes in structure were put into effect. In 1916 Woodrow Wilson proposed that Congress authorize the arming of American merchant vessels against possible attacks from German submarines. The "little band of willful men," led by Senators La Follette and Borah, succeeded in defeating the President's request through a filibuster, but this did not deter Wilson from pursuing his noble ideals. He ordered the ships armed and instructed them to fire on sight at any German submarines. In overriding Congressional recalcitrance, Wilson did not hesitate to point out that he knew he was courting war with Germany.

Wilson's ability to move *against* Congress was bolstered by three separate but related developments. First, his demand for "security" arrangements drew support because he was already carrying on an undeclared war with

---

12/This is to be found in the House Foreign Affairs Committee document put out by the Library of Congress. It is listed in the Appendix to this book.

Mexico. Second, institutional preparations for war had been made with leaders of the major corporate groupings; once it was clear the corporate class was ready to make war, Congress became a mere appendage. To legitimize his actions, Wilson used the Army Appropriations Act of 1916, which provided for the creation of an advisory body to coordinate industries and resources for the "national security and welfare." The Council of National Defense was told by Wilson at the time of its appointment (but before the Congress had declared war) to unite the forces of the country "for the victories of peace as well as those of war."[13] By 1917, the purpose of this committee was to set up the means for purchasing munitions, to rationalize the supply of war materials, and to control prices.

Finally, under the Overman Act, the President was given "more freedom than any of his predecessors had in disposing the Executive establishment to suit himself."[14] In this process, Wilson gave up any pretense of reform or control over the industrial class, since it was held that the cooperation of industry was crucial to the State's effort to make the world safe for a democratic America.

Wilson himself, surrounded by an array of Executive agencies of unprecedented scope, was finally at the center of an organism no man, however vigorous, could in any real sense direct. It was during this period that the limitations of a one-man Presidency began to appear so serious as to call in question the whole institution.[15]

Wilson's "reformism" was felt in the armed forces. Before 1916 the President had been limited in his ability to use the militia. It was Congress which had the power to

13/Rexford Guy Tugwell, *The Enlargement of the Presidency* (Doubleday, 1961), pp. 363–367.
14/*Ibid.*
15/*Ibid.*

call up the militia (now the Army and Air National Guard). Both branches were constrained by the Constitution, which limited use of the militia to executing "the laws of the Union, to suppress insurrections and to repel invasions."[16] According to one Attorney General, George Wickersham, such constitutional language meant that the militia could not be sent into a foreign country. To circumvent this limitation, Wilson developed the idea that the President should have the power to incorporate the National Guard into the Army. The power was granted by the National Defense Act of 1916, which greatly increased the Executive's ability to make war on its own. In the late winter of 1916, Wilson incorporated the National Guard into the regular Army for use against Mexico.

After World War I, American, French, and British interests turned to the question of containing and destroying the Bolshevik revolution. This required Allied intervention, which United States armed forces joined. It did not seem appropriate to think that the United States was at war, or that significant constitutional precepts had been breached. No internal ideological or political forces were organized to stop the American intervention; on the contrary, the Palmer raids against "anarchist," "communist," and socialist dissidents within the United States made the intervention in Russia even more credible. And vice versa. The Democratic intervention in Russia set up the repression at home which saw 10,000 people arrested and deported over one weekend.

But it was Franklin Roosevelt who sealed the casket on Congressional power. Before American entrance into World War II, Roosevelt expanded American interest by taking ninety-nine-year leasing rights from the British in bases at Newfoundland, Bermuda, the Bahamas, Jamaica,

---

16/*Ibid.*

St. Lucia, Trinidad, Antigua, and British Guiana, in trade for fifty old U.S. destroyers. Roosevelt *informed* the Congress of this transfer of American vessels and the extension of American imperial power. There was no treaty and hardly an explanation. Edward Corwin has noted that Roosevelt's action violated two statutes "and represented an exercise by the President of a power which by the Constitution is specifically assigned to Congress."[17]

Presidential power was greatly enhanced by 1941 when, through lend-lease authorization, the Selective Service Act of September 1940, and the Priorities Statute of May 1941, the President could direct the manufacture of weapons for war and "sell, transfer title to, exchange, lease, lend, or otherwise dispose of"[18] materials to any country in the world which met his terms. Further, he could bring industry under Presidential control—or so it was thought. Roosevelt believed that the war effort would facilitate the implementation of his plans for agriculture. In 1942, when it appeared that Congress would not support his proposed price controls for farm products, he made it clear that he thought parliamentary bodies were of limited usefulness in the twentieth century.

> I ask the Congress to take this action by the first of October. Inaction on your part by that date will leave me with an inescapable responsibility to the people of this country to see to it that the war effort is no longer imperiled by the threat of economic chaos. In the event that the Congress shall fail to act, and act adequately, I shall accept the responsibility, and I will act. . . . The American people can also be sure that I will . . . accomplish the defeat of our enemies in any part of the world where our own safety demands such defeat. When the war is won, the powers

---

17/Edward Corwin, *President: Office and Powers,* 3rd ed. (New York University Press, 1961), p. 289.

18/Tugwell, *op. cit.,* p. 452.

under which I act automatically revert to the people—to whom they belong.[19]

There are profound ironies in this message. The "war" never stopped, although it was interrupted, until 1950, and the powers have never returned to the Congress, let alone to the people. There was an attempt to uphold some of the implicit power of Congress.[20] But by 1947, in *Fleming v. Mohawk*, the Supreme Court held that when Congress appropriated funds for Executive agencies which the President consolidated on his own authority, such action was considered as "confirmation and ratification of the action of the Chief Executive."[21]

The Supreme Court has not helped to preserve Congressional prerogatives against Executive power. Under the *Pink* case[22] and *Missouri v. Holland*,[23] executive agreements have the same force of law as treaties which have gone through the advice and consent of the Senate. Needless to say, there is little bureaucratic incentive to have "agreements" sent to the Senate for ratification when there is no operational effect on their binding meaning.

The final blow against Congressional power came with the passage of the National Security Act of 1947. Its purpose was similar to that of the legislation Wilson had recommended to Congress when America was going *into* war, not supposedly coming out of it. The preamble to

---

19/*Papers of Franklin Roosevelt, 1942*, pp. 364–365. Cf. Tugwell, *op. cit.*, p. 454.

20/In *Ex Parte Endo*, a majority of the Supreme Court held that the fact that Congress appropriated funds for detention camps for American-Japanese citizens did *not* mean that Congress was ratifying every administrative policy of the detention camp program. According to Justice Douglas, who wrote the majority opinion, support of appropriations by Congress does not ratify all the activities which the Executive might pay for with appropriated funds. Ratification can only occur where there is "precise authority" for a particular purpose. (323 U.S. 283–1944)

21/331 U.S. 111, 118 (1947).

22/315 U.S. 203 (1942).

23/252 U.S. 416 (1920).

the 1947 Act told the story: It was to "provide an integrated program for the future society of the United States to provide for the establishment of integrated policies and procedures relating to the national security."[25] James Forrestal, who was to become the first Secretary of Defense under the new law, told Congress at the time that legislation provided for the integration of foreign policy with national policy, "of our civilian economy with military requirements."[26]

Secretary of State Dean Acheson, who had promised in 1949 that no troops were to be sent to Europe as part of the NATO treaty (a direct lie), also told the Senate Foreign Relations Committee at the time of the Korean intervention in 1950 that the President had the authority to use armed forces as he saw fit in carrying out American foreign policy and "this authority may not be interfered with by Congress."[27] The Acheson view coincided with his interpretation of the Truman Doctrine which, as he explained to Congress, was an extension of the Monroe Doctrine; wherever "freedom" was threatened, the military had a right to go on Executive initiative. In 1950 Congress also passed the Central Intelligence Act, which empowered the CIA to keep its budget hidden and to distribute it through other agencies of government. This caused the transformation and pollution of civilian pro-

---

25/National Security Act of 1947:61 Stat. 495.

26/The reader should note that the clause is not reversed. The policy of the leaders at that time was that peacetime military requirements were more important than the economy. This view had the effect of transferring power from Congress and the corporate elites to a military and national security bureaucracy. Those on Wall Street and in the corporations who intended to exercise power for their class would have to do so within the national security machinery. But that machinery had purposes, interests, and goals which in many instances were anticapitalist and irrational as related to a traditional definition of corporate capitalism.

27/Hearings, National Military Establishment, 80th Congress, 2nd Session, p. 28. Also note "The Making of the National Security State," by Robert Borosage, in *The Pentagon Watchers* (Doubleday, 1970), pp. 3–63.

grams, because the legislature could no longer tell whether funds which it voted for particular departments of the government were, in fact, for those departments or for covert CIA or paramilitary operations.

Congress thus found that it was no longer in a position to protect itself from the onslaught of Executive authority and illegal activity. The Senate Foreign Relations Committee has lamented that the Executive now has power of life and death over every living American, to say nothing of millions of other people in the world. It is true, of course, that Congressional power did not erode without Congressional complicity. The Senate had tried to protect its prerogatives with a concurrent resolution on April 4, 1951, which stated that it was unconstitutional to send troops abroad without Congressional approval. But the Executive Office of the President has pointed out that the Congress is responsible for its own abdication of power when it passes legislation requested by the President to create a national emergency. National emergencies allow the President "to take action which would have been possible only under a declaration of war."[28]

Such proclamations were signed by Presidents Truman,[29] Eisenhower,[30] Kennedy,[31] and Johnson.[32] One must remember that Johnson invariably pointed to the Gulf of Tonkin Resolution and to various appropriations bills as proof that Congress had supported and indeed encouraged the actions of the Executive. War, however, is made by those who have operational and political control over armed forces and their supplies. The fact that Con-

---

28/"Background Information on the Use of United States Armed Forces in Foreign Countries," GPO, 1970. Report of the House Committee on Foreign Affairs, prepared by George L. Millikan and Sheldon Kaplan.

29/No. 2914 on December 16, 1950, and reaffirmed on April 28, 1952.

30/Executive Orders Nos. 10896 and 10905.

31/Executive Order No. 11037.

32/Executive Order No. 11387.

gress appropriated funds did not mean that it exercised control over the war or the Executive's power to make war. The Senate's National Commitments Resolution meant that the Senate was a petitioner to the President. The Cambodian invasion of April 1970 meant that the President knew resolutions hardly affected war policies of the Executive and the bureaucracy. And the Department of State's comment on the proposed commitments resolution on March 10, 1969, made clear that it was too late to talk about constitutional controls. The Department stated its opinion to the Senate in these terms:

> As Commander-in-Chief, the President has the sole authority to command our Armed Forces, whether they are within or outside the United States. And although reasonable men may differ as to the circumstances in which he should do so, the President has the constitutional power to send U.S. military forces abroad without specific Congressional approval.[33]

This view not only eroded the explicit constitutional power of war declaration which was reserved to Congress by the Constitution, but it went one step further: It also meant that Congress no longer had the power under the Constitution "To make Rules for the Government and Regulation of the land and naval forces."[34] The idea, so simple and so profound, that there is a distinction between diplomatic and military policy could not be maintained once the national security state saw all forms of diplomacy as a variant of military threat, intimidation, and the actual use of force.

But what about the President? There was an irony to Executive usurpation. While Congress had lost its governing status by the end of World War II, the President also found that his surfeit of newly acquired power had

33/Statement by J. William Fulbright, June 1970.
34/Article I, Section 8.

to be delegated to others. The result was creation of a huge bureaucratic apparatus. It took a considerable act of Presidential will to find out what was going on and what sorts of commitments, criminal and otherwise, had been made by the Executive agencies of which the President was nominally in charge. The President and his immediate entourage became, in effect, the brokers for the illegitimate power wielded by such agencies as the CIA.[35] Ad hoc committees threaded the lines of legitimacy and illegitimacy, legality and illegality, in an almost seamless web.[36]

President Kennedy set up the 303 Committee, which reviewed the covert operations that were developed and carried out by the CIA and military in the field, in an attempt to create within the Executive a system of control—*a common law of illegal activities*, as it were—on the basis of "broader" purposes and objectives than the acts themselves. The President's purpose was to control and rationalize the illegal activities which seemed to be bureaucratically rather than Presidentially controlled. Yet the dialectical result of this activity was to force a legitimation of the illegitimate. Furthermore, as the President grasped power for his own survival, it matured into a leadership system that was authoritarian in its purpose and operation. Citizens did not learn of such activities

---

35/Secretary Rusk described such activities as fighting for freedom in the back-alleys of the world.

36/Whereas bureaucratic military and economic barons need Presidents as their instruments for long-term institutional interests, Presidents think tactically and see bureaucracies as instruments for their policies. During the Eisenhower period, for example, a de-emphasis on formal control over the military (that is, control over defense budgets, pact-making without commitment of troops except in Lebanon) caused the Eisenhower group to rely on the CIA. In one sense, bribery and the threat of total war were the Eisenhower mode of statecraft. Covert activities fit with the Republican need to appear capitalist. What Eisenhower's team was unable to do publicly because of its anti-labor and seemingly anti-intellectual ideology, it did covertly through the CIA. The CIA became the conduit and polluter of cultural institutions and labor unions.

or structural change except through accident, blunder, stealth, or the need of one particular group within the national security apparatus to obtain support from the "outside" for its battles at the bargaining table of power; this occurred, for example, when reports were leaked to the press in 1967 about internal debates regarding a new round of military escalation in Vietnam. The Executive branch is ensnared when it must invent rules and "commitments" to protect various parts of the bureaucracy and institutional elements who insist on their view of interest. The President must obtain funds from the Congress by manufacturing arguments and transforming error into para-law and state necessity.

CONGRESSIONAL APPROPRIATIONS AND THE DELIBERATIVE PROCESS

The power of Congress is greatest when the government is small. As the government grows, the role of Congress decreases. There is a separation between administrative and legislative authority. Legislative authority invariably transfers power of administration to the Executive. When a nation decides that it must have social welfare and military programs, the legislative branch, by voting money for such programs, invariably subsidizes huge social systems and classes that depend directly on the managers of the state machinery. Hence, the more money Congress allocates to spend, the less power it wields, since those who spend the money decide how and where it is to be spent. (It is true, however, that the Congressional seniority system permits some members—those who have attained committee chairmanships—to share in the power and direction of resources. Under the present committee and seniority system, members of both houses of Congress act like permanent undersecretaries in the British bureaucracy. In Washington after-hours places, it is said that Presidents come and go, but committee heads stay on forever.)

In the last sixty years, the power of Congress over the appropriations process has been severely curtailed. Prior to enactment of the Budget and Accounting Act of 1921, Congress seemed to have had the power to dictate the shape of the federal budget and the amounts needed by each department. This power, of course, had been conferred in the Constitution. Congress was able to raise and levy taxes, and "all bills for raising revenues" were to "originate in the House of Representatives; but the Senate may propose or concur with Amendments as on other Bills."[37]

The reality of Congressional control has long since evaporated. The Executive now clearly believes it can wage war even in the absence of Congressional appropriations. But the myth of Congressional power proved durable—at least in Congress. In 1967, during one of the many recent Senate debates on resolutions to limit the power of the Executive, Senator George Aiken of Vermont told his colleagues:

> I do not think we can excuse Congress from the situation which exists today. . . . We have reached the point now that if we are interested in retaining our form of government of which we boast so freely and fluently, *we have to do something*; . . . I do not blame the executive branch so much for doing this. I blame them for some of their recent mistakes in the last few years, but nevertheless, Congress has to share the guilt with them because we have been too negligent and too tolerant. (emphasis added)[38]

Aiken insisted that senior members of Congress were at least complicit, and that some had a far more direct

---

37/Article I, Section 7, of the U.S. Constitution.
38/S10502, July 31, 1967.

responsibility. There was, he suggested, no way to vote funds for the war or advise on it without assuming responsibility for its consequences. By June 11, 1968, however, Congressmen were denying that their vote for appropriations to the military and for the prosecution of the Indochina war meant that they supported the war. Because of that doubt, the Chairman of the House Appropriations Committee, George Mahon of Texas, declared on the House floor that a vote for a supplemental appropriations amendment in support of soldiers who were hurled into battle "does not involve a test as to one's basic views with respect to the war in Vietnam. The question here is that they are entitled to our support as long as they are there, regardless of our views otherwise."[39] A senior Republican member of the House, Paul Findley of Illinois, echoed this view:

> Mr. Chairman, I hope no one reading the *Congressional Record* on this last amendment will jump to the conclusion that the division vote denotes enthusiastic endorsement of present policies in Viet Nam. There is ample evidence not only within the conversation of Members on the floor here today but also in the newspapers of the utter bankruptcy of what is presently being attempted in Vietnam.[40]

Such reticence was hardly new. It can be found in each of the appropriations debates during the years from 1964 to 1971. It was annoying to the Executive, but hardly a crucial problem. There was, however, a political need to keep complaints within bounds, since the Executive was not prepared to open up its policy of continuing military and covert intervention—and the governing structure supporting that policy—to Congressional hectoring and con-

39/Representative George Mahon, June 11, 1968, *Congressional Record* H4824.

40/Representative Paul Findley, June 11, 1968, *Congressional Record* H4828.

trol. Executive strategy was to present Congress with a *fait accompli* so that it had no choice but to support actions in which American troops had already been committed.[41] Each time Congress accepted this result, its power was reduced even further. Nevertheless, most members of Congress cannot be absolved of complicity. They voted for the construction of bases in Vietnam, conforming to the intentions of the American bureaucratic and military leaders. And, of course, they voted for the weaponry which was used.

The leading members of the House and Senate Armed Services Committees toiled long hours to increase the American military commitment in Indochina. They were not reluctant to prod the Executive apparatus forward, joining with the Joint Chiefs of Staff from time to time in such encouragement. The Special Subcommittee on National Defense Posture of the House Armed Services Committee had long proposed that bombing restrictions on North Vietnam be removed and that Haiphong be destroyed. The House and Senate Armed Services Committees favored the use of greater force more quickly and constantly spoke out against "gradualism," hoping that a knockout blow could be struck against the "enemy" in Southeast Asia.[42]

The costs of the Indochina war made it necessary for President Johnson to obtain Vietnam supplemental appropriations. This was the legislative means that the Congress used to express its dissent or assent to the war.

41/There is an incredible cynicism here. Concern for American troops manifests itself so long as they are under attack. According to the Cranston hearings on Veterans' Hospitals, the tears of concern very quickly dry up. The unemployment rate is 20 percent among black returned veterans and 13 percent among whites.

42/*Review of the Vietnam Conflict and Its Impact on U.S. Military Commitments Abroad: Report of the Special Subcommittee on National Defense Posture,* House Armed Services Committee, GPO, August 24, 1968, pp. 6–16.

There was no way that Congress could regard the money authorized, appropriated, and spent except as funds for building bases which serve as weapons and manpower centers for American supplies. Yet there was colossal naïveté and dazzling ignorance in Congress. Few members comprehended that the activity of the national security bureaucracy was criminal. Blinded by imperium, the Cold War, and the assumption that all governing processes are legitimate, members were oblivious to legal standards which did exist and which could have been enforced. And because those standards were not enforced, there was a presumption of legality to the illegal. There was the acceptance of idealistic pretension in which the citizen and the Congress clothed the national security apparatus, masking the obvious from themselves.

CONGRESS AND PARA-LEGAL PRINCIPLES

As we have seen, the Constitution does not endow Congress with the right to sign over the war power to the Executive, nor does it indicate that appropriation of funds in fact ratifies any action of the Executive. To overcome these obstacles, the bureaucracy developed the language, color, and appearance of legality and ratification as substitutes for constitutional legality and ratification. The language of complicity and ambiguity allows men of power to fool or coopt those who have legitimate authority to say "yes" or "no" but who, in fact, lack the power to do so. To wage aggressive war it became necessary to cloak it in legality that would prove acceptable to Congress and the people.

The national security apparatus (including the President) bombarded Congress and the people with the para-legal idea that the United States had a solemn com-

mitment in Vietnam. Who made that commitment? Was
it the CIA or AID?[43] Did it come through solemn treaty?[44]
Did it originate in a letter?[45] Was it an afterthought of

43/A report prepared by four senators, including Mike Mansfield, said
in 1963: "It should also be noted, in all frankness, that our own bureaucratic tendencies to act in uniform and enlarging patterns have resulted
in an expansion of the U.S. commitment in some places to an extent which
would appear to bear only the remotest relationship to what is essential,
or even desirable in terms of U.S. interests." Quoted in *The Viet-Nam
Reader,* eds. M. Raskin, B. Fall (Vintage, 1965), p. 193.

44/Eugene Rostow, former Undersecretary of State, has insisted that
the United States is in Indochina because of the SEATO treaty. The
treaty was signed by Australia, New Zealand, France, Pakistan, the
Philippines, the United Kingdom, and the United States. Although South
Vietnam was not a party to the treaty, a separate protocol was added for
its defense. The basis of any treaty is reciprocity. Except for the Philippines, which sent a detachment of troops, paid for by the United States,
other nations have done virtually nothing. Furthermore, none has
attempted to revivify the SEATO treaty or set in motion any meetings
which would result in using the treaty as the justifying instrument for
intervention. France has specifically exempted itself from involvement in
any of the treaty provisions. Under the treaty the only obligation of the
parties is to "consult immediately in order to agree on the measures
which should be taken for the common defense." Article IV, paragraphs
1 and 2, SEATO treaty.

45/An objective reading of the famous Eisenhower letter to Diem,
which became a coat rack on which to hang every future tragedy in
Southeast Asia, leaves plenty of room for a decision to give *no* aid to the
South Vietnamese government. Letter and following comments below are
from *Vietnam and Beyond,* by Don R. and Arthur Larson (Durham, N.C.:
Rule of Law Research Center, Duke University, 1965), as reprinted in
The Viet-Nam Reader, op. cit., pp. 100–101:
"We have been exploring ways and means to permit our aid to Viet-
Nam to be more effective and to make a greater contribution to the wel-
fare and stability of the Government of Viet-Nam. I am, accordingly,
instructing the American Ambassador to Viet-Nam to examine with you
in your capacity as Chief of Government, how an intelligent program of
American aid given directly to your Government, can serve to assist
Viet-Nam in its present hour of trial, provided that your Government is
prepared to give assurances as to the standards of performance it would
be able to maintain in the event such aid were supplied.
" 'The purpose of this offer is to assist the Government of Viet-Nam in
developing and maintaining a strong, viable state, capable of resisting
attempted subversion or aggression through military means. The Government of the United States expects that this aid will be met by performance
on the part of the Government of Viet-Nam in undertaking needed
reforms. It hopes that such aid, combined with your own continuing
efforts, will contribute effectively toward an independent Viet-Nam

the Joint Chiefs of Staff? Was this a commitment which flowed from the Gulf of Tonkin Resolution,[46] which seemed to give the President power to respond to attack from the North Vietnamese?

According to the Undersecretary of State, Nicholas Katzenbach, the resolution was the "functional equivalent" of a Congressional declaration of war, even though the floor debate in the Senate and the House made clear that the resolution itself was not "an advance declaration of war." Indeed, the Chairman of the House Foreign Affairs Committee, Thomas Morgan, said the Committee had been "assured by the Secretary of State that the

---

endowed with a strong government. Such a government would, I hope, be so responsive to the nationalist aspirations of its people, so enlightened in purpose and effective in performance, that it will be respected both at home and abroad and discourage anyone who might wish to impose a foreign ideology on your free people.'

"There are six sentences. The first says that we have been 'exploring' ways and means. The second relates that our Ambassador is being instructed to 'examine' a program with Diem, subject to a condition relating to Vietnamese performance. The third states the purpose of 'this offer,' which can only refer to the offer to 'examine' the assistance program; that purpose is to help build a viable state, which in turn would be capable of resisting subversion and aggression. The fourth sentence is another condition, the making of needed reforms. The fifth sentence expresses a hope, and so does the sixth—hopes for a strong, enlightened, effective, and respected government—hopes that seem poignant indeed today in view of the sordid story that began with the assassination of Diem.

"Where in this highly tentative, highly conditional opening of negotiations and statement of hopes is the 'commitment,' the 'obligation,' the pledging of our word? Even if we seem to have indicated a willingness to do something to help, what is that something—beyond aid in developing a strong, viable state?"

46/The purpose of the Gulf of Tonkin Resolution was to show that "there was no division among us" at a time "when we are entering on three months of political campaigning." The resolution carried the House 414 to nothing and the Senate 88 to 2. The resolution read that Congress "approves and supports the determination of the President as Commander in Chief, to take all necessary measures to repel any armed attack" on U.S. forces, and to prevent any further aggression. Congress also left it up to the President to determine what necessary steps were needed, "including the use of armed forces," to assist any member of SEATO or protocol state covered by SEATO. Public Law 88–408, August 11, 1964.

constitutional power of Congress in this respect will continue to be scrupulously observed."[47]

By 1967, after some 600,000 troops were in Indochina, the Senate Foreign Relations Committee sought to define the meaning of the word "commitment,"[48] which the Executive now felt could only be met through a great war in Asia. Just as the U.S. delegation to the United Nations refused to define the word "aggression" for more than a decade in the International Law Committee, Katzenbach argued that the meaning of "commitment" should be left vague. Because of the kinds of international involvement which might be deemed necessary by the Executive, he said, it was better to leave formal actions of the United States in the hands of the Executive. Congress would be informed on a continuous basis of the arrangements that had been made. Any policy problems that might arise with regard to fulfilling American "commitments" abroad would be worked out on an ad hoc basis among the senior members of Congress and the Executive departments. They would be settled "by the instinct of the nation and its leaders for political responsibility."[49]

This "sweetheart" arrangement hardly comported with the struggles between Congress and the Executive with regard to the use of troops abroad. By the time the United States took military charge of the Indochina war, "creative tensions" could no longer be resolved by telephone calls between the leaders of the several branches of government. Irritations became policy differences. And policy

---

47/100 *Congressional Record* 18, 539 (1964).

48/In 1969 the Senate adopted the National Commitments Resolution, which expressed the sense of the Senate that "a national commitment by the United States results only from affirmative action taken by the Executive and Legislative Branches of the U.S. Government by means of a treaty, statute or concurrent resolution of both Houses of Congress, specifically providing for such commitment." Senate Resolution 85.

49/*U.S. Commitment to Foreign Powers*, Committee on Foreign Relations, GPO, 1967, p. 72.

differences uncovered realities that only such conservatives as Senators Bricker and Taft had been prepared to face fifteen years earlier, at the time of the Korean intervention and the decision to send American troops to Europe.

The struggle in Indochina pointed up structural defects in the American governing apparatus which developed from twentieth-century imperial pretensions. It exposed the dirty little secret which had been hidden by bipartisan foreign policy and the phrase that "politics stops at the water's edge."[50] By 1967, Congress was forced to acknowledge that its power with regard to issues of war and peace was ornamental. The most influential legislators, whose military loyalties were unquestionable and who *seemed* to exercise control over the appropriations of the national security bureaucracy, agreed that the United States had no interest in war on mainland Asia. They advised against it. Senators Stennis of Mississippi and Russell of Georgia —as well as Ellender of Louisiana—followed the position of Senator Robert Taft, who advised Presidents against military engagement in Asia.[51] Yet, during Kennedy's administration, once the President ratified the conclusions and operations of the national security apparatus, virtually no Senators, save Gruening and Morse, were prepared to exercise their vote to stop American-initiated war in Vietnam. The powerful, impeccable hawks opposed to the adventure were prepared to override their own sentiments and constitutional responsibilities.

This should not come as a surprise. In the twentieth century the natural inclination of any legislative body

---

50/Given the geographic extension of the United States, it was hard to know what the meaning of "water's edge" was. Did the Pacific Ocean become an inland lake of the United States because of Hawaii?

51/These Senators were ever mindful of Senator John Bricker's attempts to limit the arrangement which the Executive made without the consent of Congress. In Bricker's case, his strong move from the right did not develop momentum because of Eisenhower's opposition.

dealing with foreign and national security policy is to go along lest it be attacked as unpatriotic. Its major interest is to maintain privilege for its members and act as a broker between constituents and the bureaucracy. Senators and representatives are prepared to barter power for information, service to constituents, and the security of feeling that they are part of the "ruling club." Legislators must also contend with the narcotic attraction of imperial action for its own sake—a craving which is even stronger among Executive leaders. Once such interests predominated, it was not likely that legislators would challenge Executive national security power with the vigor necessary to defeat Executive usurpation.

As a result, the President was able to fashion or, as bureaucrats say, "orchestrate," the Congress as an instrument ready to accept his national security policies. Except as a debating point against opponents who might stir up the citizenry, the Executive no longer needed to rely on Congressional resolutions for authority to act. If Congress disagreed, the Executive was free to act on its own initiative. For example, Eisenhower, while he sought and received a Middle East resolution from Congress at the time of the American intervention in Lebanon in 1958, did not count on that action as anything but support for an *independent* exercise of power taken on his own initiative.[52] The same was true of Kennedy in the Cuban missile crisis, though a resolution was passed by Congress.[53] The Gulf of Tonkin Resolution was used by Johnson as legitimizing language for actions which came after 1964, although the substance of the resolution had been drafted months before the "provocative incident," and the incident itself was manufactured.[54] Presidential advisers such

52/Millikan and Kaplan, *op cit.*, p. 28.

53/*Ibid.*

54/"Extensive interrogation of all potentially knowledgeable sources reveals that they have no information concerning a NVN attack on U.S.

as McGeorge Bundy wanted a Congressional resolution to legitimate their plan of wide-scale escalation. The bureaucrats waited for an opportune, and *manufactured,* moment to obtain their resolution. By 1967 there was much grumbling in the Senate that the resolution was obtained fraudulently. And the Fulbright hearings, dealing with the Gulf of Tonkin incident, would seem to bear out that contention. In any case, President Johnson saw the resolution as a way of getting people into line. Had Congress voted no, the President would still have gone ahead. Indeed, the State Department has argued that repeal of the resolution did not change the legal power of the military and the Executive to engage in war.

As long ago as 1951, the State Department enunciated the doctrine that whenever the President determines it is necessary to send troops around the world, he may do so even if that action should involve the United States in war:

> As this discussion of the respective powers of the President and the Congress in this field has made clear, constitutional doctrine has been largely molded by practical necessities. *Use of the Congressional power to declare war, for example, has fallen into abeyance, because wars are no longer declared in advance.* (emphasis added)[55]

---

ships on 4 Aug. 1964. (the USS Turner Joy)" This statement of the Senate Foreign Relations Committee was contradicted by Secretary McNamara. A later captive naval officer of North Vietnam "contradicted" the earlier report. McNamara said that this captive proved the Defense Department contention that the August 4 attack had taken place. Fulbright then sent for this report. But examination showed that this "source never said that there had been an attack on August 4." The Department of Defense chose not to respond to Fulbright's implication that McNamara fabricated the meaning. It was, of course, the second attack which engendered support in Congress for the Gulf of Tonkin Resolution. Note *Gulf of Tonkin, the 1964 Incidents, Part II, Supplementary Documents to February 20, 1968 Hearing with Secretary of Defense Robert S. McNamara.* Committee on Foreign Relations, GPO, December 20, 1968.

55/Document of the Congress, entitled *Powers of the President to Send the Armed Forces Outside the United States,* February 28, 1951.

These, however, are formal considerations. During the Cold War period, as one Senate Foreign Relations report pointed out, the people and the Senate accepted the notion "that the President has the authority to commit the country to war but that the consent of Congress is desirable and convenient."[56] Political considerations impose still further constraints on legislative objections.

Even when declarations of war are sought from an assembly, they seem to constitute mere technicalities. "Before such a declaration can take place, the country will have been brought to the very brink of war by the foreign policy of the Executive."[57] Once the war declaration is demanded, the managers of the State have already deceived the people and the legislators. If the Congress were to deny the Executive and his bureaucracy a requested declaration of war, once it was requested the Executive would be in the position of a band of thieves who up to that point had engaged in a criminal enterprise. They would have to be stopped, but who would stop them? And where would the alternate source of legitimacy and power to the Executive government be found? If the answer is "the people," then the nation and society are set immediately on a revolutionary course. For its purposes the Executive merely requires complicity from Congress, not agreement. Members of Congress will comply rather than risk internal revolution to stop a war abroad. As a result of Congressional compliance the Executive is able to transform its private war into the *Zeitgeist* of the State and is justified in shedding the people's blood.

Such complicity has made progressives and populists doubt whether Congress can be anything but a collaborator in war-making activity. From time to time (as in 1924

56/Report of Foreign Relations Committee, S. Res. 85, April 16, 1969, pp. 7–34, at p. 9.

57/Randolph S. Bourne, *War and the Intellectuals* (Harper & Row, 1964), p. 82.

and 1937) they have argued that even Congress should not have the war power: that the war power should reside with the people. The idea that a people should vote to go to war, as a people, as a body, becomes an intimidating concept because it assumes personal responsibility and active citizenship. In such a framework the personal act of voting means the de-mystification of State power and the end of docile acquiescence to that power. The State becomes identical to the people. The more refined classes are reluctant to offer the less refined a choice on questions of mystic communion, such as war by frolic, mistake, or design, offering them instead a choice of different brands of toothpaste.

But if the people do not have the power to declare war and the power of Congress to declare war is dubious, the question of *how* the war-making power is exercised by the Executive has remained one which can be drawn for re-examination by critics and nags at a moment's notice, as a rhetorical lance against the warriors or the Executive. A legal or moral defect is ascribed to the Executive bureaucratic adventure by Congressional critics and popular shirkers when the war is going badly, when too many are informed about it, and when dissidents attempt to capture all legitimate symbols to discredit the war-makers. The dissidents are successful when the war actively poisons the everyday concerns of people. It is then that notions of principle, definition, responsibility, guilt, and punishment become central to the debate of citizens— when they begin to wonder about the political principles which govern their state.

We may note another example of how the para-legal[58] approach distorts perception and undermines democratic

58/The para-legal system operates in all nations which flirt with authoritarianism and imperialism. It assumes that there are no limits of behavior for officials in their public role if they are able to adduce a rationale.

principles. On May 4, 1965, the President sent Congress a message asking for a supplementary appropriation. He outlined the actions he had already taken—increasing the armed forces in Vietnam to 35,000, sending supplies and helicopters, increasing the bombings to 1,500 sorties a month, even sending medical supplies to the Vietnamese people. He asked Congress for "prompt support of our basic course . . . resistance to aggression, moderation in the use of power and a constant search for peace. Nothing will do more to strengthen your country in the world than the proof of national unity which an overwhelming vote for the appropriation will clearly show. To deny and delay this means to deny and delay the fullest support of the American people and the American Congress to those brave men who are risking their lives for freedom in Vietnam." But he began this attempt at ratification by saying, "I do not ask complete approval for every phase and action of your Government." In effect, he asked the Congress to vote $700 million retroactively for equipment and forces, and his request was granted through a joint resolution of Congress which authorized the President to transfer $700 million of unappropriated funds to any existing military account. As Francis Wormuth has pointed out, the President asked for a vote of confidence. But there is no such thing as a vote of confidence in an Executive form of government, since there is no way, save impeachment, to give *no* vote of confidence. Furthermore, there is no way that a member of Congress can do more than support a general direction, especially when that direction is described in words that are nonspecific, nonreferential, and imprecise. Can it be legally possible for Congressmen to underwrite a course that does not exist except in the minds of war-makers?

The para-legal method gives the appearance of participation to Congress without reaching the basic questions of law and reality. The military and the national security bureaucracy can report on the success of the war (filling their formal obligations with para-legal language) to the Congressional committees and to the people by using statistical analyses of body counts, number of bombs dropped, number of people moved from one area to another, and so forth. It did not dawn on anyone within the governing apparatus or the Congress (until 1970) that such modes of behavior were, by their nature, criminal enterprises.

Treatment of "refugees" is instructive in this regard. While occasional Congressional committees pointed up the dreadful refugee situation caused by American policy, no one bothered to suggest that the policy was criminal in nature. (And where the policy was not criminal in nature, it had elements of criminal negligence which were undeniable.) By May of 1968, the Senate Judiciary Committee estimated the number of refugees generated by the war at close to four million. Three years later the number was closer to six million. The U.S. budget for fiscal 1968 for care of refugees was approximately $43 million.[59] A Judiciary subcommittee asked the General Accounting Office to conduct a spot check of conditions in the camps in 1967, picking them at random. Less than one percent had sanitation facilities. Less than 45 percent had housing facilities. As the GAO report said, "In large sections of Saigon there are hundreds of thousands of people living in squalor, in subhuman conditions. They sleep in the alleys and in the streets, in courtyards and halls, even in graveyards and mausoleums where bodies have been removed to allow more room."

The question is: Who is responsible? Once Congress

59/The amount per capita was approximately $11 per person, but this figure is deceptive. For example, after each refugee left the camps he was supposed to receive $43. The Senate Judiciary Committee noted that a "top U.S. adviser to the refugee program [estimated] that 75 percent of this amount was being siphoned off before it reached the people."

learns of such matters, do its members have a positive obligation to correct them and to stop supporting policies which generate such conditions? And if Congress does not assume its responsibilities, does it become complicit? If the power of Congress is not merely an ornamental one, it is not relieved of responsibility. Congress has the right to call Executive officials to testify, under oath, about their activities.

In democratic theory, election absolves the individual official of personal responsibility where he is acting in the name of the state or in an official capacity. In theory he is acting in behalf of the people and their interests. When they discover he is acting against them, they are able to turn him out of office. But this theory does not go to the question of criminal behavior. From time to time, Congress has been graced with criminals or scoundrels, and it has been held that they can be tried under the criminal laws of the United States. It has been held that the Congress may decide the basis of membership in its body, developing and applying any rules that it deems consistent with its constitutional prerogatives. Congress is, therefore, on notice that laws of the land will apply to criminal behavior, and that elected members are not exempt from those laws. It has the power to set its standards of membership. It has developed a code of ethics to which others within the government are expected to adhere. It is able to develop a series of self-limiting actions and laws which will purge it of being drawn into such criminal enterprises as the Indochina war.

The present situation within American society is such that Congress could reassert its constitutional authority to protect the people against the Executive penchant to wage war. There are specific considerations relating to Congress which the public may wish to take into account as it ponders means of controlling and curbing the governing elite's potential for war-making. I will explore these in the context of the impulse for personal responsibility and antimilitarism which emerged in American law and policy at the end of World War II.

It is well, however, to close this chapter on reaffirming Congress's *limited* power to make war. It would seem that even if Congress assented to the Vietnam war, there is nothing in the Constitution to suggest that Congress has unlimited power to vote funds and commit *lives* to military adventures for the purpose of ideological or bureaucratic vindication. As Chief Justice Taney pointed out, it is the genius of American government to be peaceful and not wage war for conquest, aggrandizement, acquisition, or aggression. The people, then, retain those residual rights to resist usurped power on the part of the Executive or Congressional acquiescence to frolics of war and militarism.

2 /

AMERICA'S MANICHEAN APPROACH TO MILITARISM

The people are told that responsibility for the Indochina war cannot be assigned and that we must take care not to search for scapegoats. Members of both political parties insist that everyone is responsible—that anyone in a position of responsibility in the government would have done the same.[1] Whether one is the Senator from Mississippi on the Armed Services Committee, the President, a general, a tenant farmer, a special assistant to the

---

1/Liberal Americans who think of problem-solving—that is, technical solutions to questions that one would rather not regard as having moral consequences—find it difficult to think of guilt and innocence, right and wrong. It is rarely up to a citizen to decide under what form of government he will live. Yet with modern weapons the question of responsibility to decide moral questions becomes even more crucial. It becomes a citizen's responsibility to alter the consequences of despotism. And where he fails it may be said that he shares a generalized form of guilt—the guilt of nonfeasance. But this form of guilt and responsibility is hardly the same as the kind of guilt shared by those who hold operating power and use it to destroy others. They have more than a "metaphysical" guilt; it is legal and criminal. When a society averts its eyes and refuses to understand why such men are specifically guilty, so that such deeds can happen again almost immediately, the guilt of the society becomes collective.

President, a soldier, or a taxpayer, he is responsible. Some say the policies of the Indochina war are a natural extension of American foreign policies since 1940; others say, since the beginning of the United States. And to some extent such statements are true.

Yet we know that the leaders who directed the State did not see Americans as either wanting to be involved in Indochina or wanting to develop a situation which would result in colossal moral and political failure. Dean Rusk has made clear that the responsibility did not rest with the Georgian tenant farmer or, for that matter, even with the racist ax-handle wielder:

> Scratch the skin of any American and you find he wants to take care of his own affairs and not get involved. . . . There is no imperium in Americans—at least not in the post-war period. . . . Acts of will since World War II have not erased the institution of isolationism.[2]

Rusk is correct, of course. The imperium was built into the structure by its governing leaders. To make the "internationalist" (read "imperialist") response automatic, leaders knew they would have to "scare hell" out of Americans and build a bureaucratic apparatus which, by its nature, would be engaged all over the world. The apparatus created the day-to-day commitments and interests that people felt they had to maintain and protect. The "acts of will" to which Rusk referred were actions and policies taken by men operating as a government behind the shield of state necessity.[3] It was no longer possible to advocate the law of imperialism in the age of decoloniza-

---

2/Henry P. Graff, *The Tuesday Cabinet* (Prentice-Hall, 1970), p. 135.

3/It should be noted that the State is made of papier-mâché when it comes to absolving an individual of acts performed in the State's name. As Quincy Wright has said, "The State cannot protect its agent from the consequences of his act if he acted outside the State's competence under international law." There is no legal competence to commit wars of aggression. 42 American Journal of International Law (AJIL) 410 (1948).

tion. And since no moral or legal case for imperium could be made, American imperial leaders resorted to ersatz law and morality as the cover for their actions. Para-law and pseudomorality became important ingredients in their attempts at "educating" others to their view of imperial responsibility. Law became a shield in justifying action, since people would not consciously believe they were performing illegal and immoral actions—for whatever cause. People and power crave legitimacy.

Armed with para-law, the leaders took the people to places they did not want to go and caused them to perform acts from which they will not easily recover.[4] Yet it would be wrong to think that the men who decided did so hoping for disaster and evil results, at least as they related to the United States.

The actions of American leaders and the structures they maintained were designed to rationalize military and economic requirements to ensure American imperial "responsibility" and dominance.[5] Attempts were made to arrange governing so that the State's wars would not impinge on the rest of the government or on the people and their ways of life. American foreign policy has sought to avoid war among the Great Powers, if possible, without yielding the position of American dominance. Fighting continuous war in the lands of the poor and wretched was

---

4/Senator Hatfield inserted into the Congressional Record of April 6 and April 7, 1971, testimony of soldiers in Vietnam who claimed they committed or were forced to commit atrocities. E2825-E2902 and E2903-E2936.

5/When we analyze the national security apparatus, we see that those involved by their roles and functions are responsible for: (1) setting of manpower and material requirements, (2) the acquisition of resources, (3) the development of a technology, (4) the operational plans for the use of such forces and material, (5) the certifying of external threat and interest, (6) their actual use, and (7) the setting in motion of forces within the society which keep the imperial direction going. These seven purposes are the fundamental activities of the national security apparatus.

acceptable, and to some extent was the way the ruling elite thought American dominance would be maintained. The nagging policy problem was to find a legal rationale for such behavior. By John Kennedy's term it was decreed that to prevent the big war the American imperium would have to fight a series of "little" wars. It was not expected that such wars would be harmful to the American society; indeed, they would be useful economically and socially— even prestigious. Johnson also adhered to the idea of continuous limited war. According to Eugene Rostow, Johnson was impressed by the example of the British, who for so long were able to fight wars at the edge of their empire. "We have to get used to the idea," he said.[6] He did not want to make war total; to have "parades or bond drives." For Johnson and his advisers, as for Kennedy, it was to be a hip-pocket war in which the privileged would maintain their privilege and the poor would find advantage and opportunity by fighting in Vietnam.

As Secretary McNamara assured one historian, the American escalation was "an automatic response to North Vietnam's counter efforts to achieve its objectives."[7] There is no escape, as Eugene Rostow has said; there is no easy escape from the kind of policy we have pursued since 1947. The para-legal rationale for the policy would be found somewhere in the propaganda sections of USIA, the Defense Department, and the CIA.

The blacks would achieve equality of opportunity through joining the armed forces, learning to strut, as Daniel Moynihan suggested. For the middle class, sacrifice was not to be "real" but merely rhetorical, and the entrepreneurial-minded might find a way to make money, whether in leasing slot machines in Vietnam or in making

---

6/Eugene Rostow, "LBJ Reconsidered," *Esquire*, April 1971.
7/Graff, *op. cit.*, p. 32.

special floodlights for jungle lighting. The war itself would be a sport, a diversion at most. And it would be presented to the people as a daily television "news" spectacular. The frolic of the leadership, with its talk of "freedom" and "determinism" and "fighting to maintain justice and freedom in Southeast Asia," was to be shored up by an ever-ready brush-fire war armed force. The droning of everyday life would be relieved with the purpose and determination of the leaders. The will of the leaders would remove the private tedium of a society which, many privileged mandarins thought, was too caught up in personal pursuits. The national purpose, which the ruling mandarins wrote about in the pages of *Life* magazine (1959) and William Bundy sought as the Secretary of the Eisenhower National Goals Commission, was to be found in the rice paddies of Vietnam and the bawdy houses of Saigon.

War, however, has a way of getting out of control, especially when it is institutionalized through "firepower," high technology, and orders issued in language which obscures the consequences. The people who were the objects and instruments of this policy found that all of their petty but somewhat rational compulsions, desires, and interests were turned inside out in the name of a purpose and rhetoric which had only mystical meaning. The bubble burst and that primary taskmaster, Reality, interfered with the dream sequence sold by an American ruling elite.

It is at such a point that people who favor traditions grounded in everyday life attempt to set the framework of political and legal discussion. The logical and moral search for generality and symmetry is not easily denied. What might have been described as an heroic war is reevaluated in the light of the stubborn judgments which Americans made upon others a generation ago. Thus, even American war-makers become murderers, and heroes become villains. As the American prosecutor at the Tokyo trials, Joseph B. Keenan, said,

> It may seem strange to include charges of murder in an indictment before an international tribunal. But it is high time, and indeed was so before this war began, that the promoters of aggressive, ruthless war and treaty breakers should be stripped of the glamour of national heroes, and exposed as what they really are—plain, ordinary murderers.[8]

We should not fear such a reality principle, since without it there is ever-greater likelihood of violent degeneration in American society.

OFFICIAL WAR CRIMES AND DEMILITARIST PRINCIPLES

The problem of America's imperial structure and its present propensity for continuous war-making can only be resolved if the United States proves able to develop public conscience and power which build on positive aspects of American life. Radical changes in national security policy and structure do not require an overwhelming, convulsive change in American domestic life, since the national security state itself has few roots in the society. It is of no value to the blacks in Harlem, the Chicanos of the Southwest, or the upper middle class in Westchester County that the United States has a CIA, TAC, SAC, and MIRV. The business elite now doubts that the national security apparatus is "responsible"— that is, that it has a business consciousness.[9] As Governor of Wisconsin Pat Lucey said,

---

8/Department of State Bulletin, May 19, 1946, pp. 846–847.

9/In his testimony before the Senate Foreign Relations Committee, Thomas Watson, the head of IBM, on the effects of the Indochina war on business, stated: "Let me illustrate the point concretely by giving you a rundown of actions against IBM properties in various parts of the world during the last six weeks. In West Berlin, nearly all the windows in one of our buildings were broken by young rioters. Then gasoline was poured about it and it was set on fire. The windows in one of our Dutch facilities

if Melvin Laird had to get the Defense budget through the people of Wisconsin, he would most probably fail. To democratize defense and security functions which have been viewed as mystical, "too complex," and beyond the comprehension of the people, would have the effect of breaking the power of the national security apparatus. The dismantling of this apparatus could be accomplished through political and legal means. Perhaps the Indochina war can be the basis of a citizen-initiated corrective process which stems from the kind of power and conscience that is crucial to reconstructive change.

These are not new concerns for American society. At the end of World War I leading American pragmatists in politics and philosophy sought ways of holding elites personally responsible for their actions. John Dewey argued that people should outlaw war and eliminate the government's power to wage it. Senator William Borah, as Chairman of the Senate Foreign Relations Committee, proposed a resolution in the Senate

> . . . that it is the view of the Senate of the United States that war between nations should be outlawed as an institution or means for the settlement of international controversies by making it a public crime under the law of nations, and that every nation should be encouraged by solemn agreement of treaty to bind itself to indict and punish its own international war-breeders or instigators and war profiteers under powers similar to those conferred upon our Congress under Article I, Section 8 of our Federal

---

were broken by students. Our branch office in Cologne was attacked by protesters against the Vietnam war and the windows smashed. A powerful bomb was discovered just before it was timed to explode in an IBM Argentina office. Just a few days ago, we received bomb threats at our Amsterdam and Paris data centers. And here at home we've had many bomb threats and one actual bombing at 425 Park Avenue in New York City—our eastern regional headquarters." *Impact of the War in Southeast Asia on the U.S. Economy,* Senate Committee on Foreign Relations, April 15 and 16, 1970, pp. 21–23.

Constitution, which clothes the Congress with the power to define and punish offenses against the law of nations. . . .[10]

It was this resolution which led to the Kellogg–Briand Pact (also known as the "Pact of Paris" of 1928), the treaty that sealed the fate of the defendants at Nuremberg. One of the counts against the German leaders was planning an aggressive war, an action specifically prohibited under the "Pact of Paris." War was outlawed as an "instrument of national policy," and the treaty specified "that such a war is illegal in international law and that those who plan and wage such a war, with its inevitable and terrible consequences, are committing a crime in so doing."[11] The Pact categorically outlawed all forms of war. The American Secretary of State, Frank Kellogg, refused to accept a French proposal which would have limited the pact to wars of aggression. He said that if the pact "were accompanied by definitions of the word 'aggressor' and by expressions and qualifications stipulating when nations would be justified in going to war, its effect would be very greatly weakened and its positive value as a guaranty of peace virtually destroyed."[12]

The Allied and especially the American position at Nuremberg was that "any resort to war—to any kind of war—is a resort to means that are inherently criminal." As Jackson said, war by its nature leads to killings, deprivations and destruction, although "honestly defensive war is, of course, legal and saves those lawfully conducting it from criminality."[13]

10/Senate Resolution 45, December 12, 1927. 69th Congress, 477, Part 1, as quoted in *Being and Doing*, by Marcus G. Raskin (Random House, 1971), p. 72.

11/Nuremberg Tribunal Judgment found at 41AJIL (1947), pp. 172–333.

12/Note to the French Ambassador, February 27, 1928. This view should be compared to John Dewey's view as found in *Intelligence in the Modern World* (Modern Library, 1939).

13/Found at 41AJIL (1941), p. 64.

By World War II, American leaders attempted to define war crimes and responsibility for war-making. Yet they were caught in the contradiction of nation-states: that of making war to stop war, that of fighting militarism with incipient militarism. Revisionist historians have seen in World War II roots of American efforts to exert imperial control over the world's falling empires and those vanquished in that war. But such a reading is not sufficient to understand the positive aspects of American social thought and action. There was another impulse in American statecraft at the end of World War II—an impulse which carried forward the populist, antimilitarism strain in American public life. War was still viewed as a crime in the United States. This ethic, this sensibility, found its way into expressions on war crimes and the need to end militarism which, until the Cold War began, dominated American thought. The international law espoused by the United States at the end of World War II meant that war was proscribed as a method of settling disputes. And by incorporation, leaders and bureaucrats were to be held in strict account. In 1945–1946 American leaders argued that it was only through personal responsibility, through the acceptance of objective legal and political standards, that leaders could be held responsible. Imperialism was not seen as the fundamental purpose of American statecraft, and tests were to be applied that would assure an antiimperialist mode. When he signed the Charter establishing the Nuremberg Tribunal, Justice Jackson used striking language in this regard:

> The legal posture which the United States will maintain, being thus based on the common sense of justice, is relatively simple and non-technical. We must not permit it to be complicated or obscured by sterile legalisms developed in the age of imperialism to make war respectable.[14]

14/Department of State Bulletin, Vol. XII, No. 311 (June 10, 1945), p. 1076.

Francis Biddle, the American member of the Nuremberg Tribunal, in late fall of 1946 proposed to President Truman that the time had come for the drafting of a code of international law which would affirm the principles of the Nuremberg Charter. Biddle told the President that although war is not outlawed by "such pronouncements," men learn to detest war more than they otherwise might because they see its criminal character. "Aggressive war was once romantic; now it is criminal," he said. "For nations have come to realize that it means the death not only of individual human beings, but of whole nations, not only with defeat, but in the slow degradation and decay of civilized life that follows defeat."[15]

> I hope that the United Nations, in line with your proposal, will reaffirm developing the principles of the Nuremberg Charter in the context of a codification of offenses against the peace and security of mankind.[16]

In December 1946, the U.S. delegation proposed to the United Nations General Assembly the principles of international law recognized by the Charter of the Nuremberg Tribunal and its judgment:

> The Committee on the Codification of International Law established by the resolution of the General Assembly of December 1946 to treat as a matter of primary importance plans for the formulation, in the context of general codification of offenses against the peace and security of mankind or of an international Criminal Code, of the principles recognized in the Charter of the Nuremberg Tribunal and in the judgment of the Tribunal.[17]

This remains unfinished business.

15/Department of State Bulletin, Vol. XV, No. 6 (November 24, 1946), p. 956.

16/Department of State Document No. 2783, August 1947.

17/*Ibid.*

The Cold War interrupted the development of the law of personal responsibility for leaders.[18] The ending of the Cold War could point to the reassertion of that interrupted direction in international and domestic affairs. A new generation seems to have turned totally against the militaristic ethic and craves a definition of personal responsibility. The end of militarist values leaves a clear void in American public life which could be filled by the ethic of personal and group responsibility.

After World War II, members of the American government persuaded (or forced) the Japanese and Germans to do more than punish the guilty for war crimes. They attempted to move these societies—including Austria—to renounce militarism and ultranationalism as their dominant mode of life. Militarism and ultranationalism were seen as the conditions which created war and war crimes. Various officials were purged or retired from areas of responsibility. Unless means are found within the United States to do the same, without bloodshed and with an understanding of why this is required, we will find a society in which the values will so greatly diverge and the practice of morality will be so clearly vitiated as to lead to the kind of total degeneration and decay which Biddle said was the inevitable result of war as an instrument of national policy.

It is useful to review some of the standards which the U.S. government applied to both Germans and Japanese

---

18/In 1947, Lord Wright, the Chairman of the United Nations War Crimes Commission, stated in his foreword to the fifteen-volume series on War Crimes, "I cannot sufficiently emphasize what I regard as the great importance of these reports from the point of view of the future development of International Law as applied to war crimes. . . . These reports will show, for the practitioner or the student, the particular problems which had arisen and how in practice they have been dealt with and also show to the historian of the laws of war the practice of courts in applying those laws to particular cases." But these volumes are virtually nonexistent in the United States and have had no impact on American law. This state of affairs was a result of the Cold War.

to build a society which would be free from militarism and ultranationalism. I will refer to only a few of those rules, laws, and directives which could help in examining the present condition within the United States. Some of those standards (inspired and insisted upon by Americans) should be applied internally as our own society finds itself in the hands of a militarized governing elite whose major response to the problems of the world seems to be a continuous violent engagement with it.

The entire American governmental system embraced the standards of war crimes which were promulgated at the end of World War II. As Telford Taylor put it,

> . . . the United States Government stood legally, politically and morally committed to the principles enunciated in the charters and judgments of the tribunals. The President of the United States, on the recommendation of the Departments of State, War and Justice, approved the war crimes program. Thirty or more American judges drawn from appellate benches of the states . . . conducted the later Nuremberg trials and wrote the opinions.[19]

Americans believed that only through the imposition of war-crime standards would it be possible to stop statesmen who embarked on war for whatever motive or purpose. "But the ultimate step in avoiding periodic wars, which are inevitable in a system of international lawlessness, is to make statesmen responsible to law."[20] The Yamashita case contemplated that such personal responsibility would apply internally to American officials. Whatever the wartime leaders of the United States were, they were not fools. As Justice Jackson said, "while this law is

---

19/Telford Taylor, *Nuremburg and Vietnam* (Quadrangle Books, 1971), p. 34.

20/Opening statement at Nuremburg, 1945, by Robert Jackson, Department of State Document No. 2783, 1947. Note Appendix to this book.

first applied against German aggressors, the law includes, and if it is to serve a useful purpose it must condemn, aggression by any other nations, including those which sit here now in Judgment."[21] But most important, as it applies to the present internal domestic situation, he noted that *"We are able to do away with domestic tyranny and violence and aggression by those in power against the rights of their own people only when we make all men answerable to the law."* (emphasis added)[22]

THE OPERATIONS OF DEMILITARIST PRINCIPLES BY THE UNITED STATES GOVERNMENT

The avowed purpose of the occupation of Germany was to destroy Nazism and German militarism. President Roosevelt outlined the American policy in a series of wartime addresses, declaring that the militarists who bred war would have to be removed from public life:

> We shall not be able to claim that we have gained total victory in this war if any vestige of Fascism in any of its malignant forms is permitted to survive anywhere in the world.[23]

In one of his last speeches, Roosevelt outlined the need for the "eradication of militaristic influence from public, private, and cultural life." This policy included war-crime trials, the dismemberment of the military, and the transformation of the laws and institutions of Germany, Japan, and Austria. There was a strict proscription of militarism, whether it came in uniform or mufti. The concern at Potsdam was the same on July 26, 1945:

21/*Ibid*.
22/*Ibid*.
23/Department of State Document No. 2783, August 1947, p. 2.

There must be eliminated for all time the authority and influence of those who have deceived and misled the people of Japan into embarking on world conquest, for we insist that a new order of peace, security, and justice will be impossible until irresponsible militarism is driven from the world.[24]

These were not, according to John Montgomery, "partisan declarations" or "inspirational readings." Militarism and Nazism were defined, and there was a concerted attempt to develop a concept of justice and a political theory.

The fundamental directive by which the United States attempted the transformation of Germany was JCS 1067, which outlined a plan and general objectives for a non-Nazi, nonmilitaristic Germany:

Essential steps in the accomplishment of this objective are the elimination of Nazism and militarism in all their forms, the immediate apprehension of war criminals for punishment, the industrial disarmament and demilitarization of Germany, with continuing control over Germany's capacity to make war, and the preparation for an eventual reconstruction of German political life on a democratic basis.[25]

In Japan, directives were issued with the same purpose:

. . . persons who have been active exponents of militarism and nationalism will be removed and excluded from public office and from any position of public and substantial private responsibility.[26]

The Joint Chiefs of Staff directive noted:

Any persons who held key positions of high responsibility since 1937 in industry, finance, commerce or agriculture . . .

24/*Ibid.* Note Appendix to this book.

25/JCS 1067 found in Department of State Document No. 2783, p. 82.

26/*Political Reorientation of Japan, September 1945–September 1948,* Report of the Government Section, Supreme Commander for the Allied Powers, GPO.

[were assumed to be] . . . active exponents of militant nationalism and aggression.[27]

In effect, the military government was to bring with it as representatives of the victorious nations a social transformation which would replace the war-making elites.[28] U.S. occupation authorities prepared a six-page questionnaire covering the public and private lives of individuals under investigation. Any falsification was held to be grounds for prosecution by the American military government court, and could be punished with sentences of two to five years' imprisonment. By June 1, 1946, more than 1.6 million Germans—one out of ten in the American Zone —were processed. According to the original author of the denazification program, Elmer Plischke, some 23 percent of those who filled out the questionnaires were removed or excluded from office.[29]

On March 5, 1946, the uniform "Law for Liberation from National Socialism and Militarism" was set forth by the German leaders in the American Zone. It had the full support of the American military government. The purpose of this program was to develop the legal and social processes needed to transfer authority from those who had been part of the German regime between 1933 and 1945 to

. . . those who will establish a free, peaceful and democratic society. . . . The only way to develop the roots of a free

---

27/Department of State Document No. 2783, op. cit., p. 82.

28/No elite will admit to aggressive war. Each will invent a threat that has to be dealt with through military means which leads to great war. For example, it is entirely likely that the Executive Committee of the National Security Council at the time of the Gulf of Tonkin will reply that they were reacting to aggression. But such a view can be disproved. More important, we begin to understand aggression when we note the relations between Germany and Poland at the time of the outbreak of war in 1939. Quincy Wright, A Study of War, II (University of Chicago Press, 1942).

29/Denazification Law and Procedure, 41AJIL 805 (1947), p. 811.

society was to destroy the influence and authority of those who favored Nazism and militarism.[30]

The first article called for liberation from national socialism and militarism so that a "lasting base of German democratic life could be initiated." According to this article, this could only be accomplished by

. . . excluding from public life all those who are guilty of having violated the principles of justice and humanity, or having selfishly exploited the conditions thus created.[31]

According to the principles laid out in the March 5, 1946, law, the Allied purpose was to eliminate militarism, its conduct and ideas, from the public economic and cultural life of the people (Article II). Five categories were established under Article IV: (1) major offenders (2) offenders (activists, militarists, and profiteers), (3) lesser offenders, (4) followers, and (5) persons exonerated. The October 12, 1946, directive of the Allied Control Council ordered the

. . . punishment of war criminals, Nazis, militarists and industrialists who encouraged and supported the Nazi regime. Their internment, imprisonment, or restriction of their activities.[32]

In examining the criteria used to identify offenders, one finds that the strict standards applied by Americans to other societies are fully applicable to American conduct in Asia. In other words, the idea that standards of international legality or morality do not exist within the bureaucratic or legal context turns out to be patently false.

Under Part 2, Article II, of Control Council Directive No. 38, ten criteria were used to define a major offender. A

30/*Occupation of Germany—Policy and Progress, 1945–46*, Department of State, p. 9. Note Article I, March 5, 1946.

31/*Ibid*. See Appendix to this book.

32/*Ibid*. See Appendix to this book.

major offender was one who could be charged with war crimes of the most serious nature. Several of these criteria seem directly applicable to our present situation. Anyone who

> . . . in the occupied areas treated foreign civilians or prisoners of war contrary to international law; anyone who is responsible for outrages, pillaging, deportations, or other acts of brutality, *even if committed in fighting against resistance movements.* (emphasis added)[33]

This clause is of importance since some commentators have attempted to justify an all-is-fair philosophy against resistance movements, whose combatants do not identify themselves as such. The Americans promulgated a view in Germany that resistance movements had to be treated with the same attention to rules of war as armies in "proper" insignia and badge. The callous idea that the NLF could be destroyed through the Phoenix program by murder of the infrastructure, by direct assassination, burnings, etc., could not be countenanced under America's own standards as applied to the Germans. Under Section 8 of the Major Offenders clause:

> Anyone who in any form whatever, participated in killings, tortures or other cruelties in a concentration camp, a labor camp or a medical institution of asylum. . . .[34]

qualified as a major offender. As of May 1971, the U.S. government had admitted to between 5 and 6 million refugees in a country of seventeen million people as a result of its own policies in Vietnam. In October 1967, the *New England Journal of Medicine* carried an article saying:

> The destruction of villages, the uncontrolled movement of groups of people and the squalid conditions in the camps

---

33/*Ibid.*
34/*Ibid.*

have broken the natural barriers to the spread of disease
. . . a rising incidence of under-nutrition, especially among
children . . . tuberculosis . . . intestinal parasites, leprosy
. . . malaria have been major causes of morbidity . . .;
plague . . . cholera also have grown greatly in number.[35]

Under Article III, Number 2, a war crimes offender
was deemed to be "anyone who exploited his position,
his influence or his connections to impose force and utter
threats, to act with brutality and to carry out oppressions
or otherwise unjust measures." The national security
managers saw threat, force, and brutality as their primary
means of carrying out their purposes in Vietnam. It is not
possible to conclude otherwise from such memoranda
as those which passed between staff and cabinet officers
in the White House, Department of Defense, CIA, and
State Department.

Militarists were viewed as offenders who caused and
made war. The Control attempted to establish

. . . a common policy covering . . . the complete and lasting
destruction of Nazism and *militarism* by imprisoning and
restricting the activities of important participants or adherents to these creeds. (emphasis added)[36]

Militarists were those who "sought to bring the life of
the German people into line with a policy of militaristic
force." They included "anyone who advocated or is responsible for the domination of foreign peoples, their
exploitation or displacement" as well as those who "promoted armament" for these purposes. They also included
those who "disseminated militaristic programs . . . serving
the advancement of militaristic ideas." Profiteers who

35/CIVILIAN CASUALTY AND REFUGEE PROBLEMS IN SOUTH VIETNAM,
*Findings and Recommendations of the Subcommittee to Investigate Prob-
lems Connected with Refugees and Escapees, of the Committee on the
Judiciary,* United States Senate, May 6, 1968, p. 9.

36/Control Council Directive No. 38, found in *Occupation of Germany,* Department of State, 1947, p. 123. See Appendix to this book.

presented minorities or made "disproportionately high profits in armament or war transactions" were also viewed as offenders.

In each of the categories (major offenders, minor offenders, lesser offenders, and followers) the sanctions were stringent, ranging from death, imprisonment for life, and fifteen years at hard labor for major offenders to probation, jail terms, and loss of public employment for the lesser categories. To be "exonerated" it was necessary for those who had been in power or in the Nazi Party to show that they "actively resisted . . . and thereby suffered disadvantages."[37] The civil service was to be patterned on basic American democratic models, which meant that "the new civil service system will prohibit the maintaining of secret personnel files."[38]

In Germany, the United States insisted on a denazification process which resulted in 50,000 cases a month being heard by about 545 tribunals in the American Zone. These were basically kangaroo administrative courts which offered little, if any, chance for response, although a "defendant" who was not cleared by such tribunals was unable to occupy any position of importance. As of June 1949, some 947,000 cases had been processed in the American Zone. Montgomery suggests that the denazification system was a "gentler means" than would have been used if a natural revolution had taken place in Germany. He points out that

> . . . in a genuine revolution, the victims of tribunals have to be buried; in Germany they merely suffered fines or temporary employment restrictions or, at worst, a brief internment period.[39]

37/*Ibid.*, pp. 127–129.

38/*Ibid.*, p. 187.

39/John Montgomery, *Forced to Be Free* (University of Chicago Press, 1957), p. 25.

The State–War–Navy directives to General Mark Clark pertaining to Austria[40] followed the antimilitarist, anti-ultranational and anti-Nazi directions applied to Germany and Japan. The basic American objective was to develop a "free, independent and democratic state," which meant the elimination of "Nazism, Pan-Germanism, militarism, and other forces opposed to the democratic reconstitution of Austria." It was concluded that war criminals would have to be apprehended and that all political and social service organizations which were Nazi- or militarist-inspired would have to be dissolved. Those who actively supported "organizations promoting militarism or who have been active proponents of militaristic doctrines" were to be excluded or removed from government service. In this task the American occupying force was to effectuate "the total dissolution of all military and para-military organizations together with all associations which might serve to keep militarism alive in Austria." The purge extended to those who "took an active and prominent part in the undemocratic measures of the pre-Nazi regime." Procedures were set up to "facilitate the conversion of industrial facilities to non-military production" and to abolish "all semi-official or quasi-public business and trade organizations of an authoritarian character." This directive also called for a "policy prohibiting cartels or other private business arrangements" which controlled the economy.

A White House press release on September 22, 1945, stated the policy which the United States government intended to adopt toward Japan:

> Japan will be completely disarmed and demilitarized. The authority of the militarists and the influence of militarism will be totally eliminated from her political, economic and social life. Institutions expressive of the spirit of militarism

---

40/Department of State Bulletin, September 1945.

and aggression will be vigorously suppressed . . . The Japanese people shall be afforded opportunity to develop for themselves an economy which will permit the peacetime requirements of the population to be met.

The demilitarization policy followed by the Americans in Japan was more benign than the one followed in Germany. In the first post-surrender directives it appeared that the United States would imprison various Japanese who would have qualified as militarists and ultranationalists, if not as war criminals, but this approach was rejected on grounds that the changes the United States was interested in making in Japan fell within the preventive rather than the punitive category. The major purpose was "the removal of leadership tainted with war responsibility from the political, economic, and social life of Japan—that under a new leadership not so tainted, democratic growth might be possible."[41] Seven categories were established.

In the major directive laid down by the American military government in Japan,[42] the Japanese government was required to remove officials of the national government and

Bar from reappointment and from election to the coming Diet, anyone who falls within the following categories . . .:

A. War Criminals.

B. Career and Special Service Military Personnel; and Special Police Officials; Officials of War Ministries.

C. Influential Members of Ultranationalistic, Terroristic or Secret Patriotic Societies.

D. Persons Influential in Imperial Rule Assistance Association, Imperial Rule Assistance Political Society, etc.

41/Hans Baerwald, *The Purge of Japanese Leaders Under the Occupation* (University of California Press, 1959), p. 16.

42/*Political Reorientation of Japan, op. cit.*, "Removal and Exclusion of Undesirable Personnel from Public Office," SCAPIN 550, January 4, 1946. See Appendix to this book.

E. Officers of Financial and Business Concerns Involved in Japanese Expansion.

F. Governors of Occupied Territory.

G. Other militarists and ultranationalists.[43]

The immediate result was great consternation among the "old reactionary hierarchy." General Whitney, Chief of the Government Section in Japan, described the directive (SCAPIN 550):

> . . . blasting from their entrenched positions in the command posts of the government all those who planned, started and directed the war, and those who enslaved and beat the Japanese people into abject submission and hoped to do the same with all the world.[44]

The American directive and SCAPIN 448, which ordered the closing of all ultranationalistic societies and forbade the establishment of new ones, produced a Cabinet crisis in Japan. Since the military government's order was meant to provide removal by categories of individuals, the Japanese government proposed to appoint an "Executive Commission of Inquiry to determine upon *prima facie* evidence whether the careers and activities of the persons in question deserved their removal and exclusion from office" within the meaning of the directive. The Shidehara government asserted that it would move quickly in such cases:

> As the examination of each case comes to an end, the government will at once notify the person charged of the findings of the committee and if they are satisfied of his guilt, they will proceed forthwith to his removal and exclusion from office as directed, if he has not by that time spontaneously resigned.[45]

43/*Ibid.*, Volume I.
44/*Ibid.*
45/*Ibid.*, p. 17.

The report of the Government Section of the Supreme Commander of the Allied Powers noted that the Japanese proposal sought to change the administrative process of removal and exclusion to a judicial one. The result would have been to require a legal case "against each individual and trying it before a quasi-judicial body. . . ."[46] The response of the Government Section of the Allied Commander was that the directive itself was not

> . . . punitive (as the Japanese proposal implied) but, on the contrary, it is preventive. It is a necessary precaution against the resurgence of Japanese expansionist tendencies; therefore, until after the directive has been complied with, "individual guilt" (which requires inquiries into *intent* as distinguished from *act*) is irrelevant.[47]

The American government did not object to the establishment of a commission of inquiry which would make recommendations to the Japanese government, provided that the individual was first removed from public office. One case shows the extent to which the American government in Japan intended to hold to account leaders who were not viewed as war criminals. In April 1946, Hatoyama Ichiro won an election to the Diet and was thought to be the obvious choice for Premier. The Americans objected, claiming he should be excluded from public office on the following grounds:

> a. As Chief Secretary of the Tanaka Cabinet from 1927 to 1929, he necessarily shares responsibility for the formulation and promulgation without Diet approval of amendments to the so-called Peace Preservation Law which made that law the government's chief legal instrument for the suppression of freedom of speech and freedom of assembly, and made possible the denunciation, terrorization, seizure, and imprisonment of tens of thousands of adherents to minority

46/*Ibid.*
47/*Ibid.*

doctrines advocating political, economic, and social reform, thereby preventing the development of effective opposition to the Japanese militaristic regime.

b. As Minister of Education from December 1931 to March 1934, he was responsible for stifling freedom of speech in the schools by means of mass dismissals and arrests of teachers suspected of "leftist" leanings or "dangerous thoughts." The dismissal in May 1933 of Professor Takigawa from the faculty of Kyoto University on Hatoyama's personal order is a flagrant illustration of his contempt for the liberal tradition of academic freedom and gave momentum to the spiritual mobilization of Japan which, under the aegis of the military and economic cliques, led the nation eventually into war.

c. Not only did Hatoyama participate in thus weaving the pattern of ruthless suppression of freedom of speech, freedom of assembly, and freedom of thought, but he also participated in the forced dissolution of farmer–labor bodies. In addition, his endorsement of totalitarianism, specifically in its application to the regimentation and control of labor, is a matter of record. His recommendation that "it would be well" to transplant Hitlerite anti-labor devices to Japan reveals his innate antipathy to the democratic principle of the right of labor freely to organize and to bargain collectively through representatives of its own choice. It is a familiar technique of the totalitarian dictatorship, wherever situated, whatever be its formal name, and however be it disguised, first to weaken and then to suppress the freedom of individuals to organize for mutual benefit. Whatever lip service Hatoyama may have rendered to the cause of parliamentarianism, his sponsorship of the doctrine of regimentation of labor identifies him as a tool of the ultranationalistic interests which engineered the reorganization of Japan on a totalitarian economic basis as a prerequisite to its wars of aggression.

d. By words and deeds he has consistently supported Japan's acts of aggression. In July 1937 he traveled to America and Western Europe as personal emissary of the then Prime Minister Konoye to justify Japan's expansionist pro-

311

gram. While abroad he negotiated economic arrangements for supporting the war against China and the subsequent exploitation of that country after subjugation. With duplicity, Hatoyama told the British Prime Minister in 1937 that "China cannot survive unless controlled by Japan," and that the primary motive behind Japan's intervention in China involved the "happiness of the Chinese people."

e. Hatoyama has posed as an anti-militarist. But in a formal address mailed to his constituents during the 1942 election in which he set forth his political credo, Hatoyama upheld the doctrine of territorial expansion by means of war, referred to the attack on Pearl Harbor as "fortunately . . . a great victory," stated as a fact that the true cause of the Manchuria and China "incidents" was the anti-Japanese sentiment (in China) instigated by England and America, ridiculed those who in 1928 and 1929 had criticized the Tanaka Cabinet, boasted that the cabinet had "liquidated the (previous) weak-kneed diplomacy toward England and America," and gloated that "today the world policy drafted by the Tanaka Cabinet is steadily being realized." This identification of himself with the notorious Tanaka policy of world conquest, whether genuine or merely opportunistic, in and of itself brands Hatoyama as one of those who deceived and misled the people of Japan into militaristic misadventure.

4. Accordingly, in view of these and other considerations not herein recited, the Imperial Japanese Government is directed to bar Ichiro Hatoyama from membership in the Diet and to exclude him from government service pursuant to SCAPIN 550.[48]

The Japanese position seemed designed to protect individual rights but also to destroy militarism and ultranationalism. Justice Minister Yoshio Suzuki said:

It is our solemn duty to purge those who led the people into waging war. Needless to say, we must do so voluntarily.

48/*Ibid.*, Vol. II, pp. 494–495. See Appendix to this book.

If anyone disapproves of this, he does not know the present position of Japan. It is regrettable that there are people in this country who do not consider the purge question sternly enough. In Germany 100,000 people have been thrown into jail and one million fined, sentenced to menial labor, their property confiscated, deprived of their civil rights or sentenced to hard labor. In our country, however, those who precipitated the nation into war are only barred from public office, which, we must explicitly bear in mind, is due to General MacArthur's generous occupation policy. For this reason, although we are sorry for them, those who fall under the purge directive must be brave enough and have enough sense of honor voluntarily to assume the moral responsibility. There is no other means, I am convinced, to restore international confidence in our country.[49]

In Japan, only 210,287 persons were removed and excluded from office, as opposed to 418,037 in the U.S. Zone in Germany.[50]

As can be seen from the number of people excluded from office, the American government went to great lengths to purge other countries of militarism. American leaders believed that certain elite groups, namely the militarists and ultranationalists, were responsible for warmaking, and that unless modes of exclusion from the political life of the nation occurred, there was no way that a meaningful transformation of the society could occur which would allow for more humane and pacific impulses to achieve any support in the government.

One may disagree with the negative and simplistic view of the transformation of society embodied in these postwar measures, but such disagreement does not connote that in America no penalties need attach to people who make and threaten war. One can object, too, to the cynicism of the victor who forces his way on the vanquished

49/*Ibid.*, Vol. I, p. 45. Statement part of article in the *Yomiuri Shimbun*, December 5, 1947.

50/Montgomery, *op. cit.*, p. 26.

and attempts to set the terms of life for him. Indeed, wars and revolutions are not usually instruments of justice. In war and revolution, people, justice, and public moral virtue are the casualties. As Hans Baerwald has pointed out,

> The key has not been found which might open the secrets to the manner in which the liberal democratic way of life (and its political, social, and economic institutions) might be transferred to societies in which it did not emerge as part of an indigenous process.[51]

Fortunately, we are not concerned with that question here. *We are, rather, concerned with how citizens within their own society, of their own free will,* undertake the transformation of their own elite groups and set rules of punishment and restitution when their elites operate outside the law .

Democracy degenerates when its leaders and bureaucratic elites are drawn continuously from a pool of people who have been consistently wrong, politically and morally, about their values and purposes. A society which consistently draws on such leaders invariably deprecates—and punishes—those who have made correct judgments from the beginning. Opponents of America's war in Indochina have paid heavily for their opposition with trials, jail sentences, police surveillance, detention, and blacklisting. As the war continued, the government escalated its repression of critics, including those in the military who rebelled against insane orders and requests—until it became impossible to order them about. The federal employees who now openly oppose the war and American imperialism are invariably on the edges of the government even as their position proves correct in an assessment of the American relationship to the world, and even as the Senate itself favors a nonimperialist turn and at-

---

51/*Op. cit.*, p. 106.

tempts to end the war through cutting off appropriations.

Repression directed against those who have been correct in their instincts and views on the war is likely to continue and cause greater conflict between large segments of the people and the governing structures, unless a new public policy results in promulgation of a series of laws for civilians, government workers, and policy-makers which reassert the proposition that governments must not become criminal enterprises. America must publicly and legally affirm the principle that those who were morally and legally wrong were those who generated and prosecuted the war—not those who struggled against it. From this point of view, it would be intolerable to permit criminal wrongdoers to benefit from their actions and continue their control over governmental life. In the *Constitution of Athens*, Aristotle pointed out that the friends of the tyrants, "with the usual leniency of a democracy," allowed them to remain in the city of Athens. *But even there they were not rewarded with continued control over the democracy.*

The present war will not end until forces within the United States are able to overcome the elite groups and institutions which assume continuation of the war in one form or another and the established habit of mind which assumes that aggressive war-making is a legally accepted way of conducting foreign policy. The present war (and its offshoots, Laos and Cambodia) will not end without the transformation of those institutions that allowed the war to be made, and the deposition of those elites who manned the institutions. Conversely, if the war does end, American society will be far different from what it is today. The elite groups which made the war and benefited from it cannot be expected to emerge from such a ten-year conflagration with their power intact. New groupings in American society will bring forward their own leadership and values, pushing aside, at least for a time, present elite groups. It is only natural that such changes should occur.

Elites which control societies can be expected to suffer punishment if they lose at war or revolution. The question American society now has to face is whether it is possible to move aside an elite group that enforced institutions of war-making on the American people, without resorting to totalitarian revolution.

An important legal step to be taken is the development of a system of enforceable standards which can be applied to bureaucrats and men of power. In the literature of revolution, it is taken for granted that when elites lose the will to rule, they can be overthrown. But democratic reconstruction requires different standards. When elites rule badly, without moral purpose or wisdom, without any sense of understanding of what they are doing, they must be compelled by popular and legal means to stand aside. The first step in creating a revitalized democratic society must be the development of a system of laws which sets the limits of action for leaders of the state. Such rules must be clearly stated and understood as having real meaning; they must be supported by a system of enforcement procedures. The second must be the adoption of procedures for removing from office those who breach that system of laws. In the proposed code for discussion I am suggesting a standard for prospective behavior. It is based on American law and directives applied to other societies. The sanctions, however, might be seen as reflective of an older "American" culture.

The question of what is to be done with this leadership will be a test of whether or not American society is creative and humane and whether those groups which were denied justice can do justice to others while they dismantle those institutional structures which developed war and genocide to the point that they have reached in the world culture.

Lévi-Strauss, in his remarkable book, *Tristes Tropiques*, talks about the North Plains Indians who were known as the most cruel of societies. Nevertheless, they developed a humane form of punishment which did not sever the social links of the individual. An Indian who broke the laws of his tribe was sentenced to the destruction of his belongings, his tent and his horses. Yet, when that occurred, the police were indebted to the law-breaker. They were required to compensate him for the harm he had been made to suffer. In this way, the criminal was put back in debt to the group and he was obliged to acknowledge the way the community undertook to help him.

> These reciprocities continued, by way of gifts and counter gifts, until the initial disorder created by the crime and its punishment had been completely smoothed over and order was once again complete.[52]

TOWARD A FUTURE ACCOUNTING

After World War II, the American government forced and persuaded the Japanese and Germans to renounce militarism and ultranationalism as their dominant way of life. To this end, hundreds of thousands of persons were purged or retired from areas of responsibility in the Japanese and German governments. The United States now finds itself in a similar position. It now must find the means, within strict legal limits, to retire from public life bureaucrats and policy-makers who see violence as the primary means of American policy-making. Unless such means are found, we will find that American society is one in which there are no communal values that tie the society together. The values will be so different among groups and the practice of morality so personal as to

---

52/Claude Lévi-Strauss, *Tristes Tropiques* (Adler, 1968).

clearly vitiate the chance for a peaceful society. Instead, the chances for total degeneration will geometrically increase.

New standards must be found to deal not so much with what has happened, as with what will happen in the *future*. We may reject laws which have an *ex post facto* quality, or which become bills of attainder. There is no need for such purge tactics in the United States. It is crucial, however, that we devise standards which tell government officials in reasonably precise terms what they can and cannot do. The Uniform Code of Military Justice and the field manuals define such limits for the military. Civilian officers of the government who deal with foreign policy and national security must not be left without standards to which they are held.

As a political matter, officials of the government who served in high positions during previous administrations, who acted to fan the flames of war and disaster, and who developed bureaucratic structures which allowed for such a situation to develop, need not be reappointed. Indeed, any political party platform should now include a clear statement that it will not appoint those who pursued a policy of war in Southeast Asia to any future cabinet, subcabinet, or policy-making position. The Senate Foreign Relations Committee could begin to serve notice on any Presidential aspirant or President that there is little likelihood that any person directly involved in the Indochina war will be recommended by that Committee for Senate confirmation.

The issue is not a partisan issue. It is a question of the standards of citizenship within the body politic. During the occupation of Germany after World War II the United States insisted that the various parties of Germany—and then the Germans themselves—develop a code of behavior which would be applicable to all Germans as citizens of Germany. The German representatives of the various

political parties—Christian Social Union, Social Democratic Party, Communist Party, Economic Reconstruction
Party, and Free Democratic Party—all joined with the
German government to support the Law for Liberation
from National Socialism and Militarism. They drew a
proclamation which developed a definition of citizenship
that separated itself from the national socialist and militarist period of German life. It is this lesson upon which
we can draw.

The power to declare war and the power to define offenses against the Law of Nations is left, constitutionally
speaking, with the Congress. In 1947, when the public debated the meaning of war crimes, international lawyers
argued for the development of laws which would make
such crimes punishable within national courts. As one
commentator wrote, the government of the United States
"should not allow the slow processes of international
agreement to defeat its sincerity of purpose."[53] Now, in
the 1970's, the question of such a code cannot remain an
item of unfinished business.

Some have argued that States are incapable, by definition, of keeping the peace, and that citizens must find a
means for doing so.[54] John Dewey contended that the institutions of the state are so saturated with the war men-
tality that to regard the state as a major instrument
for maintaining peace is a contradiction which can never
be resolved in practice. But, as we have seen, there was
an antimilitarist mood within the American government
after World War II. Many officials were convinced then
that another war had to be avoided, and that leaders had
to be controlled. But those who took that position either
resigned or were driven out by the new militarism which

53/George Finch, *The Nuremberg Trial and International Law*, AJIL
(1947).

54/Anti-war students have pursued the pragmatist tradition of direct
action independent of the state by promoting a separate peace treaty.

mushroomed during the Cold War years.

In 1947, with the National Security Act, the American government blurred the distinction between civilian and military operations in national security and foreign policy. Foreign policy became an instrument of conflict, and national security was judged in terms of military and para-military strength and the government's willingness to engage in their use. The federal government became an instrument of the national security state as the militarized civilians employed the resources of the society for covert operations, forced refugee programs, bombing missions, and nuclear war tactics. The militarized civilians escaped any code of law under which they could be held account-able by the citizenry or the Congress. Americans found that their leaders took the fork in the road which was marked by the flag of imperialism and paved with sign-posts which said that raw power was law.

Since 1963 the transformation of values within the American society has meant that there is a conscious wish on the part of an active public to retrace those steps, be-cause of its own heritage and hopes and because of what has become obvious to all: that war is a crime in itself, that murder or organizing for it on a small or grand scale can no longer pass as high policy. The people are con-concerned with how the State is to be held in check and how power is to be held accountable. Those who have argued that the nation-state system is obsolete, and by its nature immoral, may be theoretically correct. But there is nothing to suggest that in the present there is a believ-able alternative. The question remains as to how the sev-eral branches of government within the United States, and the people, are able to end criminality masking as government. This can and should be done through lawful means. What recourse do the people have against elites other than law?

*The following outline for a law reenforces demilita-
rizing aspects of American society. It uses standards the
American government applied to others and reasserts the
tradition of personal responsibility for American government officials.*

PROPOSED CONCURRENT RESOLUTION OF THE CONGRESS
OF THE UNITED STATES/NO. I/

The Speaker and President Pro Tempore of the Senate
shall appoint four members of the House Judiciary Committee and four members of the Senate Judiciary Committee who shall constitute a Special Committee of the
Congress to review the decisions and directives of the
United States in Germany and Japan between September
30, 1945, and December 31, 1948, which concern militarism and ultranationalism. The Special Committee shall
study whether any or all such directives are the basis of
legislation which has been or should be incorporated
into the domestic laws of the United States.

The Committee shall report back with proposed legislation to the House and Senate no later than 90 business
days after the passage of this Resolution.

PROPOSED CONCURRENT RESOLUTION OF THE CONGRESS
OF THE UNITED STATES/NO. II/

The Speaker and President Pro Tempore of the Senate
shall appoint four members of the House Judiciary Committee who shall constitute a Special Commission of the
Affairs, four members of the Senate Judiciary Committee,
and four members of the Senate Foreign Relations Committee who shall constitute a Special Commission of the
Congress. The Commission shall investigate whether any
agencies of the government of the United States are, by
their nature, day-to-day activity, and mission, illegal or

criminal in the light of international law, the Uniform Code of Military Justice, the Field Manuals of the armed forces, the Charter of the United Nations, the Nuremberg and Asian War Crimes Tribunals, and such directives of the United States in Germany and Japan between May 30, 1945, and December 31, 1948, which may apply.

The Commission shall make public its findings. It shall report and make recommendations to the House and Senate no later than 120 business days from the passage of this Resolution.

Where the Commission determines that any agencies of the government of the United States are or may be breaching any of the aforesaid rules, laws, decisions, and directives, the report and recommendations of the Commission shall take precedence over all Congressional business and will be taken up by the Congress over all other matters on the Calendar.

An Act for the establishment of a code of uniform justice for public officials whose responsibilities include, but are not limited to, national security policy of the United States.

A PROPOSED AMENDMENT TO THE
NATIONAL SECURITY ACT OF 1947:

Section 11.   Nothing in this Act shall be construed as denying any individual his Constitutional rights.

Section 22.   Nothing in this Act shall be construed as applying to anyone who advocates or teaches militarism, ultranationalism, or genocide, and who is not in an official position of the government of the United States or is on contract to the United States.*

---

*For the purposes of this act:
Militarism is defined as the organization of all or part of the human

Section 33.   Officials of the United States shall not be entitled to preach and advocate militarism or genocide.

Section 44.   An offender of this Act shall be anyone who:

A/   treats or causes others to treat foreign civilians or prisoners of war contrary to International Laws, including but not limited to treaties of the United States, executive agreements, the Uniform Code of Military Justice, and the Charter of the United Nations;

B/   approves or causes plans to be developed for or carries out outrages, pillages, deportations, mass defoliations, or other acts of brutality against civilians, insurgent groups, and resistance movements;

C/   in any form whatever, participates in mass murders masking as defense or strategy, killings, maimings, planning or causing to be planned assassinations, tortures, or developing concentration camps, labor camps, and detention camps, cruelties and conscious policies of neglect and abuse of populations of another land;

D/   undertakes military or covert frolics on his own initiative or with others.

Section 44a.   For the purposes of this Act, anyone above GS 14 or FSO 4, including members of the White House Staff, the Executive Office of the President, and all individuals holding policy-making positions, including and above the rank of Deputy Assistant Secretary, shall

---

and material resources of the United States as instruments of threats and force in order to dominate and terrorize the people of other nations.

A *militarist* is anyone who uses his official position for these purposes.

Genocide is defined as the attempt on the part of individuals and agencies of the government to destroy a race, religion, class, group, or people by killing, causing serious mental or bodily harm, or deliberately inflicting upon the group conditions of life resulting in their destruction.

Ultranationalism is defined as the defiance of international law, the United Nations Charter, and resolutions of the United Nations Security Council and General Assembly while instead resorting to force, domination, and unilateral action through the government of the United States, its agencies, or third party agents.

be held directly accountable as offenders for any and all plans and policies signed by them in writing or by orders given orally which cause to be developed plans, policies, or actions of:

1/ assassination within the United States or in other lands;

2/ mass bombing in an undeclared or aggressive war;

3/ the use of remote control weapons of mass destruction;

4/ the destruction of crops, livestock, and the natural habitat of another nation, people, or land;

5/ the overthrow by force, violence, bribe, or stealth of the leadership of another nation;

6/ the use of weapons of mass destruction such as nuclear weapons of whatever kilotonnage or megatonnage;

7/ the use of chemical, biological, and radiological weapons in any form;

8/ the forcible removal of populations of other lands;

9/ the use of weapons declared illegal under the Hague conventions of 1899 and 1907;

10/ entering into agreement with corporate or other leaderships for the purpose of making war or developing a militarist economy;

11/ threatening and provoking other nations and lands with U.S. or third-party military and paramilitary forces.

Section 44b. The Freedom of Information Act is hereby revised to include all information pertaining to the national security, thus making such information available to the public no later than six months after it is considered within the government.

Section 55.   Sanctions—Anyone who violates Section 55B
and 55C of this Act shall be suspended from
government service but with pay. He shall
be tried under the federal criminal laws of
the United States by the Department of Justice and in the federal courts, including the
U.S. Court of International and National
Security Law.

A/   Planning—Anyone above the Civil Service rank of
GS 14 or FSO 4, or in a policy-making position, who plans
or causes to be planned actions which violate the Constitution, international law, the Uniform Code of Military
Justice, the United Nations Charter, the Field Manuals of
the Armed Forces, the directives and rules of the U.S.
government in Germany, Japan, and Austria which deal
with proscribed activities, the Nuremberg and Asian war-
crime trials, and the amendments to the National Security
Act of 1947 will be liable to the following sanctions:

1/   reduction in Civil Service rank;
2/   discharge from the Civil Service;
3/   retirement from the Civil Service;
4/   ineligibility to hold any Civil Service position,
including that of Schedule C, for a period of not less
than 10 years from the time of dismissal.

B/   Ordering—Any official above the rank of GS 14
having committed or caused to be committed specific war
crimes will be liable to the following sanctions:

1/   confiscation of property beyond the amount necessary to guarantee a reasonable living standard for the
accused and his family as defined by the Bureau of
Labor Statistics;
2/   custodial imprisonment for 7 years at socially
useful work as aides in the helping professions.

C/   Carrying Out—Anyone who carries out or commands others to carry out plans specifically proscribed
under the amended National Security Act of 1947 shall be:

1/ subject to an imprisonment of 12 years at socially useful work as defined under the law;

2/ subject to confiscation of property or income beyond the amount necessary to guarantee a reasonable living standard for the accused and his family as defined by the Bureau of Labor Statistics.

Section 66. Failure to have a program or policy affirmed by the Office of the National Security Solicitor shall result in:

A/ immediate suspension of bureau chiefs and supergrade civil service employees responsible for passing the plan or program to the National Security Solicitor.

Section 77. Any government official who attempts to impede investigation by the Solicitor's office of both houses of the Congress, the Executive, and duly-authorized citizen committees shall be suspended from government service without pay.

Section 88. Where plans are implemented and where the planners cause the plans to be implemented, planners may be liable under subsections A/, B/, and C/ of Section 55.

Section 100. The Legal Office for National Security Affairs is hereby established in the Executive Office of the President which will give advisory opinions to the President and the Congress on the legality of any contemplated military or national security action, program, or weapons acquisition.

A/ Executive privilege shall not apply to the Legal Office.

Section 101. Copies of the opinions of the Legal Office will be published in a public series on a regular basis upon completion of each opinion of the Legal Office.

Section 102. Copies will be sent as a matter of course to

the Legal Adviser of the Congress.

Section 103. Issues may be presented for investigation to the Legal Office by the President, agencies of the government, and private citizens of the United States.

Section 104. The Legal Office shall have investigatory power over all aspects of United States national security affairs including subpoena power.

Section 105. The Legal Office shall have the power of swearing witnesses within the government of the United States.

A/ It shall have the power with their consent to accept testimony from individuals who are not U.S. citizens.

B/ It shall have the power to take testimony, and to subpoena and swear witnesses.

Section 106. The Legal Office shall use international law and domestic law to judge the legality and illegality of any governmental actions. Such law shall be the Constitution, the Charter of the United Nations, treaties entered into by the United States, international law, the Uniform Code of Military Justice, Field Manuals of the Armed Forces, the standards of conduct developed at the Nuremberg and Asian war-crime trials, and directives of the United States in Japan and Germany which defined and developed standards for the dismantling of militarism and ultranationalism.

Section 107. The Legal Office shall have advisory and investigatory power.

Section 108. The Legal Office shall be directed by the National Security Solicitor Legal Adviser. The term of Solicitor Legal Adviser shall be 15 years. He shall be nominated by the President with the advice and consent of the Senate.

A/ Compensation for the National Security Solicitor Legal Adviser shall be at the rate of a Federal District Court Judge.

B/ Members of the Office of the National Security Solicitor Legal Adviser shall be known as Assistant Solicitor Legal Advisers. They shall be compensated for at a super-grade level. In certain instances, and for special assignments, the Solicitor Adviser is empowered to hire research and legal staff on a contractual and consultant basis.

1/ As a matter of day-to-day business the National Security Solicitor Legal Adviser shall designate open hearings in which presentations are made by individuals and groups on any matters of foreign and national security policy which may be in violation of Section 44, 44A, and 44B of this Act.

2/ The National Security Solicitor Legal Adviser shall recommend for prosecution to the Department of Justice individuals who are in violation of this Act.

3/ On the basis of its own study and the recommendation of the National Security Solicitor, the Department of Justice shall bring criminal cases before a Grand Jury. A Grand Jury shall indict on the basis of its own study.

4/ Cases will be brought in the United States District Courts.

Section 109. The National Security Solicitor Legal Adviser's Office shall be broadly representative of the racial and sex composition of the United States.

Section 110. According to its respective rules of appointment, the House and Senate of the United States shall appoint as officers of each body a National Security and International Law Solicitor of the Senate and a National Security and International Law Solicitor of the House.

A/ The Solicitor of the Senate and the House, respectively, shall advise members of the House and Senate, including committees and groups of members, on any policy, bill, or recommendation which may be introduced by them in the normal course of transacting legislative business. This advice will be based on ascertaining the legality of any proposed legislation from the framework of international law, the Constitution, the Uniform Code of Military Justice, the Law of Land Warfare, the Hague Conventions, international treaties of which the United States is signatory, the Nuremberg Trials, Tokyo trials, and United States directives in Germany and Japan between 1945 and December 1, 1948, which pertain to directives against militarism and ultranationalism.

B/ The Solicitor of the Senate and House, respectively, shall advise both houses on aforementioned questions which may cause actions to be brought against the President, the Vice President and all civil officers of the United States under Article II, Section 4, of the Constitution.

Section 111. There shall be chosen a citizens' committee broadly representative of the United States which shall be responsible for holding public reviews of the Office of the National Security Solicitor Legal Adviser.

A/ The Committee shall be comprised of 12 jurors chosen at random by the Speaker of the House and the President Pro Tempore of the Senate from the Federal Jury lists of each of the Federal Judicial Circuits of the United States including the District of Columbia.

B/ The Committee shall meet for a term of 90 official days of business over two years and issue its own reports on the work of the Office of the National Security Solicitor

Legal Adviser, including recommendations to Congress.

C/ A new committee shall be chosen from the Jury lists every two years.

D/ Compensation shall be at the rate of federal jurors.

E/ The Committee shall be provided with adequate funds for six professional staff members chosen by the Committee with the advice of the Office of the Solicitor of the House and Senate.

Section 112. Judicial and Administrative Procedures: Any civil servant or policy-maker charged under Section 33, Section 55A, Section 66, or Section 77 of this Act by the Department of Justice or the Civil Service Commission shall have the right of public administrative hearing. Twelve jurors shall be chosen from the list of the federal district courts of the site where the federal official resides. Any individual who holds public office and is removed from that office for probable cause, shall receive an administrative jury hearing within 30 days of his removal except where the individual is unable to prepare his case in time. The individual shall have available to him all files of the federal government upon which the Department of Justice or the Civil Service Commission bases its case against the individual for his defense.

A/ He shall have the right of appeal to the U.S. Court of National Security and International Law.

Section 113. There is hereby established a nine-judge Court of National Security and International Law.

A/ This Court shall be on a level equal to the U.S. Court of Appeals, the U.S. Court of Claims, and the U.S. Court of Tax Appeals.

1/ The appeal jurisdiction of the Court shall be:

(a) actions brought by the United States against officials and former officials of the United States, who are charged with breaching Section 44, Section 44a, and Section 44b of this Act, not including members of the Cabinet, the President, the Vice President, and judges of the federal courts.

(b) appeals from judgments of the administrative jury by a defendant or defendants.

(c) appeals from judgments of the federal courts.

2/ Original jurisdiction shall be exercised in all cases which include elected officials of the United States.

(a) This section does not detract from the power of Congress to discipline its own members.

(b) Nothing in this Act shall be construed as infringing on the power of the Congress to bring charges of impeachment against the President, the Vice President, and all civil officers, or the power of the Senate to decide any impeachment proceeding.

(c) The Chief Judge of the United States Court shall make public annual reports to the Congress and the people of the United States.

(d) The Judges of the U.S. Court for National Security and International Law shall be appointed by the President with the advice and consent of the Senate for terms of 15 years.

Section 114. A decision of the U.S. Court of National Security and International Law shall have the force of law on the government of the United States.

A/ Any official of the United States or member of the armed forces of the United States shall be automatically on notice that he or she will be liable for violations of this Act if he or she continues to plan, order, or carry out actions specifically related to the case before the Court;

1/ An injunction may include positive relief for the

citizen including but not limited to an order enjoining the Collector of the Internal Revenue Service from collecting taxes from the plaintiff or plaintiffs.

2/ An injunction may include positive relief for an individual of draft age including but not limited to an order enjoining the Director of the Selective Service System from issuing draft calls until the federal government complies with the Court order.

B/ Any citizen may apply for an injunction in the U.S. Court of National Security and International Law against that agency or official who continues activities held by the Court as illegal under the terms of this Act.

Section 115. Army National Guard and Air Militia—Under Article I, Section 8, of the U.S. Constitution, authority for calling up the Guard and Reserves shall revert to the Congress.

A/ In no case shall they be used outside of the United States.

MODELS FOR DEMILITARIZATION AND PERSONAL ACCOUNTABILITY OF PUBLIC OFFICIALS: Selected Documents from the American Occupation of Japan and Germany

Appendix A: Official U.S. Actions Toward Demilitarization, Ending Ultranationalism, and Building Democracy in Japan

----

Part I: Potsdam Declaration—Proclamation by Heads of Governments; United States, United Kingdom, and China   *July 26, 1945*

4) The time has come for Japan to decide whether she will continue to be controlled by those self-willed militaristic advisers whose unintelligent calculations have brought the Empire of Japan to the threshold of annihilation, or whether she will follow the path of reason.

6) There must be eliminated for all time the authority and influence of those who have deceived and misled the

people of Japan into embarking on world conquest, for we insist that a new order of peace, security and justice will be impossible until irresponsible militarism is driven from the world.

10) We do not intend that the Japanese shall be enslaved as a race or destroyed as a nation, but stern justice shall be meted out to all war criminals, including those who have visited cruelties upon our prisoners. The Japanese Government shall remove all obstacles to the revival and strengthening of democratic tendencies among the Japanese people. Freedom of speech, of religion, and of thought, as well as respect for the fundamental human rights, shall be established.

11) Japan shall be permitted to maintain such industries as will sustain her economy and permit the exaction of just reparations in kind, but not those which would enable her to re-arm for war. To this end, access to, as distinguished from control of, raw materials shall be permitted. Eventual Japanese participation in world trade relations shall be permitted.

Part II: Removal of Japanese Militarists and Ultranationalists from All Positions of Power

SECTION I: POLITICAL

1. Disarmament and Demilitarization

Disarmament and demilitarization are the primary tasks of the military occupation and shall be carried out promptly and with determination. Every effort shall be made to bring home to the Japanese people the part played by the military and naval leaders, and those who collaborated with them in bringing about the existing and future distress of the people.

Japan is not to have an army, navy, air force, secret police organization, or any civil aviation. Japan's ground, air and naval forces shall be disarmed and disbanded and the Japanese Imperial General Headquarters, the General Staff and all secret police organizations shall be dissolved. Military and naval materiel, military and naval vessels and military and naval installations, and military, naval and civilian aircraft shall be surrendered and shall be disposed of as required by the Supreme Commander.

High officials of the Japanese Imperial General Headquarters, and General Staff, other high military and naval officials of the Japanese Government, leaders of ultra-nationalist and militarist organizations and other important exponents of militarism and aggression will be taken into custody and held for future disposition. Persons who have been active exponents of militarism and militant nationalism will be removed and excluded from public office and from any other position of public or substantial private responsibility. Ultra-nationalistic or militaristic social, political, professional and commercial societies and institutions will be dissolved and prohibited.

Militarism and ultra-nationalism, in doctrine and practice, including para-military training, shall be eliminated from the educational system. Former career military and naval officers, both commissioned and non-commissioned, and all other exponents of militarism and ultra-nationalism shall be excluded from supervisory and teaching positions.

2. War Criminals

Persons charged by the Supreme Commander or appropriate United Nations agencies with being war criminals, including those charged with having visited cruelties upon United Nations prisoners or other nationals, shall be arrested, tried and, if convicted, punished. Those wanted by another of the United Nations for offenses against its nationals, shall, if not wanted for trial or as witnesses or otherwise by the Supreme Commander, be turned over to the custody of such other nation.

3. Encouragement of Desire for Individual Liberties and Democratic Processes

Freedom of religious worship shall be proclaimed promptly on occupation. At the same time it should be made plain to the Japanese that ultra-nationalistic and militaristic organizations and movements will not be permitted to hide behind the cloak of religion.

The Japanese people shall be afforded opportunity and encouraged to become familiar with the history, institutions, culture, and the accomplishments of the United States and the other democracies. Association of personnel of the occupation forces with the Japanese population should be controlled, only to the extent necessary, to further the policies and objectives of the occupation.

Democratic political parties, with rights of assembly and public discussion, shall be encouraged, subject to the necessity for maintaining the security of the occupying forces.

Laws, decrees and regulations which establish discriminations on ground of race, nationality, creed or political opinion shall be abrogated; those which conflict with the objectives and policies outlined in this document shall be repealed, suspended or amended as required; and agencies charged specifically with their enforcement shall be abolished or appropriately modified. Persons unjustly confined by Japanese authority on political grounds shall be released. The judicial, legal, and police systems shall be reformed as soon as practicable to conform to the policies set forth in Articles 1 and 3 of this Part III and thereafter shall be progressively influenced, to protect individual liberties and civil rights.

1. Economic Demilitarization

The existing economic basis of Japanese military strength must be destroyed and not be permitted to revive.

Therefore, a program will be enforced containing the following elements, among others; the immediate cessation and future prohibition of production of all goods designed for the equipment, maintenance, or use of any military force or establishment; the imposition of a ban upon any specialized facilities for the production or repair of implements of war, including naval vessels and all forms of aircraft; the institution of a system of inspection and control over selected elements in Japanese economic activity to prevent concealed or disguised military preparation; the elimination in Japan of those selected industries or branches of production whose chief value to Japan is in preparing for war; the prohibition of specialized research and instruction directed to the development of war-making power; and the limitation of the size and character of Japan's heavy industries to its future peaceful requirements, and restriction of Japanese merchant shipping to the extent required to accomplish the objectives of demilitarization.

The eventual disposition of those existing production facilities within Japan which are to be eliminated in accord with this program, as between conversion to other uses, transfer abroad, and scrapping will be determined after inventory. Pending decision, facilities readily convertible for civilian production should not be destroyed, except in emergency situations.

2. Promotion of Democratic Forces

Encouragement shall be given and favor shown to the development of organizations in labor, industry, and agriculture, organized on a democratic basis. Policies shall be favored which permit a wide distribution of income and of the ownership of the means of production and trade.

Those forms of economic activity, organization and leadership shall be favored that are deemed likely to strengthen the peaceful disposition of the Japanese people, and to make it difficult to command or direct economic activity in support of military ends.

To this end it shall be the policy of the Supreme Commander:

(a) To prohibit the retention in or selection for places of importance in the economic field of individuals who do not direct future Japanese economic effort solely towards peaceful ends; and

(b) To favor a program for the dissolution of the large industrial and banking combinations which have exercised control of a great part of Japan's trade and industry.

3. Resumption of Peaceful Economic Activity

The policies of Japan have brought down upon the people great economic destruction and confronted them with the prospect of economic difficulty and suffering. The plight of Japan is the direct outcome of its own behavior, and the Allies will not undertake the burden of repairing the damage. It can be repaired only if the Japanese people renounce all military aims and apply themselves diligently and with single purpose to the ways of peaceful living. It will be necessary for them to undertake physical reconstruction, deeply to reform the nature and direction of their economic activities and institutions, and to find useful employment for their people along lines adapted to and devoted to peace. The Allies have no intention of imposing conditions which would prevent the accomplishment of these tasks in due time.

Japan will be expected to provide goods and services

338

to meet the needs of the occupying forces to the extent that this can be effected without causing starvation, widespread disease and acute physical distress.

The Japanese authorities will be expected, and if necessary directed, to maintain, develop and enforce programs that serve the following purposes:

(a) To avoid acute economic distress.

(b) To assure just and impartial distribution of available supplies.

(c) To meet the requirements for reparations deliveries agreed upon by the Allied Governments.

(d) To facilitate the restoration of Japanese economy so that the reasonable peaceful requirements of the population can be satisfied.

In this connection, the Japanese authorities on their own responsibility shall be permitted to establish and administer controls over economic activities, including essential national public services, finance, banking, and production and distribution of essential commodities, subject to the approval and review of the Supreme Commander in order to assure their conformity with the objectives of the occupation.

4. Reparations and Restitution

Reparations

Reparations for Japanese aggression shall be made:

(a) Through the transfer—as may be determined by the appropriate Allied authorities—of Japanese property located outside of the territories to be retained by Japan.

(b) Through the transfer of such goods or existing capital equipment and facilities as are not necessary for a peaceful Japanese economy or the supplying of the occupying forces. Exports other than those directed to be shipped on reparation account or as restitution may be made only to those recipients who agree to provide necessary imports in exchange or agree to pay for such exports in foreign exchange. No form of reparation shall be exacted which will interfere with or prejudice the program for Japan's demilitarization.

Restitution

Full and prompt restitution will be required of all identifiable looted property.

5. Fiscal, Monetary, and Banking Policies

The Japanese authorities will remain responsible for the management and direction of the domestic fiscal, monetary, and credit policies subject to the approval and review of the Supreme Commander. . . .

Part III: Extension of the Purge   *October 31, 1946*

My dear General:

Further to my letter of October 22nd enclosing copies of the Government proposals, I have received a letter dated October 23rd from General Whitney, copy of which is enclosed herewith.

Before proceeding with the points raised by the General, I would like to state some of the principles with which the Japanese Government have so far dealt with the Purge.

A. I feel that the purge should be carried out in accordance with the actual and real conditions which existed or exist today in the country. I realize fully that your Purge Directive is linked with the Potsdam Declaration and also realize that the execution of the Directive in letter and spirit, particularly the latter, is so essential in order that the country should restore the respect and friendship of the Allied Powers and be made a member of the democratic world. But at the same time, the purge should be applied where it is due and although some cases of injustice could not be helped, the Government should feel its great responsibility towards the people in trying its utmost to minimize these unjust cases.

B. I am keenly aware of the fact that the most important work before the Government today is the rehabilitation of the ruined country. Before the rehabilitation is definitely set on its smooth way, the confusion and chaotic, economic as well as social, conditions must be taken care of. In this connection, I feel that to purge a man simply because he had some connection, however remote and superficial, with the military regime, would cause uninvited antagonism and disappointment among the people, thereby increasing the difficulties of the rehabilitation, formidable as they are, by creating feeling of dissention which must inevitably follow the purge unjustly applied.

C. I believe the regimentation of the military regime had been engineered by a clique of professional soldiers, of government officials, of right wing reactionary and of some members of Zaibatsu, and the people were merely the target of their scheme of regimentation. To accuse some portion of the people, who were actually regimented to do something without having been given any chance of voicing their opinion, the refusal of which would have probably meant self destruction in some form, of regimenting other people, is not, I think, reasonable. Take the case of Imperial Rule Assistance Association. There is no doubt that some executive members of the central organization should be held responsible for misleading the people to misery and unhappiness but local "influential members" of the association shared neither "ideals" nor feeling of comradeship with the central executives. I think it is similar to the case of one accidentally helping a burglar escape from the police pursuit by running into the police car by mistake.

D. With regard to the Purge, the important thing is for the people to realize its justification. The purge should be carried out with thorough conviction of the people that

341

"justice is being done where it is due" and when it goes beyond the limit, it is bound to cause distrust of the Government and the purge. The Government should not give a moment of doubt to the people that it might be-doing the purge for the sake of doing it and not for a real and high objective.

While keenly appreciating the fact that General Whitney has studied the Government's proposal with such care and understanding, I would venture to make the following comments:

1. "That persons deemed undesirable from any public office shall be barred from all public service." The Government, in close cooperation with the Government Section, set a certain "standard" for your Purge Directive and it was applied to the Cabinet Ministers, members of the House of Peers, Officers of Chokunin Rank or higher of the Government Services, candidates for the House of Representatives and holders of other important "public offices." In other words, the interpretation of your Purge Directive was definitely arrived at and made known to the people. My original intention was to adhere to this "standard" throughout, whether central or local, and I am still of the opinion that this is the legitimate and reasonable course to adopt. But having been advised of the disapproval of my intention, the Government proposal has been altered to set another "standard" for your Purge Directive to be applicable to local "public offices" but proposed that these two "standards" should, be strictly adhered to each respective "sphere." It has now been instructed that this discrimination should not exist and any one barred from local "public office" should also be barred from all other "public offices." Supposing the instruction were taken into effect, it would mean excluding or removing quite a number of the present members of the Diet, who held some local "public offices" at one time. I think the consequence would be most serious because

the very question of faith and integrity of the Government would be involved. Based on your Purge Directive, the Government officially approved of their "qualifications" one day and still basing on the same directive, the Government could not, on another day, disapprove of their "qualifications."

2. "That local government and quasi-government office-holders shall not be permitted to perpetuate themselves in office." The Government's proposal is to screen, on the basis of the new standard of Your Purge Directive, all candidates for the mayors of cities and their deputies, town and village headmen and their deputies and leave the rest to the freely expressed will of the people and I think this is the sound and reasonable course to follow. As to the block heads (Chonaikaicho and Burakukaicho), the Government's proposal is to regard these positions as "public offices" and to prevent "undesirable" persons from holding these "offices." As explained officially before, these blocks are entirely voluntary organizations and have no official or legal status. Their "sphere of influence," if any, is necessarily confined to routines of daily life of the people, such as distributing foodstuffs, advising the people of medical injection dates, etc., and to accuse them of any political influences in regimenting the people towards the war is considered unreasonable. It is probably true that a few block heads, mostly Chonaikai heads, took advantage of their position and swindled some portion of food rations during the war but most of these undesirable heads resigned on their own accord at the end of the war for their own "safety." It is also true that the Communists are agitating for their removal but I am convinced that the great majority of the people have no misconception as to the "duties" they performed during the war. I know in some districts the block heads were "elected" in rotation as no one wanted the job which demanded a great deal of time and attention without remunerations. I am for the

idea that these block heads should be elected by adult universal suffrage, but before embarking on such a course, these blocks should have legal status for which a law should be promulgated by the Diet.

3. With regard to "influential members of the Imperial Rule Assistance Association," it seems to me that the "definition" for the "influential members" was decided by the original interpretation of your Purge Directive but in view of the opinion of the Government Section, the Government proposed to exclude those chiefs of cities, towns and villages who happened to be the local chiefs of the Imperial Rule Assistance Association, ex officio, although I am still of the opinion that the part they played in dragging the country to war is almost nil, if any. But to include other local "influential members," which actually means small functionaries, under the Purge is not only unreasonable but also unjust.

I may add that I seriously question the contention that "it was on the lowest level that direct pressure in the shaping of the thoughts and actions and daily lives of the people was to be found in the gearing the country for war." As you must be aware, these people "in the lowest level" were so completely unlike the agents of the Nazi or Fascist Party and I know for fact that they had no real hand in the matter. In fact, I look to them to achieve the rehabilitation of the country, establishment of democracy and the continuation of the Emperor institution. They are the people who are now leading the country back to peace and order as they are and have always been the backbone of the peace loving people who hate and despise anarchy and chaos. Besides, to do them this injustice would be taken as injustice done to most of the healthy agricultural population and it would certainly reflect in such a way that they would be annihilated from their own government whereas they are now looking towards the Government for guidance and leadership.

No doubt you are getting many letters urging the headquarters to extend the purge and I must confess that I get many of them myself. But I feel certain that majority of the "middle of the road" people share my views as I have stated here.

I earnestly appeal to you to let the Japanese Government handle the whole matter as we have proposed to you officially and I am sure that you will not have any chance to regret it. It is of such paramount importance to the people and the government of this country, as well as for the future of democratic and uncommunistic Japan, I take the privilege of addressing this letter of appeal to you.

Yours most sincerely,

(S) SHIGERU YOSHIDA.

GENERAL OF THE ARMY DOUGLAS MACARTHUR
General Headquarters, Tokyo

Part IV: General MacArthur's Comment on *Newsweek* Article Entitled "Behind the Japanese Purge— American Military Rivalries" *January 27, 1947*

. . .

"It was these very persons, born and bred as feudalistic overlords, who held the lives and destiny of the majority of Japan's people in virtual slavery, and who, working in closest affiliation with its military, geared the country with both the tools and the will to wage aggressive war. This, to the end that a large part of the earth's surface and inhabitants might be brought under the same economic bondage they had so long maintained over a majority of the Japanese people—and that Japan might weld from conquered nations and peoples of the world a vast totalitarian economic Empire, designed further to enrich them. Those are the persons who, under the purge, are to be removed from influencing the course of Japan's future economy.

"Petitions and letters have been received by the thousands from the people of Japan calling for the extension of the purge to which "Newsweek" objects, and since its announcements the press of Japan has been practically unanimous in applauding its purpose. The only dissenting views thus far heard are from that small minority to be adversely affected by its application, such as the anonymous Japanese sources which are quoted in the article's support.

"The details of the purge program have been carefully evolved so as not to disturb the ordinary businessman, nor the technicians whose skill and brains did not influence formulation of the policy which directed Japan's course toward aggressive war. It is fantastic that this action should be interpreted or opposed as antagonistic to the American ideal of capitalistic economy. In my opinion, and I believe in the opinion of truly responsible Japanese as well, the action will not unduly disturb the development of a future peaceful industrial economy. But even if this should prove not the case—even if, as "Newsweek" avers, this cleansing of the economy of Japan of undesirable influence is destined seriously to handicap industrial revival for lack of essential leadership—or even if such revival is wholly impossible without the guidance of those several thousand persons involved who directly contributed to leading the world into a war taking a toll of millions of human lives and effecting destruction of hundreds of billions in material resources—then, in that event the interests of those other hundreds of millions of people who want and seek peace leave no alternative than that Japan must bear and sustain the consequences, even at the expense of a new economy geared down to the capabilities remaining."

Appendix B: Official U.S. Actions Toward Demilitarization, Denazification, and Building Democracy in Germany

Part I: 5. Law for Liberation from National Socialism and Militarism (U.S. Zone) *March 5, 1946*

Excerpt

Principles

ARTICLE 1

1. To liberate our people from National Socialism and Militarism and to secure a lasting base for German democratic national life in peace with the world, all those who have actively supported the National Socialist tyranny, or are guilty of having violated the principles of justice and humanity, or of having selfishly exploited the conditions thus created, shall be excluded from influence in public, economic and cultural life and shall be bound to make reparations.

2. Everyone who is responsible shall be called to account. At the same time he shall be afforded opportunity to vindicate himself.

ARTICLE 2

1. The individual shall be judged by a just consideration of his individual responsibility and his actual conduct, taken as a whole. In accordance therewith there shall be determined in just gradation the extent of sanctions and of exclusion from participation in the public, economic and cultural life of the people, in order to eliminate permanently the influence of National Socialistic and Militaristic conduct and ideas.

2. External criteria, such as membership of the NSDAP, any of its formations or other organizations, shall not be

decisive by themselves alone for the degree of responsibility under this law. They may be taken as important evidence as to a person's conduct as a whole, but may be overcome, wholly or partly, by evidence to the contrary. Conversely, non-membership by itself is not decisive to absolve one of responsibility.

Registration Procedure

ARTICLE 3

1. In order to seek out all persons responsible and to carry out this law, a registration procedure is hereby established.

2. Every German above the age of 18 will fill out and submit a registration form.

3. Detailed regulations will be issued by the Minister for Political Liberation.

Groups of Persons Responsible

ARTICLE 4

In order to make a just determination of responsibility and to provide for imposition of sanctions, the following groups of persons shall be formed:
(1) Major Offenders,
(2) Offenders (activists, militarists and profiteers),
(3) Lesser Offenders (probationers),
(4) Followers,
(5) Persons exonerated.

———————

Part II: 6. Control Council Law No. 2 (*Providing for the Termination and Liquidation of the Nazi Organizations*)   *October 10, 1945*

The Control Council enacts as follows:

1. The National Socialist German Labour Party, its formations, affiliated associations and supervised agencies, including paramilitary organisations and all other Nazi institutions established as instruments of party domination are hereby abolished and declared illegal.

2. The Nazi organisations enumerated in the attached Appendix, or which may be added, are expressly abolished.

3. The reforming of any of the organisations named herein, whether under the same or different name is forbidden.

ARTICLE II

All real estates, equipments, funds, accounts, records and other property of the organisations abolished by this law are confiscated. Confiscation is carried out by Military Commands; general directives concerning the distribution of the confiscated property are given by the Control Council.

ARTICLE III

Until such time as the property mentioned is actually placed under the control of the Military Commands all officers and other personnel, including administrative officials and others accountable for such property, are held personally responsible for taking any action necessary to preserve intact all such property and for complying with the orders of the Military Commands regarding such property.

Part III: 5. Press Release Omgus (*Civil Service Codes*)
August 28, 1946

Press Release

A civil service system patterned in its basic democratic conceptions after that in the United States will be adopted shortly by each of the three U.S. Länder in occupied Germany. . . .

. . . the new system is in line with the U.S. policy of decentralization and the strengthening of the Länder. Although each Land—Bavaria, Greater Hesse and Wuerttemberg-Baden—was instructed to adopt its own civil service code, all three will embrace the basic principles of democratizing civil service in Germany. In devising their own system, German civil service officials have been given considerable freedom but have been required to completely denazify the civil service and introduce democratic ideas.

Each code will place German civil service on a strictly merit basis, enabling all officials and employees who are employed full time by the German governmental unit or agency to qualify for permanent civil service positions. At the same time, everyone who has a reasonable chance of performing duties of a government position will be given equal opportunity for appointment or promotion to that position. The new system will bring about 80% of government employees under civil service. During the Nazi regime, only about 20% were so classified.

. . . the codes will provide machinery whereby every civil service employee may have his grievances given fair and impartial consideration. This is an innovation in Germany where every civil servant had to "kow-tow" to his superior.

The new codes will prohibit civil servants from engaging in political activities except membership in a political party, the right to express an opinion as a citizen, and to vote. A civil servant may run for an elective office providing he resigns or takes a leave of absence from his civil service position.

The new codes also will prohibit any discrimination because of sex, religion, or race. Provision also shall be made by every official agency, no matter how small, to make sure that the press and other agencies of public information are afforded the opportunity to inform themselves and have adequate access to policy-making officials.

The new civil service system in each Land also will prohibit the maintaining of secret personnel files. Under the Weimar constitution, secret personnel files were prohibited, but they were used extensively during the Nazi regime.

The code in each Land will be administered by a Civil Service Department in which will be a commission whose members will be persons in sympathy with the application of merit principles to public employment and not politicians. The commission will determine policy. A personnel director will be appointed to administer the personnel system.

In addition, each code defines the rights and privileges of civil servants, the method of their removal, release or retirement, and the organization powers and duties of the Land Civil Service Department.

One of the results of the newly-adopted system will be the conferring of permanent civil service status on thousands of emergency German appointees of Military Government throughout the American Zone of Germany. In conferring civil service status on employees appointed since the occupation, qualifying, and not competitive, examinations will be given these candidates.

The new civil service codes abstract all Nazi and militaristic philosophies from civil service in Germany. Under the old system, civil service was broken up into five categories and, in large, limited promotions of the worker to jobs within his respective category. The five grades were: Lower Service (*Der einfache Dienst*), Intermediate Service (*Der mittlere Dienst*), Upper Service (*Der gehobene Dienst*), Higher Service (*Der Hochere Dienst*), and, for "preferred" employees, Political Civil Servants (*Politische Beamte*).

A Prussian ordinance of 11 July 1849, perpetuated by the Nazi Regime, created the class of public officials later to be known as Political Civil Servants. They held key positions connected with the execution of policy and were, therefore, given special confidence of the political party or parties in power. Political civil servants held office at the pleasure of the Fuehrer and were subject to immediate removal without cause and without hearing or investigation.

Positions coming under this "privileged class" included: State Secretaries (*Staatssekretaere*), Ministerial Directors (*Ministerialdirektoren*), press officials at higher government agencies (*Pressereferenten*), Oberburgermeister and City President of Berlin, State Prosecutors (*Staatsanwaelte*), Police President (*Polizeipraesidenten*), and Police Directors (*Polizeidirektoren*).

Candidates for positions in the Higher Service, which included key jobs in government administration down to, for example, administrative head of a city tax district, were required to have the equivalent of a PHD degree. Higher civil service was much coveted because it provided a lifetime job and considerable prestige.

The old German system offered military personnel special privileges in appointments and promotions:

1. Intermediate: Military candidates had to be placed in nine out of ten vacancies, and a severely-wounded candidate in every fifth vacant position.

2. Upper: Every third vacant position had to be filled by a military candidate.

3. Higher: Military personnel were eligible if they possessed Certificate No. 2 of the Wehrmacht Technical School, and were proficient in German shorthand. (The latter requisite was required of all candidates).

4. Political: Categories of Wehrmacht officials designated by Hitler, received "privileged" appointments. Special civil service treatment also was granted former noncommissioned officers of the German armed forces and labor service with honorable discharges, and to children from large families within these two groups. NCO's

among those so-called "special candidates" who served twelve or more years in the armed or labor services took precedence.

The newly-adopted civil service codes provide no special privileges for former German military personnel, or other categories.

In the United States it has been estimated that one out of every nine persons works for the Government. In Germany . . . [the percentage was much greater] because the government controlled almost every phase of activity that was a part of the community's basic existence: All public utilities (gas, electric, water, transportation systems, including the U-Bahn); had very heavy holdings in industry (the Hermann Goering Works, employing some 600,000 workers, was almost totally owned by the Reich); operated all opera houses and even some movie houses and breweries.

Part IV: Extracts from the Charter of the International Military Tribunal Convened at Nuremberg
August 8, 1945

Excerpt

. . .

JURISDICTION AND GENERAL PRINCIPLES

Article 6. The Tribunal established by the agreement referred to in Article 1 hereof for the trial and punishment of the major war criminals of the European Axis countries shall have the power to try and punish persons who, acting in the interests of the European Axis countries, whether as individuals or as members of organizations, committed any of the following crimes.

The following acts, or any of them, are crimes coming within the jurisdiction of the Tribunal for which there shall be individual responsibility:

(a) Crimes against peace: Namely, planning, preparation, initiation or waging of a war of aggression, or a war in violation of international treaties, agreements or assurances, or participation in a common plan or conspiracy for the accomplishment of any of the foregoing;

(b) War Crimes: Namely, violations of the laws or customs of war. Such violations shall include, but not be limited to, murder, ill-treatment or deportation to slave labor or for any other purpose of civilian population of or in occupied territory, murder or ill-treatment of prisoners of war or persons on the seas, killing of hostages, plunder of public or private property, wanton destruction of cities, towns or villages, or devastation not justified by military necessity;

(c) Crimes against humanity: Namely, murder, extermination, enslavement, deportation, and other inhumane acts committed against any civilian population, before or during the war, or persecutions on political, racial or religious grounds in execution of or in connection with any crime within the jurisdiction of the Tribunal, whether or not in violation of the domestic law of the country where perpetrated.

Leaders, organizers, instigators and accomplices participating in the formulation or execution of a common plan or conspiracy to commit any of the foregoing crimes are responsible for all acts performed by any persons in execution of such plan.

Part V: 7. Control Council Directive No. 33 (*The Arrest and Punishment of War Criminals, Nazis, and Militarists, and the Internment, Control, and Surveillance of Potentially Dangerous Germans*)   October 12, 1946

Excerpts

The Control Council directs as follows:

1. Object.

The object of this paper is to establish a common policy for Germany covering:

a) The punishment of war criminals, Nazis, Militarists, and industrialists who encouraged and supported the Nazi Regime.

b) The complete and lasting destruction of Nazism and Militarism by imprisoning and restricting the activities of important participants or adherents to these creeds.

c) The internment of Germans who, though not guilty of specific crimes, are considered to be dangerous to Allied purposes, and the control and surveillance of others considered potentially so dangerous.

. . .

2. The Problem and General Principles.

It is considered that, in order to carry out the principles established at Potsdam, it will be necessary to classify war criminals and potentially dangerous persons into five main categories and to establish punishments and sanctions appropriate to each category. We consider that the composition of categories and the nature of penalties and sanctions should be agreed in some detail but without limiting in any way the full discretion conferred by Control Council Law No. 10 upon Zone Commanders.

4. A clear definition of Allied policy with regard to the obviously dangerous as well as to only potentially dangerous Germans is required at this time in order to establish uniform provisions for disposing of these persons in the various Zones.

5. Categories and Sanctions.

Composition of categories and sanctions are treated in detail in Part II of this Directive. They shall be applied in accordance with the following general principles:

a) A distinction should be made between imprisonment of war criminals and similar offenders for criminal conduct and internment of potentially dangerous persons who may be confined because their freedom would constitute a danger to the Allied Cause.

b) Zone Commanders may, if they so desire, place an individual in a lower category on probation, with the exception of those who have been convicted as major offenders on account of their guilt in specific crimes.

c) Within the categories, Zone Commanders will retain discretion to vary the sanctions if necessary to meet the requirements of individual cases within the limits laid down in this Directive.

d) The classification of all offenders and potentially dangerous persons, assessment of sanctions and the review of cases will be carried out by agencies to be designated by the Zone Commanders as responsible for the implementation of this Directive.

e) The Zone Commanders and tribunals will have the authority to upgrade or downgrade individuals between categories. Zone Commanders may, if they wish, use German tribunals for the purpose of classification, trial and review.

f) In order to prevent persons dealt with under this Directive avoiding any of the consequences of the Directive by moving to another Zone, each Zone Commander will ensure that the other Zones know and understand the methods employed by him in endorsing the identity documents of classified individuals.

g) To implement this Directive, it is recommended that each Zone Commander will issue Orders or Zonal Laws conforming in substance to the provisions and principles of this Directive in his own Zone. Zone Commanders will supply each other with copies of such Laws or Orders.

h) Provided that such Zonal Laws are in general conformity with the principles here set forth, full discretion is reserved to the individual Zone Commanders as regards their application in detail in accordance with the local situation in their respective Zones.

i) In Berlin the Allied Kommandatura will have the responsibility for implementing the principles and provisions of this Directive and will issue such regulations and orders as are required for that purpose. Whatever discretion in the implementation of this Directive is left to Zone Commanders will be exercised by the Allied Kommandatura in Berlin.

j) Apart from the categories and sanctions set forth in Part II of this Directive, persons who committed war crimes or crimes against peace or humanity as defined in Control Council Law No. 10 will be dealt with under the provisions and procedures prescribed by that Law.

PART II

Article I
Groups of Persons Responsible

In order to make a just determination of responsibility and to provide for imposition (except in the case of 5. below) of sanctions the following groupings of persons shall be made:

1. Major offenders;
2. Offenders (activists, militarists, and profiteers);
3. Lesser offenders (probationers);
4. Followers;
5. Persons exonerated. (Those included in the above categories who can prove themselves not guilty before a tribunal).

Article II
Major Offenders

Major Offenders are:

1. Anyone who, out of political motives, committed crimes against victims or opponents of national socialism;

2. Anyone who, in Germany or in the occupied areas, treated foreign civilians or prisoners of war contrary to International Law;

3. Anyone who is responsible for outrages, pillaging, deportations, or other acts of brutality, even if committed in fighting against resistance movements;

4. Anyone who was active in a leading position in the NSDAP, one of its formations or affiliated organizations, or in any other national socialistic or militaristic organization;

5. Anyone who, in the government of the Reich, the Laender, or in the administration of formerly occupied areas, held a leading position which could have been held only by a leading national socialist or a leading supporter of the national socialistic tyranny;

6. Anyone who gave major political, economic, propagandist or other support to the national socialistic tyranny, or who, by reason of his relations with the national socialistic tyranny, received very substantial profits for himself or others;

7. Anyone who was actively engaged for the national socialistic tyranny in the Gestapo, the SD, the SS, or the Geheime Feld- or Grenz-Polizei;

8. Anyone who, in any form whatever, participated in killings, tortures, or other cruelties in a concentration camp, a labour camp, or a medical institution or asylum;

9. Anyone who, for personal profit or advantage, actively collaborated with the Gestapo, SD, SS, or similar organisations by denouncing or otherwise aiding in the persecution of the opponents of the national socialistic tyranny;

10. Any member of the High Command of the German Armed Forces so specified.

. . .

Article III
Offenders

A. *Activists*

I. An activist is:

1. Anyone who by way of his position or activity, sub-

stantially advanced the national socialistic tyranny;

2. Anyone who exploited his position, his influence or his connections to impose force and utter threats, to act with brutality and to carry out oppressions or otherwise unjust measures;

3. Anyone who manifested himself as an avowed adherent of the national socialistic tyranny, more particularly of its racial creeds.

II. Activists are in particular the following persons, insofar as they are not major offenders:

1. Anyone who substantially contributed to the establishment, consolidation or maintenance of the national socialistic tyranny, by word or deed, especially publicly through speeches or writings or through voluntary donations out of his own or another's property or through using his personal reputation or his position of power in political, economic or cultural life;

2. Anyone who, through national socialistic teachings or education, poisoned the spirit and soul of the youth;

3. Anyone who, in order to strengthen the national socialistic tyranny, undermined family and marital life disregarding recognised moral principles;

4. Anyone who in the service of national socialism unlawfully interfered in the administration of justice or abused politically his office as judge or public prosecutor;

5. Anyone who in the service of national socialism agitated with incitement or violence against churches, religious communities or ideological associations;

6. Anyone who in the service of national socialism ridiculed, damaged or destroyed values of art or science;

7. Anyone who took a leading or active part in destroying trade unions, suppressing labour, and misappropriating trade union property;

8. Anyone who, as a provocateur, agent or informer, caused or attempted to cause, institution of a proceeding

to the detriment of others because of their race, religion or political opposition to national socialism or because of violation of national socialist rules;

9. Anyone who exploited his position or power under the national socialistic tyranny to commit offences, in particular, extortions, embezzlements and frauds;

10. Anyone who by word or deed took an attitude of hatred toward opponents of the NSDAP in Germany or abroad, towards prisoners of war, the population of formerly occupied territories, foreign civilian workers, prisoners or like persons;

11. Anyone who favored transfer to service at the front because of opposition to national socialism.

III. An activist shall also be anyone who after 8 May 1945 has endangered or is likely to endanger the peace of the German people or of the world, through advocating national socialism or militarism or inventing or disseminating malicious rumors.

B. *Militarists*

I. A Militarist is:

1. Anyone who sought to bring the life of the German people into line with a policy of militaristic force;

2. Anyone who advocated or is responsible for the domination of foreign peoples, their exploitation or displacement; or

3. Anyone who, for these purposes, promoted armament.

II. Militarists are in particular the following persons, insofar as they are not major offenders:

1. Anyone who, by word or deed, established or disseminated militaristic doctrines or programs or was active in any organization (except the Wehrmacht) serving the advancement of militaristic ideas;

2. Anyone who before 1935 organized or participated in the organization of the systematic training of youth for war;

3. Anyone who, exercising the power of command, is responsible for the wanton devastation, after the invasion of Germany, of cities and country places;

4. Anyone without regard to his rank who, as a member of the Armed Forces (*Wehrmacht*), the Reich Labor Service (*Reichsarbeitsdienst*), the Organization Todt (OT), or Transport Group Speer, abused his official authority to obtain personal advantages or brutally to mistreat subordinates;

5. Anyone whose past training and activities in the General Staff Corps or otherwise has in the opinion of Zone Commanders contributed towards the promotion of militarism and who the Zone Commanders consider likely to endanger Allied purposes.

C. *Profiteers*

I. A profiteer is:

Anyone who, by use of his political position or connections, gained personal or economic advantages for himself or others from the national socialistic tyranny, the rearmament, or the war.

II. Profiteers are in particular the following persons, insofar as they are not major offenders:

1. Anyone who, solely on account of his membership in the NSDAP, obtained an office or a position or was preferentially promoted therein;

2. Anyone who received substantial donations from the NSDAP or its formations or affiliated organizations;

3. Anyone who obtained or strove for advantages for himself or others at the expense of those who were persecuted on political, religious or racial grounds, directly or indirectly, especially in connection with appropriations, forced sales, or similar transactions;

4. Anyone who made disproportionately high profits in armament or war transactions;

5. Anyone who unjustly enriched himself in connection with the administration of formerly occupied territories.

. . .

Article IV
Lesser Offenders
Probationers

I. A lesser offender is:

1. Anyone including former members of the Armed Forces who otherwise belongs to the groups of offenders but because of special circumstances seems worthy of a milder judgement and can be expected according to his character to fulfil his duties as a citizen of a peaceful democratic state after he has proved himself in a period of probation.

2. Anyone who otherwise belongs to the group of followers but because of his conduct and in view of his character will first have to prove himself.

II. A lesser offender is more particularly:

1. Anyone who, born after the first day of January 1919, does not belong to the group of major offenders, but seems to be an offender without however having manifested despicable or brutal conduct and who can be expected in view of his character to prove himself;

2. Anyone, not a major offender, who seems to be an offender but withdrew from national socialism and its methods, unqualifiedly and manifestly, at an early time.

Article VI
Exonerated Persons

An exonerated person is:

Anyone who, in spite of this formal membership or candidacy or any other outward indication, not only showed a passive attitude but also actively resisted the national socialistic tyranny to the extent of his powers and thereby suffered disadvantages.

Article VII
Sanctions

In accordance with the extent of responsibility the sanctions set forth in Art. VIII-XI shall be imposed in just selection and gradation, to accomplish the exclusion of national socialism and militarism from the life of the German people and reparation of the damage caused.

Article VIII
Sanctions against Major Offenders

I. Major Offenders having committed a specific war crime will be liable to the following sanctions:

a) Death;

b) Imprisonment for life or for a period of five to fifteen years, with or without hard labour;

c) In addition, any of the sanctions listed in para. II of this Article may be imposed.

II. The following sanctions may be imposed upon other Major Offenders:

a) They shall be imprisoned or interned for a period not exceeding 10 years; internment after 8 May 1945 can be taken into account; disabled persons will be required to perform special work in accordance with their capability;

b) Their property may be confiscated. However, there shall be left to them an amount necessary to cover the bare existence after taking into consideration family conditions and earning power;

c) They shall be ineligible to hold any public office, including that of notary or attorney;

d) They shall lose any legal claims to a pension or allowance payable from public funds;

e) They shall lose the right to vote, the capacity to be elected, and the right to be politically active in any way or to be members of a political party;

f) They shall not be allowed to be members of a trade union or a business or vocational association;

g) They shall be prohibited for a period of not less than ten years after their release:

1) To be active in a profession or, independently, in an enterprise or economic undertaking of any kind, to own a share therein or to supervise or control it;

2) To be employed in any dependent position, other than ordinary labour;

3) To be active as teacher, preacher, editor, author, or radio commentator;

h) They are subject to restrictions as regards living space and place of residence, and may be enlisted for public works service;

i) They shall lose all licenses, concessions and privileges granted them and the right to keep a motor vehicle.

Article IX
Sanctions against Offenders

1. They may be imprisoned or interned for a period up to ten years in order to perform reparation and reconstruction work. Political internment after 8 May 1945 can be taken into account.

2. Their property may be confiscated (as a contribution for reparation), either as a whole or in part. In case the property is confiscated in part, capital goods (*Sachwerte*) should be preferred. The necessary items for daily use shall be left to them.

3. They shall be ineligible to hold any public office, including that of notary or attorney.

4. They shall lose any legal claims to a pension or allowance payable from public funds.

5. They shall lose the right to vote, the capacity to be elected, and the right to be politically active in any way or to be members of a political party.

6. They shall not be allowed to be members of a trade union or business or vocational association.

7. They shall be prohibited, for a period of not less than five years after their release:

a) To be active in a profession or, independently, in an enterprise or economic undertaking of any kind, to own a share therein or to supervise or control it.

b) To be employed in any dependent position, other than ordinary labour.

c) To be active as a teacher, preacher, editor, author, or radio commentator.

8. They are subject to restriction as regards living space and place of residence.

9. They shall lose all licenses, concessions and privileges granted them and the right to keep a motor vehicle.

10. Within the discretion of Zone Commanders sanctions may be included in zonal laws forbidding offenders to leave a Zone without permission.

Article X
Sanctions against Lesser Offenders

If the finding of the tribunal places an individual in the category of lesser offenders, he may be placed on probation. The time of probation shall be at least two years but, as a rule, not more than three years. To which group a person responsible hereunder will be finally allocated will depend on his conduct during the period of probation. While on probation, the following sanctions will apply:

1. They shall be prohibited, during the period of probation:

a) To operate an enterprise as owner, partner, manager or executive, supervise or control an enterprise or to acquire any enterprise in whole or in part, or any interest or share therein, in whole or in part;

b) To be active as teacher, preacher, author, editor or radio commentator.

2. In the event the lesser offender is the owner of an independent enterprise, or any share therein, at the time of his classification, his interest in such enterprise may be blocked.

3. The term enterprise as used in paragraph 1 a) and 2 of this Article need not include small undertakings of craftsmen, retail shops, farms and like undertakings, having less than 20 employees.

4. Property values, acquisition of which rested upon use of political connections or special national socialistic measures such as aryanization and armament shall be confiscated.

5. For the period of probation additional sanctions, taken from those set forth in Article XI hereof may be imposed, with just selection and modification, more particularly:

a) Restrictions in the exercise of an independent profession, and prohibition to train apprentices;

b) In respect of civil servants: reduction of retirement pay, retirement or transfer to an office with lesser rank or to another position with reduction of compensation, rescission of promotion, transfer from the civil service relationship into that of a contractual employee.

6. Internment in a labor camp or confiscation of the whole property may not be ordered.

7. Within the discretion of Zone Commanders sanctions may be included in zonal laws forbidding the lesser offenders to leave a Zone without permission.

8. Within the discretion of Zone Commanders sanctions may be included in zonal laws denying them the capacity to be elected and the right to be politically active in any way or to be members of a political party. They may also be denied the right to vote.

9. They may be required to report periodically to the police in the place of their residence.

Article XI
Sanctions against Followers

The following sanctions against followers may be applied at the discretion of the Zone Commanders:

1. They may be required to report periodically to the police in the place of their residence;

2. They will not be permitted to leave a Zone or Germany without permission;

3. Civilian members in this category may not stand for election at any level but may vote.

4. In addition, in the case of civil servants, retirement or transfer to an office with lesser rank or to another position, possibly with reduction of compensation or rescission of a promotion instituted while the person belonged to the NSDAP, may be ordered. Corresponding measures may be ordered against persons in economic enterprises including agriculture and forestry.

5. They may be ordered to pay single or recurrent contributions to funds for reparations. When determining contributions, the follower's period of membership, the fees and contributions paid by him, his wealth and income, his family conditions and other relevant factors shall be taken into consideration.

Article XII
Exonerated Persons

No sanction will be applied against persons declared to be exonerated by a tribunal.

Article XIII

Persons in the categories defined in Articles II to VI above who are guilty of specific war crimes or other offences may be prosecuted regardless of their classification under this Directive. Imposing of sanctions under this Directive shall not bar criminal prosecutions for the same offence.

Done at Berlin on the 12th day of October 1946.

R. NOIRET
Général de Division

P. A. KUROCHKIN
Colonel General

LUCIUS D. CLAY
Lieutenant General

G. W. E. J. ERSKINE
Major General

for B. H. ROBERTSON
Lieutenant General

Part VI: 3. Statement by Justice Jackson (*Opening Address for the United States of America by Robert H. Jackson, Representative and Chief of Counsel for the United States of America at the Palace of Justice, Nuremberg, Germany*)　November 21, 1945

Excerpt

May It Please Your Honors,

The privilege of opening the first trial in history for crimes against the peace of the world imposes a grave responsibility. The wrongs which we seek to condemn and punish have been so calculated, so malignant and so devastating, that civilization cannot tolerate their being ignored because it cannot survive their being repeated. That four great nations, flushed with victory and stung with injury, stay the hand of vengeance and voluntarily submit their captive enemies to the judgment of the law is one of the most significant tributes that Power ever has paid to Reason.

This tribunal, while it is novel and experimental, is not the product of abstract speculations nor is it created to vindicate legalistic theories. This inquest represents the practical effort of four of the most mighty of nations, with the support of 17 more, to utilize International Law to meet the greatest menace of our times—aggressive war. The common sense of mankind demands that law shall not stop with the punishment of petty crimes by little people. It must also reach men who possess themselves of great power and make deliberate and concerted use of it to set in motion evils which leave no home in the world untouched. It is a cause of this magnitude that the United Nations will lay before Your Honors.

In the prisoners' dock sit twenty-odd broken men. Reproached by the humiliation of those they have led almost as bitterly as by the desolation of those they have attacked, their personal capacity for evil is forever past. It is hard now to perceive in these miserable men as captives the power by which as Nazi leaders they once dominated much of the world and terrified most of it. Merely as individuals, their fate is of little consequence to the world.

What makes this inquest significant is that those prisoners represent sinister influences that will lurk in the world long after their bodies have returned to dust. They are living symbols of racial hatreds, of terrorism and violence, and of the arrogance and cruelty of power. They are symbols of fierce nationalisms and militarism, of intrigue and war-making which have embroiled Europe generation after generation, crushing its manhood, destroying its homes and impoverishing its life. They have so identified themselves with the philosophies they conceived and with the forces they directed that any tenderness to them is a victory and an encouragement to all the evils which are attached to their names. Civilization can afford to compromise with the social forces which would gain renewed strength if we deal ambiguously or indecisively with the men in whom those forces now precariously survive.

What these men stand for we will patiently and temperately disclose. We will give you undeniable proofs of incredible events. The catalogue of crimes will omit nothing that could be conceived by a pathological pride, cruelty, and lust for power. These men created in Germany, under the *Führerprinzip*, a National Socialist despotism equalled only by the dynasties of the ancient East. They took from the German people all those dignities and freedoms that we hold natural and inalienable rights in every human being. The people were compensated by inflaming and gratifying hatreds toward those who were marked as "scape-goats." Against their opponents, including Jews, Catholics, and free labor the Nazis directed such a campaign of arrogance, brutality, and annihilation as the world has not witnessed since the pre-Christian ages. They excited the German ambition to be a "master race," which of course implies serfdom for others. They led their people on a mad gamble for domination. They diverted social energies and resources to the creation of what they thought to be an invincible war machine. They overran their neighbors. To sustain the "master race" in its war making, they enslaved millions of human beings and brought them into Germany, where these hapless creatures now wander as "displaced persons." At length bestiality and bad faith reached such excess that they aroused the sleeping strength of imperiled civilization. Its united efforts have ground the German war machine to fragments. But the struggle has left Europe a liberated yet prostrate land where a demoralized society struggles to survive. These are the fruits of the sinister forces that sit with these defendants in the prisoners' dock.

In justice to the nations and the men associated in this prosecution, I must remind you of certain difficulties which may leave their mark on this case. Never before shoulder to shoulder with these prison-

...ing party at your bar is Civilization. ...s it is still a struggling and imperfect ...ot plead that the United States, or any ...has been blameless of the conditions which ...German people easy victims to the blandish- ...d intimidations of the Nazi conspirators.

...ut it points to the dreadful sequence of aggressions and crimes I have recited, it points to the weariness of flesh, the exhaustion of resources, and the destruction of all that was beautiful or useful in so much of the world, and to greater potentialities for destruction in the days to come. It is not necessary among the ruins of this ancient and beautiful city, with untold numbers of its civilian inhabitants still buried in its rubble, to argue the proposition that to start or wage an aggressive war has the moral qualities of the worst of crimes. The refuge of the defend- ants can be only their hope that International Law will lag so far behind the moral sense of mankind that conduct which is crime in the moral sense must be regarded as innocent in law.

Civilization asks whether law is so laggard as to be utterly helpless to deal with crimes of this magnitude by criminals of this order of importance. It does not expect that you can make war impossible. It does expect that your juridical action will put the forces of International Law, its precepts, its prohibitions and, most of all, its sanctions, on the side of peace, so that men and women of good will in all countries may have "leave to live by no man's leave, underneath the law."